D1271880

THE STRUGGLE
FOR THE
MEDITERRANEAN
1939 - 1945

THE STRUGGLE
FOR THE
MEDITERRANEAN
1939-1945

By *RAYMOND DE BELOT*
Rear Admiral, French Navy (ret.)

Translated by JAMES A. FIELD, JR.

GREENWOOD PRESS, PUBLISHERS
NEW YORK

Introduction

ALTHOUGH final victory over the Axis was gained in northern Europe, the importance of the Mediterranean theater was second to none. Longer than any other area, it was the scene of continuous action. For twelve months, from the fall of France to the German attack on Russia, it was the only theater in which Axis armies could be engaged; for four years, from the evacuation of Dunkirk to the landings in Normandy, it was the only area in which Britain and her western allies could bring ground forces to bear.

Nor are the massive and decisive campaigns of 1944-1945 necessarily more important than the early battles, fought though these were with the slimmest of resources and without hope of gaining a permanent decision. Indeed, a case can be made that the reverse is true, and that there is danger in the tendency of the victors to remember only the final campaigns, the more so in view of the chronic unpreparedness of democracies and the advantages possessed by the aggressor in modern war. It is one thing to win a war when overwhelming strength is available; it is quite another, more difficult but no less vital, to avoid losing one when strength is lacking and the weapons are still on paper. Even if final victory was not gained in the Mediterranean, final defeat was here avoided.

In this theater there were great operations on land: the battles in the Libyan Desert, the landings in North Africa, the invasion of Italy. But always the invading forces were brought from across the oceans, and war in the desert was dependent on control of the sea. For the Axis in Africa, as for the Allies throughout the war, armies and factories were separated by water passage, and logistic support was impossible lacking maritime control. Nor is this all. The land battles in Africa were fought to gain further areas of maritime dominance: to make the Mediterranean an Axis lake, or to open it as a path for an Allied return to the continent of Europe. The implications of either of these alternatives necessarily made the Mediterranean a theater of supreme strategic importance.

To some, the fact of American participation in the North African landings, or in the Italian campaign, may appear an historical oddity, a temporary but unnatural involvement properly abandoned for more reasonable preoccupation with northern Europe. But the importance of the Mediterranean to the United States is no new thing; at widely different times in our history it has been an object of national interest. During Jefferson's administration the activities of the Tripolitan corsairs led to our first overseas military campaign, a police action carried out by the executive without a declaration of war, to which almost the entire Navy was committed. And although the problem of the Barbary pirates was permanently settled in 1815, a Mediterranean Squadron of varying composition was maintained for over fifty years.

In the present century a Mediterranean crisis led to America's first involvement in the broils of Europe when Theodore Roosevelt, a Republican president, took a hand in the Moroccan dispute and in the Algeciras Conference of 1906. During the First World War United States naval forces operated in the Mediterranean, while in the Second it was in North Africa that the New World, coming again to redress the balance of the Old, first powerfully intervened in the European struggle. Since the defeat of the Axis the Mediterranean Squadron has been reestablished in the form of the Sixth Fleet, and a sizeable proportion of our naval strength has been stationed in these waters. Finally, it was here that the Truman Doctrine of underwriting the defense of free states against Communist subversion had its origin. The freedom of Greece and Turkey, and the existence of Tito's independent Communism, are today alike dependent on the power of the West to control this sea.

Indeed there appears to be an intimate connection between the independence of nations and the policy of the powers that control the seas, a relationship given classic expression in the memorandum of Sir Eyre Crowe on sea-power and British national policy. Writing in 1907, Crowe pointed out that since all maritime nations are, in a certain sense, neighbors, the state supreme at sea is in danger of finding itself the object of universal fear and hostility. This it can avoid only by a national policy designed to harmonize with the primary interests of the majority of other powers. Since, in an international system of sovereign states, the primary interest of each is the preservation of its independence, it appeared to Crowe that Britain, so long as she remained the leading naval power, would, in her own self-interest, inevitably be driven into opposition to any nation aspiring to dominate Europe. This analysis, illuminating for an understanding of British history, is equally applicable to the situation of the United States today. It is in this light that the strategic importance of the Mediterranean can be most clearly seen: the opportunity it affords to reach behind a power threatening Europe, and to sustain continental allies, has been vital to the British in their wars with the France of Louis XIV and Napoleon, and to the Western Allies in both First and Second World Wars. It is still vital today.

War, someone has said, is four-fifths geography, and so doubtless are all international affairs. The ability of British sea power to influence the course of Europe by way of the Mediterranean has always rested on possession of strategically located bases: Gibraltar since 1704, Malta since 1800, Suez and Egypt since the second half of the nineteenth century. But geography is a mutable thing: Maltas can be abandoned or defended, new oilfields create new rivalries, the railroad has moved mountains, the airplane has shrunk the seas. The political and economic developments of decades, no less than the immediate decisions of war, have powerfully affected the strategic problem of the Mediterranean in all but its prime essential, its existence as an avenue for the exertion of western power in eastern Europe.

Beginning in the late nineteenth century, the regions

along the southern shore of this sea underwent great changes owing to the expansion of the Mediterranean nations—Spain, France, Italy—onto the northern littoral of Africa. This expansion brought new life to the ports of Tripoli, Bizerte, Algiers, and Oran, and led to a cross-hatching of important Mediterranean seaways. Upon the ancient east-west passage to India was superimposed a series of north-south routes, important to Italy for the export of population, especially following American immigration restriction, and for relations with her new African colonies; vital to France for the import of colonial soldiery as a makeweight to the growing German population. And as these routes grew in importance, so the French and Italian navies grew in their defense.

In the northeastern corner of the Mediterranean the perennial Eastern Question, essentially that of distributing the pieces of the crumbling Ottoman Empire so that no one nation would profit unduly, was ultimately stabilized. This problem, which had so preoccupied the statesmen of the nineteenth century, disappeared in the twentieth with the emergence of a powerful postwar Turkey and with Russian post-revolutionary weakness.

At the same time the Eastern Mediterranean gained a new importance of its own. Its historic function as the short route to the Orient was modified by new developments: the economic maturity of Eastern Mediterranean countries which made them both exporters of raw materials and markets for manufactured goods; rising nationalism in these countries; and, above all, the immense importance, hardly less in peace than in war, of the Middle East as the prime source of Europe's oil.

It is against this shifting background that the strategies of the two World Wars must be judged. Both of these wars were fought for the control of Europe, a peninsula off the western coast of Asia with important sub-peninsulas of its own. Essentially, therefore, the questions concern the conduct of peninsular war, the continuing strategic problem of our time.

So far as the First World War is concerned, the Mediterranean was more notable as a bone of contention between the "Easterners" and "Westerners" in Allied councils than as a scene of conflict between the Allies and Central Powers. Turkey's naval strength was negligible; Austria's surface fleet was locked up inside the Adriatic, as were the German cruisers *Goeben* and *Breslau* within the Dardanelles. The only serious naval threat to the Allies came from the activities of Austrian and German submarines, and these, although costly, were held within bounds. But when the armies on the Western Front bogged down in the bloody stalemate of trench warfare, there arose in England a powerful "Eastern" school of thought which sought a strategical solution in a flanking attack in another theater. In 1915, furthermore, as in 1942, a major problem for the Western Powers was that of supplying and sustaining Russia. Despite vehement opposition from the "Western" school of strategic thought, whose adherents, possessed by belief in an early breakthrough in France, argued against all diversion of strength, these factors led to the attempt to force the Dardanelles.

Only by sea were the Western Allies neighbors to Russia; and Straits and Black Sea, the route of attack during the Crimean War, was now to be the route of succor. Admirable in its concept, the scheme was bungled in execution: divided councils, lack of strategic insight, and single-minded concentration on the Western Front led first to failure on the beaches, and ultimately to the collapse of Russia into tragic revolution. With the evacuation the great opportunity to exploit the twin advantages of the Mediterranean route to the east and of Allied naval superiority was lost. The alternative eastern effort, the Salonika expedition of October 1915, succeeded only in tying up sizeable Allied forces for a period of three years; not until September 1918 did they break out of the beachhead and advance against the crumbling Central Powers.

From the time of the evacuation of Gallipoli, therefore, the importance of the Mediterranean lay principally in its use as a convoy route. Exploitation of its true possibilities had not proved possible. The "Westerners" had won.

In the years between the wars two developments powerfully affected the strategic situation in the Mediterranean. The first of these was the increased military promise of the airplane, the second the shift of two Mediterranean powers, Italy and Spain, to the side of Germany. With the rapid advance in speed, range, and lifting power of aircraft went an even more rapid development of theoretical speculation regarding their role in any future conflict. Conservatives generally agreed that the airplane was here to stay; radicals contended that only the airplane was permanent. The arguments of the extremists found their classic formulation in the writings of General Giulio Douhet, an oddly unsceptical Italian, who affirmed the existence of an absolute weapon, and who produced an influential theory of war based less on an estimate of the capabilities of aircraft than on a faulty concept of mass psychology. The theories of Douhet, the expansionist policies of Mussolini, and the creation of a potent Italian Navy and Air Force, raised in many minds the possibility that the Mediterranean would no longer be an arm of the Atlantic and an avenue of British policy; that now, should the Italians so will it, this sea was divisible into two; indeed, that under certain circumstances it might be destined to become an Italian lake.

The likelihood of this prospect was increased when Mussolini took his country into the mutually tragic link with Germany. In 1882, when Italy had joined the Triple Alliance, her participation was limited by the proviso that it should never involve her in action against Great Britain. But the Duce, true to his definition of Fascism as "pure act," showed less strategical sophistication; like his compatriot Douhet, he seemed unable to measure probabilities and contingencies. Unable to perceive where the real interest of his country lay, urged onward by imperial aspirations, he founded long-term policy on the requirements of immediate maneuver. With the Ethiopian War he led Italy into a position of increasing political and economic depend-

ence on the northern neighbor, a neighbor not only poten-
tially much more powerful but one with antagonistic aims.

By 1939, when the disturbers of the peace linked themselves in the Pact of Steel, the Axis, unlike the Central
Powers in the First World War, extended from the Baltic
to North Africa and gripped the Mediterranean at its wasp-
like waist. And, as the Second War approached, it seemed
evident that the Axis had on its side not only the geography
of the Mediterranean narrows but also important naval
and air power. Future Allied support of an eastern front
against the nations seeking the hegemony of Europe now
appeared difficult if not impossible.

This danger was redoubled with the collapse of France.
But the Mediterranean revolution did not take place. That
it did not, as Admiral de Belot well shows, was in large part
the result of Axis military planning and strategy. For one
thing the airplane did not prove to be the absolute weapon;
for another, Italian power did not live up to its advance
notices; for a third, Italy, although desirous of driving
Britain permanently from the Mediterranean, had no strategic plan. As for the Germans, their intervention in this
theater, which might well have proven decisive, was weakened by their own indecision; by debates, reminiscent of
the struggle between Falkenhayn and Hindenburg, between those who wished to destroy Russia and those who
wished to strike down England first. The firm plan which
would have employed their preponderant force to best
advantage was notably lacking. The keys to the Mediterranean remained in British hands.

This seems the more remarkable when one remembers
the multiplicity of dangers which faced Britain in the summer of 1940. She had then to wage war on three separate
maritime fronts: on the oceans in defense of her trade
routes; in the Channel to protect the home islands against
invasion by overpowering German forces; and in the Mediterranean, where she was outnumbered by the Italians on
land, at sea, and in the air. And although the immediate
dangers on the Channel and ocean fronts—invasion and

conquest or rapid starvation—were the most pressing, loss of the Mediterranean would in the long run have been hardly less fatal. For Axis control of this sea would have linked Italy's Mediterranean possessions with those in East Africa, and led to the irruption of commerce raiders into the Indian Ocean. These events in turn, lacking naval strength at Singapore, would presumably have resulted in the immediate entrance of Japan into the war. Control of the Mediterranean would have given Germany and Italy access to Middle Eastern oil, thus alleviating a critical shortage, as well as to Balkan raw materials otherwise cut off by British dominance of the eastern basin. Finally, following the German attack on Russia, Axis control of the Mediterranean would have permitted support of that campaign by way of the Straits and Black Sea, and would have threatened if not prevented use of the Persian Gulf as the route of classical western support of the eastern front.

So long as the Axis could be confined to the Central Mediterranean these mortal dangers could be averted. Conversely, if complete control of the sea could be regained by Britain, not only would the way be opened for the return to Europe, but fleet units would be liberated for the Far East. The potential influence of events in the Mediterranean was thus worldwide.

Politically and militarily, then, the Mediterranean was vital to British success in the war. Retention of the eastern and western basins was essential to survival, while if the sea link between Italy and North Africa could be cut, great possibilities would lie open for the future. It was recognition of these facts that motivated the magnificent decision to reinforce the Army of the Nile at the moment when the invasion threat to the home island was at its height. It was this same recognition that led to the daring resolve to attempt the extremely unpromising venture of defending Malta, a small island, weakly garrisoned, completely dependent upon imports, only sixty miles from strong enemy air bases, and over two thousand miles from its own source of supply.

Brilliant though these actions were, they were defensive only. Force was lacking to gain a decision. Consequently, as the war dragged on, the old dispute between "Easterners" and "Westerners" returned in new guise, complicated by the lure of the air weapon. Where, in the previous conflict, the European front had rested on a line of trenches extending from Switzerland to the sea, it was now stabilized at the water's edge. The armies could not come to grips, and aerial bombardment replaced the trench warfare of 1914-1918 as the main reliance of the continental school of strategists. The result was that an immense productive effort was consecrated to the bombing offensive. Some forty-five per cent of British war production was devoted to the R.A.F., the balance being divided between Army and Navy. Thus it came about that in the spring of 1942, at the moment when Rommel was advancing to the gates of Egypt, the first thousand-plane bomber raid was made against Cologne. Prior to the arrival of American forces in the Mediterranean, strength was sufficient, although barely so, to hold Suez; there was never enough to drive the Axis from Africa. Thus not only were Greece and Crete lost, but it was never possible to divert sufficient naval force to intimidate Japan.

Not only did Allied emphasis on the production of bombers for the air war against Germany hamper the prosecution of the struggle for the Mediterranean, but it diminished the effectiveness of Allied naval dominance even after the tide of war had turned. In 1943, the year of the invasion of Sicily and Italy, the Mediterranean enjoyed comparatively plentiful resources, but the requirements of these operations forced the postponement of OVERLORD until 1944. In the latter year the transfer of landing craft to northern Europe led again to serious restrictions on Allied freedom of action in Italy and to delays in the invasion of southern France. Throughout the war the critical shortage of landing craft hampered the exploitation of the potentialities of dominant sea power, whether in the Mediterranean, in the Pacific and Indian Oceans, or in the planning of the cross-Channel invasion of Europe.

The strategic possibilities of the Mediterranean were thus fully exploited by neither side. But while Italian adherence to the German cause in the first instance, and the influence of Allied partisans of the doctrine of victory through air power in the second, combined to reduce the historic function of this sea, they did not destroy it. Despite all qualifications, it seems fair to say that Allied use of the Mediterranean was far superior in the Second World War to what it was in the First. The brilliant defensive strategy of the British was of prime importance, while the decision to give priority to the defeat of Germany, reached by the American Joint Board in September 1941, led inevitably to further Mediterranean operations once the United States entered the war. With active American participation, sufficient strength was brought to bear so that the great flanking operation of the Second War, the landings in North Africa, proved a brilliant success. Unlike the Dardanelles expedition, this one was both well conceived and well planned, and succeeded in its aim of expelling the Axis from Africa. Full control of the sea was thus gained; the passage to Europe was opened; Allied naval power was freed for action against the entire northern shore. The route to Russia was immensely shortened: the distance from New York to the Persian Gulf was reduced by 3,500 miles, that from Southampton by 4,800.

But although great profits were inevitable once control of the Mediterranean was gained, the indecision that had affected the mounting of the operation of 1915 now reappeared in the question of how to exploit that of 1942-1943. Alternatives constantly presented themselves: Sardinia or Sicily? Calabria or Liguria? the Balkans or western Europe? Foggia or Rome? southern France or the Ljubljana Gap and the plains of Hungary? At the great conferences and in the staff meetings these questions repeatedly obtruded themselves. In the heat of action the long view was obscured; lacking one overall decision numerous minor decisions were necessary, and were taken on largely short-term considerations.

Some of the responsibility, it would appear, must be attributed to the clamant American desire to strike Germany directly and at once, and to American suspicion of British motives in the Mediterranean. Admiral Leahy's comments on how "our persistent British friends strove mightily to create diversions in the Mediterranean area" have had many echoes. Yet it can be argued that proper British and American policy in this theater, strategic as well as political, was coincident.

For in the Joint Board Estimate of 11 September 1941, signed by General Marshall and Admiral Stark, one of the "major national objectives of the United States" was defined as the "eventual establishment in Europe and Asia of balances of power which would most nearly ensure political stability in those regions and the future security of the United States; and, so far as practicable, the establishment of regimes favorable to economic freedom and individual liberty." Applying this test, one can perhaps say that the true exploitation of the North African landings and of regained control of the Mediterranean came only in March 1947, with the proclamation of the Truman Doctrine and the extension of aid to Greece and Turkey. Policy today is a mere continuation of war by other means.

Indeed, materials for further argument between "Easterner" and "Westerner" remain: while emphasis is laid on the formation of a West European army the Near and Middle East remain a strategic prize of the first order; the Mediterranean, bypassing the Iron Curtain and bounded on both sides by friendly territory, still leads eastward; the Yugoslavs, the Greeks, and the Turks still sustain their independence. The Eastern Question has returned in a new dress. The strategic importance of the Mediterranean is undiminished.

It would be difficult to imagine an author better qualified than Admiral de Belot to write on the war in the Mediterranean. With a lifetime of training directed largely toward the problems of naval war in this arena, he found himself forced to remain a spectator and to apply his talents to the description rather than the prosecution of the struggle. A graduate of the Ecole Navale prior to the First World War, Admiral de Belot served principally in submarines during that conflict. Following the Armistice he commanded various French submarines, and attended the Naval War College. In 1937-1938 he served as chief of staff to Admiral Estéva, who was then in command of the French units aiding in the enforcement of the Nyon Agreements for the suppression of Italian submarine piracy during the Spanish Civil War. After a tour as commanding officer of the cruiser *Gloire*, he was assigned in 1940 to the command of a submarine flotilla in the North Sea, a post which he held until after the fall of France. In addition to his professional background Admiral de Belot has had personal experience with both the Italian and the British navies in wartime: in 1916-1917 he was a member of the French Adriatic Flotilla which operated with the Italian Navy; in 1940 his submarine flotilla was under the operational control of the British Admiralty.

In discussing the struggle for the Mediterranean, Admiral de Belot has applied his talents to good purpose. For although the literature of the Second World War has already reached vast proportions, it remains somewhat limited in nature. The personal narratives of the correspondents have been followed by those of the participants, and the meticulous official histories have begun to appear. But as yet there are few theater histories which cover in accurate and adequate detail the course of events in the major areas of the struggle. Most of the available literature is still either premature, or partial, or so detailed as to interest only the specialist. In a time when strategy and its consequences affect us all, and when some understanding of military affairs is more than ever essential, works such as this acquire an especial value.

JAMES A. FIELD, JR.

Preface

IN the course of the war in the Mediterranean, the British carried off some resounding victories at negligible cost to themselves. At Taranto, on 11 November 1940, they sank three Italian battleships while losing only two planes; at Matapan, in March 1941, they destroyed three heavy cruisers and two destroyers at the cost of one aircraft and its pilot. These deeds, played up by Allied propaganda, have perhaps given the general public the impression that so far as the Mediterranean was concerned the victory at sea was an easy one.

Nothing could be further from the truth, for the struggle was in fact exceedingly bitter. The accounts of the crews of the British warships and merchant vessels, which repeatedly and at terrible cost sailed through "Bomb Alley," the dangerous Sicilian Strait, have given us the plain truth about the conflict. Nor do the statistics lack eloquence: at the time of the Italian armistice, in September 1943, the British had lost as many ships in the Mediterranean as had the Italians.

Not only was the struggle arduous but the issue was long in doubt. All Frenchmen will remember the alternations of hope and despair with which they followed the fluctuations of the Libyan front, and the sensations with which they saw Rommel threaten Suez at a time when the Alexandria Fleet, weakened by heavy losses, was incapable of effective action.

Although the Mediterranean war, with its sudden changes of fortune, is fertile in lessons, a full understanding could not be gained from Allied sources alone. But today we have on the German side numerous statements of the military leaders, the Nuremberg Documents, the records of the Fuehrer Naval Conferences, and the reports of Admiral Weichold, the German naval commander in the Mediterranean. On the Italian side official publications are available, as are a mass of memoirs. Some of the latter are biased, but many are highly objective: for example, the

writings of Admiral Iachino, former commander in chief
of the Italian Fleet, and those of Admirals Bernotti and
Giamberardino, proclaim the complete intellectual honesty
of their authors.

Since Allied sources are also numerous, it is now possible
to write a history of the Mediterranean war based on docu-
mentary evidence.

The nature of the present work has made it necessary
to overlook many details which, interesting in themselves,
are of only secondary importance. What is here attempted
is a general survey. Emphasis has been laid on the actions
of the Axis, for these, being less well known in France than
those of the Allies, may have a greater interest for the
reader.

R. DE BELOT

Contents

PART I
THE FALL OF FRANCE

1. The Mediterranean Theater to 25 June 1940

The period of Italian neutrality

ON the first day of September 1939 the German armies rolled across the Polish frontier to begin the Second World War. Two days later, their ultimatums having expired without reply, Great Britain and France declared war on Germany. But although the conflict was thus broadened, it remained for some time confined to northern Europe, to Poland and to the Franco-German frontier. Peace, of a sort, continued to exist throughout the Mediterranean basin. Italy made no move.

This attitude on the part of the Italians, coming as it did after three years of Axis propaganda and the signing of an alliance, was, at the time, severely criticized in Germany. Nevertheless, in the light of the information that is now available, Italy's position with respect to her Axis partner seems to have been a strong one.

On 22 May 1939 Italy and Germany had signed the Pact of Steel. Article I specified that the two powers would remain permanently in contact and would agree on all questions of mutual interest; Article II provided for immediate consultation in the event that common interests were endangered; Article III stipulated that if one of the contracting parties became involved in military action the other would come to its aid with all its forces.

One week after the signing of the Pact of Steel, Mussolini sent Hitler a most secret memorandum by the hand of General Cavallero, an officer who, after subsequently becoming Chief of Staff, came to a tragic end: having refused his services to Germany following the Italian surrender, he was assassinated by the Gestapo and his murder disguised as suicide. The Duce's note, which is generally referred to today as the "Cavallero Memorandum," could have given Europe a breathing space, and perhaps, had the

3

respite been profitably used, might even have preserved the peace. In it Mussolini explained that, while war seemed to him inevitable, Italy would not be ready to participate for at least three years; he therefore requested the Fuehrer to postpone the outbreak of the conflict until 1942. To this suggestion Hitler agreed "in principle."

But on 11 August, at a meeting at Salzburg, Ribbentrop informed Count Ciano that Germany was about to attack Poland, and invoked the Pact. Not having been consulted in advance, the Italians could have made use of Articles I and II of the treaty to avoid the obligations of Article III. But the outbreak of war three years before the date they had expected had caught them unawares and they chose instead to act in the spirit of the Cavallero Memorandum, to attempt to delay rather than to avoid hostilities.

On 25 August, therefore, Mussolini telegraphed to Hitler that Italy could not enter the conflict unless she received substantial material assistance. He asked for six million tons of coal, two million tons of steel, seven million tons of oil, a million tons of lumber, 150,000 tons of copper; and Attolico, the Italian ambassador at Berlin, specified that delivery had to be made at once and prior to Italy's entry into war. Hitler replied on the same day that he was not in a position immediately to satisfy these demands, but that he nevertheless understood Italy's position and asked only that she should make threatening troop deployments so as to hold Franco-British forces on her frontiers. A further exchange of messages confirmed both the Italian neutrality and Hitler's acquiescence in it.

By these actions Italy laid herself open to charges of opportunism, but in fact, as is now known, the unpreparedness of her army was so shocking as wholly to justify her attitude. The upshot was the Italian proclamation of "non-belligerence," a term which to Mussolini implied a neutrality favorable to Germany. In the course of the war the Italians were to pass from this state of "non-belligerence" to one of active war against the Allies, and subsequently to "co-belligerence," or war on their side.

4

Although the expression "non-belligerence" had an alarming sound, the position taken by Italy in September 1939 was extremely fortunate for the Allies. Spain, exhausted by her civil war and disturbed by the Russo-German non-aggression pact, saw in the Italian decision a further reason for not entering the conflict and proclaimed her neutrality. In the Eastern Mediterranean things were still more favorable: there, in contrast to the situation in 1914, Turkey was now clearly partial to the Allies, and a treaty containing certain guarantees for Greece and Rumania, signed on 19 October between Turkey, France, and Britain, was followed up by staff conversations. Thus all the shores of the Mediterranean were either neutral or in the possession of the French or English; and although both powers were obliged to maintain local security forces, the war in this theater opened under the most favorable circumstances possible.

The absence of an enemy in the Mediterranean greatly facilitated the rapid transport of troops from North Africa to metropolitan France. This movement had for many years constituted one of the principal problems confronting the French staffs, and the Navy, whose particular responsibility it was, had considered all aspects of the question and had prepared for all eventualities. All students at the Naval War College had worked on this operation and many of the fleet problems had been based upon it. In the event, however, all was made easy by Italian neutrality and German naval weakness.

For the German Navy, at the outbreak of the war, was in no way capable of challenging the Allied control of the sea. In 1939 Germany possessed the two battleships *Scharnhorst* and *Gniesenau*, three pocket battleships, two heavy cruisers, five light cruisers, about sixty destroyers and escort vessels, and fifty-seven submarines of which only twenty-six were capable of operating outside the North Sea. Owing to their great numerical inferiority, the German surface forces could not hope to penetrate the Mediterranean, and the German submarines were fully occupied in the Atlantic.

5

Furthermore, since Hitler hoped that after the defeat of Poland France would accept a compromise peace, he issued orders to his submarines on 7 September to refrain from attacks on French ships; and although these instructions were revoked on 23 September, the German Navy made no attempt to dispatch submarines to the Mediterranean. Not until the autumn of 1941 did the first U-boats pass the Strait of Gibraltar.

Thus the Mediterranean situation in 1939 was as favorable to the Allies as it could possibly have been. France and Great Britain were able to send into the Atlantic much of the strength that had hitherto been held back to fight against Italy. Only a few light forces were left in the Mediterranean to protect Allied shipping against possible enemy raiders and to enforce the blockade.

At this time Allied strategy envisaged an intervention in the Balkans at some future date; with this in mind diplomatic preparations were undertaken and the 86th Algerian Division was sent to Syria. This flanking maneuver, dear to many of the French leaders, was based on the certainty that the Western front would be stabilized, an assumption which unfortunately proved to be mistaken.

Such, for the time being, were the benefits of Italian neutrality: it gave the Allies uncontested mastery of the Mediterranean; it permitted the planning of great designs for the future; and in the meantime it had a beneficial influence on relations between the Allies and the countries bordering on this sea.

The blockade

From the outset the blockade was tighter than it had been during the First World War. The lists of absolute and conditional contraband, which were at once drawn up by the Allies, were most extensive. On 8 September the control ports were designated. On 1 December the system of "navicerts" was instituted: a ship which permitted examination of its cargo in a neutral port by an Allied agent, and which carried no contraband, received a certificate

6

permitting rapid passage through the blockading cruisers. Not only did the ships themselves find real advantages in this method but it made Allied control simpler and more reliable. From the outbreak of war the imports of Germany's neutral neighbors were restricted to a reasonable amount, thus preventing any serious leakage to the enemy such as had existed in 1914-1918. In consequence of these measures the Danubian countries, which in peacetime send a large part of their exports to Germany via the Black Sea and the Mediterranean, were now restricted to the use of the Danube, and during the period when the river was frozen over were forced back on the railroads, whose capacity was still more limited.

In addition to these measures of blockade, the Allies, who possessed foreign exchange, conducted preventive buying at high prices of raw materials from Sweden, Belgium, and southeastern Europe, thus further complicating the German procurement problem. France, indeed, even supplied herself with war materials from Italy, a process of which the Reich complained bitterly. But the Italian Government replied that these sales permitted it to obtain certain supplies which were essential to its military preparedness, and that this increase in Italy's strength indirectly aided her ally. This argument seems perhaps somewhat disingenuous, but many Italians at this time were hesitant. "Win victories and we will be on your side," Ciano told the Allies.

But further steps in the tightening of the blockade adversely affected Allied relations with Italy. On 21 November 1939 the Allies announced that, in reprisal for illegal mooring of mines by Germany, they would seize all German exports no matter what the flag of the carrier. These measures, which violated the Declaration of Paris of 1856, were protested by Japan, Belgium, Holland, Denmark, and Sweden, but to no effect. On 27 November, King George signed the Order in Council providing for enforcement of the common decision beginning on 4 December, and on the 28th the French Government published a similar decree. Nevertheless no seizures were yet made of German coal exported to Italy under neutral flags.

In December, however, the Italian government sent a note to Great Britain protesting against the blockade and demanding both an end to all diversion of ships and the abolition of all controls on communication between Italy and her colonial empire. These demands the British government rejected on 9 January 1940, without, however, closing the door to further discussion. In February negotiations between Great Britain and Italy for a treaty of commerce broke down, and on the 18th Sir Percy Loraine, the British Ambassador at Rome, informed Count Ciano that all shipments of coal by sea from Germany to Italy would be stopped. In early March thirteen Italian colliers sailed from Germany for the peninsula; they were promptly intercepted in the North Sea by the British Fleet and the Italian protests were ignored.

Nevertheless, no matter how tight the blockade, it could have only minor influence on the progress of the conflict. Not only had Germany developed an autarky which diminished her vulnerability to economic warfare, but she could look to the U.S.S.R. to provide those raw materials which she lacked. On the other hand the blockade was profoundly irritating to the Italians and, while not the determining cause of their entry into war, helped Mussolini's propagandists to prepare public opinion.

Italy enters the war

IT IS a little unjust to say that Mussolini awaited the military developments of May 1939 before placing himself at the side of Germany, for his decision preceded these happenings. From the time of the collapse of Poland he had been certain of German victory. "England will be beaten," he told Ciano. "Inexorably beaten. This is a truth which you should get into your head." Furthermore, he considered intervention to be a question of honor. "We cannot be," he declared, *"gli eterni traditori*—the eternal traitors."

8

On 10 March 1940 Ribbentrop came to Rome bearing a letter from Hitler to the Duce. As a result of this visit Mussolini met the Fuehrer on the 18th at the Brenner Pass, and there promised to enter the war. On 31 March the Duce sent the King and the military leaders a most secret memorandum concerning the necessity of undertaking what he called "parallel war," a concept of which more will be heard. War was thus decided upon in Mussolini's own mind by the end of March; the fall of France merely helped him to overcome resistance at home, and led him to advance the date of hostilities.

The Italian intent was not lost upon the Allies. At the end of April Great Britain withdrew her merchant ships from the Mediterranean and, in concert with France, assumed the military dispositions which had been planned in case of war with Italy. By agreement Great Britain was responsible for the Eastern Mediterranean and for control of the Strait of Gibraltar; France was responsible for the western basin. One French battleship and three cruisers were placed under the orders of the British high command at Alexandria and, correspondingly, British submarines at Malta were put under French control. At sea all security measures were taken in good time, and at no moment did the two Allies let themselves be placed in danger of surprise by sudden Italian naval or air attacks.

In mid-May the rapid progress of the German armies on the western front caused Mussolini to move up the date of his entry into war, and the rising tone of the Italian press foreshadowed an early outbreak of hostilities. Among the complaints raised to drag the country into war, the blockade was given first place. On 11 May the press carried a report by Luca Pietromarchi, Chief of the Bureau of Economic Warfare, outlining the harm suffered by Italy from Allied naval controls and, in particular, from the way in which these had been enforced. On 8 June a new account proclaimed that Italy could no longer tolerate such a state of affairs.

9

At six o'clock on the afternoon of the 10th, Mussolini announced from the famous balcony of the Palazzo Venezia that war would begin at at one minute after midnight on the 11th. Many groups and associations—the Italian Academy, the University, the Association of War Wounded and Old Soldiers, the Corporation of Workers, and so on—had provided the Duce with messages of vigorous approval. Thus they supported what President Roosevelt was to call a stab in the back and what, still worse, was a blow struck against an already beaten combatant. Nevertheless countless Italians silently disapproved of this aggression against their kinsmen, their comrades of the Piave, the descendants of the soldiers of Magenta. A few days later, when signing the armistice with the defeated French, Marshal Badoglio said to his officers, "I have never felt more uncomfortable and unhappy than I do at this moment." The country entered the conflict profoundly disturbed in conscience and with all its hopes placed in a short war, a state of mind hardly favorable for enduring the long adversity which the future held.

On 7 June the Italian Admiralty had ordered all merchant ships which were unable to reach an Axis port to take refuge as rapidly as possible in neutral waters. In the hope of improving her balance of trade Italy had permitted her merchant marine to navigate without restriction, and the suddenness of her entry into war had prevented a timely recall of shipping. Two hundred and eighteen ships, totalling approximately 1,200,000 tons, remained abroad. This loss amounted to about a third of the entire merchant marine, and the ships thus lost were among the very best. It was a defeat the importance of which was not then fully realized, but which was later to have the most serious consequences, for a strong navy cannot exist without a corresponding merchant marine. The Italian Admiralty knew this; Mussolini's government did not. But subsequently the Duce came bitterly to regret what his Navy termed the initial tragedy of the merchant fleet.

Early skirmishes

THE Western Mediterranean theater is characterized
by its compartmentation. It is subdivided by the line of the
Balearic Islands, running from southwest to northeast, and
by the line Corsica-Sardinia-Sicily, which encloses the Tyrrhenian Sea. Because of this compartmentation, the French
naval command had divided its forces into three groups,
the Second Squadron at Toulon, the Third Squadron at
Oran, and a division of cruisers at Algiers. It had also set
up a theater command under Admiral Estéva, whose mission was to ensure the protection of convoys and to be
responsible for the establishment of security patrols. One
such patrol group was maintained in the southwest to
strengthen and to extend in depth the watch kept by the
British at Gibraltar; one group was stationed in the southeast between Sicily and Tunisia; one operated to the northeast in the upper Tyrrhenian Sea.

Admiral Estéva controlled light surface forces, submarines, and the air strength assigned to naval cooperation,
but the Squadrons were not under his orders; these reported directly to Admiral Darlan, Commander in Chief
of French Naval Forces, whose headquarters were at Maintenon. This dual organization was justified by the necessity
of shifting units between the high seas forces in the Atlantic and those in the Mediterranean, and also by the excellent
communications available to the Commander in Chief at
Maintenon, where the Navy had established a remarkably
well-organized command post. But the fact remained that
in the Mediterranean the French naval command was divided, and that the British commander in the Mediterranean was unable to treat with Admiral Estéva on all questions under his jurisdiction.

Such, briefly described, was the organization of the
French naval command and the distribution of French
naval forces in the Mediterranean at the time that Italy
entered the war. The dispositions were operative for too
short a time to be judged in the light of experience. But it

11

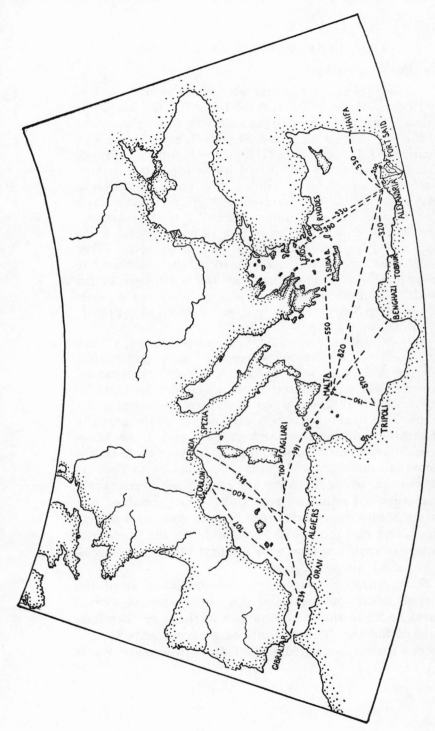

Fig. 1. The Mediterranean Theater, distances in nautical miles

seems probable that the light forces based in Tunisia would have had to be increased at the expense of those at Algiers and Oran, which were too distant to act effectively against enemy communications between Libya and Italy. In other words, it would have been necessary to shift French naval power closer to the Central Mediterranean, but this move would not have been possible without a prior reinforcement of Tunisian fighter strength.

As for the Italians, they had disposed their forces in the lower Tyrrhenian and in the Ionian Sea so as to facilitate their concentration by way of the Strait of Messina. On 5 June, prior to the declaration of war, they had given notice that a twelve-mile zone along the coasts of Italy, Albania, and the colonies was dangerous to navigation. On the 10th they announced that the Strait of Sicily was to be considered as having been mined and that neutral shipping was to use the Strait of Messina. They then proceeded to lay mines between Tunisia and Sicily, and this operation, carried out under the protection of cruisers and destroyers, went unhindered by Allied naval forces.

The only operation of importance in the Western Mediterranean was the bombardment of Genoa and Vado by the French Second Squadron. Originally planned for 12 June, this was delayed for forty-eight hours by indecision on the part of the French Government, which thought that Italy, faced with a greatly strengthened Germany, would attempt to prevent the crushing of France at the peace conference, and that she should therefore not be antagonized. In fact, of course, Mussolini was chiefly intent on seizing from France and Great Britain the greatest possible spoil at the least possible cost. On the 12th the bombardment of Bizerte by about twenty Italian airplanes persuaded the French Government, and at 2250 Admiral Darlan ordered the execution of the operation.

The Squadron, commanded by Admiral Duplat, got underway at 2100 on the 14th. At 0430 on the 15th the Vado Group (cruisers *Algérie* and *Foch*, Destroyer Divisions 1 and 5) opened fire on the fuel reservoirs and the metallurgical establishments at Savo, on the Ilva steelworks at Savona, and on the shore batteries. Enemy reaction was lively and the fire of the batteries straddled *Algérie*, but without hitting. The only Italian forces in the area were mobile coast defense units whose torpedo boats attacked twice but without result. At the same time the Genoa Group (cruisers *Dupleix* and *Colbert*, Destroyer Division 7) bombarded the gas works and metallurgical establishments at Sestri Ponente and also the shore batteries. There too, reaction was vigorous: the destroyer *Albatros* received a hit which put it temporarily out of action and killed or wounded fourteen men; and the old Italian torpedo boat *Calatafini*, which was escorting a minesweeper, happened upon the scene and made an unsuccessful torpedo attack on the French destroyers. Eight French bombers took part in these attacks, but the Italian Air Force made no appearance either at Vado or at Genoa. On the 14th, about noon, the Squadron returned to Toulon.

Meanwhile, in the Eastern Mediterranean the Alexandria Fleet, two battleships, one aircraft carrier, five cruisers, and destroyers, had sailed on 11 June and swept as far as the southern coast of Italy without meeting the enemy. On 13 June an Italian submarine sank the old British cruiser *Calypso* off Crete. The French cruisers from Alexandria carried out a search in the Aegean Sea and, in turn, the Italians sent forth their Second Squadron. On the 21st a force composed of the French battleship *Lorraine*, four British cruisers, and destroyers bombarded depots of munitions and stores at Bardia; the Italians did not reply. The opposing air forces carried out a few raids in which the Italians attacked Malta, Bizerte, Toulon, and Marseilles, and the French struck Savona, Genoa, Leghorn, Cagliari, and Palermo. All was on a small scale; these early operations at sea and in the air were little more than skirmishes.

On land on 21 June the Italian Army went over to the offensive on the Alpine front, an offensive which made little progress and which proved murderous to the attackers.

2. The Armistice and its Consequences in the Mediterranean

The Armistice and North Africa

O N 22 June 1940 the Franco-German armistice was signed at Rethondes. Although the Germans insisted on the demilitarization of the French Fleet and made the ending of hostilities conditional on the signature of the Franco-Italian armistice, which took place two days later near Rome, they made no demand for bases in the Mediterranean.

Of the various accounts that have been given of the haggling between Hitler and Mussolini prior to the armistices, the following appears probable. On 19 June the dictators met at Munich. Although Ribbentrop counseled moderation toward France, the better to isolate Great Britain, Mussolini insisted on Italian occupation of Corsica, of Tunisia, and of France as far as the Rhone. These terms were accepted by Hitler. Then on 22 June, after reflecting on Ribbentrop's arguments and seeing the German peace terms, Mussolini telegraphed to Berlin that in order to facilitate French acceptance of the armistice he would renounce his demands. Hitler replied that the Italians might do as they pleased. The upshot was that Italian territorial requirements were limited to the demilitarization of France's Mediterranean ports, of a 50-kilometer zone along the Alpine frontier, of the Mareth Line in Tunisia, and of a 200-kilometer zone along the Libyan-Algerian border. In addition Italy exacted the use of the port of Jibuti in French Somaliland and of the French section of the Addis Abbaba railroad.

The principal reason which led the Axis to make no major demands regarding French North Africa was the German desire to isolate Great Britain and force her to sue for peace by effecting a quick settlement with France. When, with the passage of time, it became clear that the

British were determined to continue the struggle, this attitude changed; but by that time the continued existence of the French Fleet had come to weigh heavily upon Axis decisions. For when it became obvious that the British would fight on, the Germans planned to reduce Great Britain first by invasion and then subsequently by block-ade. In either case the French Fleet could have been of great help to the British, and any attempt by Germany or Italy against Algeria or Tunisia would have put it back in the British camp. Thus the strength of the French Fleet contributed to the protection of North Africa; the Empire and the Fleet remained two strong cards in the hands of the French Government, each of which added to the other's value.

The Germans did not long remain satisfied with the terms of the armistice. As early as 15 July they attempted to modify its provisions, but their requests for bases in the south of France and in North Africa were evaded. Then in late summer, with the defeat of the Luftwaffe in the skies over London, both Germans and Italians saw their errors even more clearly. But they were still unable to agree on what attitude to adopt toward France. Admiral Raeder, the German naval commander, long cherished the hope of seeing the French Fleet, together with North Africa and Dakar, rally to the German side. Wholly preoccupied with the naval war, he thought such a move would prove deci-sive in the struggle against Great Britain, and with this in mind urged liberal concessions to France. On this point, however, Hitler was hesitant and Mussolini sceptical. The Duce insisted, although without success, that the French Fleet should be effectively disarmed, its personnel reduced, its fuel and ammunition unloaded.

Thus North Africa, object of the hopes and fears of the belligerents, became the occasion of a long diplomatic struggle, in which the often discordant moves of Germany and Italy were countered by those of the United States. Only with the greatest difficulty did France succeed in maintaining her position against the Axis until the moment of the Allied landings. After the war the chiefs of the O.K.W.[1] came to recognize that in neglecting North Africa at the time of the French Armistice Germany had made a major blunder. They felt that this question and that of the French Fleet could have been solved by threats or concessions and that, even had the French not given way to persuasion, North Africa could not have withstood a German attack.

Similarly, as the war dragged on, Mussolini was criticized by his countrymen for not having insisted, in June 1940, on at least the occupation of Tunisia, a step that would have wholly transformed the Italian strategic position in the Central Mediterranean. Several times the Duce vainly attempted to have the Libyan armies supplied by way of Tunisia and, failing in this, blamed his setbacks on the Germans, whom he accused of letting themselves be made fools of by the French. "In the presence of the French," he said, "the Germans are like provincials before the aristocracy, and their vision is completely warped." But at the time of the armistice it was Mussolini, unmindful of what the future might bring, who had himself renounced Tunisia.

The Axis blunder regarding North Africa might have been easily rectified by an attack on Gibraltar. For the Germans had occupied the western coast of France as far as the Pyrenees; they were thus in contact with Spain, and might logically have been expected to penetrate into the Iberian peninsula.

The Gibraltar question: German strategy and the Mediterranean

From the naval point of view no country in Europe holds a more important strategic position than Spain. From her Atlantic ports and islands Spain controls the sea lanes southwest of the continent; she has a long coastline on the Western Mediterranean, where, in addition, her Balearic

---

[1] Oberkommando der Wehrmacht, the supreme command of German armed forces.

Islands lie athwart the north-south routes; she can neutralize Gibraltar and close the Strait. The friendship or at least the neutrality of Spain is essential to both France and Great Britain.

On 22 September, five days after deciding to put off indefinitely the invasion of England, Hitler met Franco at Hendaye. According to German documents captured by the Americans, Franco here promised Hitler to enter the war on the side of the Axis, but he was careful not to specify a date and he advanced claims which the Fuehrer considered excessive. Then, on 18 November, Serrano Suñer, the Spanish Minister of Foreign Affairs, was summoned to Berchtesgaden. Prior to his departure a conference was held between Franco, Suñer, and the military leaders; all were of the opinion that involvement in the war was to be avoided at any cost. At Berchstegaden Hitler informed the Spanish minister that he had decided to attack Gibraltar: "My operation has been carefully prepared. Of 230 German divisions, 186 are now inactive." Suñer understood the hidden menace; but by arguing that capture of Gibraltar would be ineffective so long as Suez remained in British hands, that Spain was not ready, and that the Axis should first of all take Suez, he succeeded in avoiding an immediate and formal agreement. But on 7 December, Admiral Canaris, chief of the German intelligence and one of the strangest figures of the war, came to Madrid to renew pressure on the still reluctant Franco.

On 12 November Hitler had signed Directive 18 which set forth the general plans for the war, among which was the attack on Gibraltar, known by the code name of FELIX:

> Gibraltar will be taken and the Strait closed. The British will be prevented from gaining footholds elsewhere in the Iberian peninsula, or in the Atlantic Islands.

As a result of the occupation of Gibraltar, the Atlantic Islands, especially the Canaries and the Cape Verdes, will take on great importance. The Commanders in Chief of the Navy and the Air Force will study methods of reinforcing the Spanish defence of the Canaries and the possibility of occupying the Cape Verde Islands. The question of the occupation of Madeira and the Azores will also be examined and the results of these investigations submitted to me as soon as possible.

It will be seen that the question of Portuguese neutrality did not trouble the Fuehrer.

The Gibraltar operation was to be undertaken with assistance from the Spanish, who were, however, to have only a secondary role, but without any call on Italian forces. The Air Force and parachute troops were to play the leading parts in the conquest of the fortress. Naval action, limited in the beginning to submarine attacks on British vessels fleeing the port, would in the later stages of the operation become increasingly important, both for defense of the Strait and for seizure of the Atlantic islands. Admiral Raeder, for example, thought it essential to have the use of the port of Dakar to carry out the Cape Verde Islands operation.

Nevertheless, the seizure of the Portuguese islands— Madeira, the Azores, and the Cape Verdes—seemed highly problematical. Indeed, Keitel, chief of staff of the O.K.W., thought the British would occupy these islands as soon as the attack on Gibraltar was begun, and that the whole operation would thus lose most of its value since possession of the islands would permit Great Britain to avoid the threat to her communications resulting from the loss of Gibraltar. This was a strong argument, but even if the islands had been lost to Germany the conquest of Gibraltar would have prevented British access to the Mediterranean from the Atlantic, and it seems highly probable that this enterprise would have succeeded. Doubtless the Rock would have resisted valiantly, but even had the Germans failed to seize it they would nevertheless have rendered untenable the harbor and the airfield on the Bay of Algeciras. The British, who were at this time very weak, could not have seized enough Spanish territory to protect the fortress. With Gibraltar once neutralized, the Axis, holding Algeciras, Ceuta, and Tangier (which Franco had occupied at the beginning of November), would have been master of the Strait, and French North Africa would have lost much of its importance.

In any event, Franco's evasions delayed the execution of the plan. On 11 December, on instructions from Hitler, Keitel signed the following order: "Operation FELIX will not be undertaken as the desired political conditions have not been obtained. Planning will be continued . . . . preparations will be deferred."

On 31 December Hitler wrote to Mussolini: "All our preparations for entering Spain on 10 January and for attacking Gibraltar at the beginning of February had been completed. . . . I am greatly disturbed by Franco's decision, which does not correspond to the help which we—you, Duce, and I—gave him when he was in difficulties." Thus it was owing to the intransigeance of the Spanish Government that the plan fell through. The Axis never finally abandoned it, but by midwinter 1940-1941 the venture appeared less promising, and on 8 February the High Command reported: "It is clear that in view of operations MARITA and BARBAROSSA[1] the troops held in reserve for operation FELIX will have to be used in the new undertaking."

After losing the chance to dominate the Western Mediterranean from North Africa at the time of the French armistice, Germany lost a second by not seizing Gibraltar at the end of 1940. "With or without the consent of the Spanish," Mussolini said later, "it was necessary to go into Spain." Why did Hitler draw back? Reluctance to attack a friendly country, fear of repeating Napoleon's mistake and starting a guerilla war, lack of foresight—all these reasons played a part. So to the astonishment of many military leaders, and particularly of naval officers, the German troops which had reached Hendaye did not cross the frontier, and La Linea, the little Spanish village at the foot of Gibraltar, whose total destruction might well have been

[1] The projected invasions of Greece and Russia.

predicted, went through the war without receiving a scratch.

The Gibraltar question, however, was only one aspect of the larger Mediterranean problem which long divided the German high command. It is often said that the Germans are too landminded, that they do not understand naval questions, that they failed to see the importance of the Mediterranean, and that this was one of the principal reasons for their defeat. Such a view is perhaps too strong. It is obvious that the German high command, which from the instant that a war breaks out must fight against powerful land armies, is unable to look at military problems from the point of view of the British Admiralty. But Hitler's greatest error was in underestimating the difficulties of an attack on the U.S.S.R., and this can hardly be called an error of naval strategy.

It was not without great apprehension that his military commanders followed Hitler against Russia. While not fully appreciating the strength of the Russian Army, they had the traditional fear of war on two fronts and, after the defeat of the Luftwaffe over England, many of them had begun to look towards the Mediterranean. Here Goering had grandiose projects: an invasion of Spain and of Morocco followed by the conquest of Dakar, an invasion of the Balkans and of Asia Minor through Turkey, an invasion of Egypt through Tripolitania. Grand Admiral Raeder, who throughout the war was often opposed to Goering on tactical questions, had similar ideas regarding the orientation of general strategy. He was convinced that the U.S.S.R. would not dare to attack Germany and, on the contrary, that the United States would enter the war to uphold Great Britain. He therefore thought it essential to solve the Mediterranean question before having to cope with American power. In his view it was necessary to capture Suez and deploy the Italian fleet in the Indian Ocean, and, to the westward, to secure first Gibraltar and then Dakar, the latter in so far as possible with French concurrence. From Dakar it would be possible to threaten the

American continent and thus force the United States to hold back for defensive purposes a part of the resources intended for Great Britain.

It will thus be seen that naval questions were not neglected by the German commanders. Furthermore, Raeder thought that once control of the Mediterranean had been won the Russian question would appear in a different light. But Hitler felt, and with equal justification, that if he were to eliminate Russia the whole Mediterranean question and, indeed, the whole war with Great Britain, would be completely transformed. In short the problem boiled down to the decision as to whether Great Britain or Russia was to be overthrown first. Hitler chose the second alternative; according to Raeder he had decided as early as 1937 to drive the U.S.S.R. from the Baltic. But even in choosing the attack on Russia the Axis had time, prior to June 1941, to take the important precaution of eliminating Gibraltar.

As things turned out, Germany did not intervene in the Mediterranean in 1940. In 1941 she did, but this action, undertaken without a long-range strategic plan, was intended merely to sustain her failing ally and to protect the southern flank of her armies. Finally, in the spring of 1942, Hitler decided to intervene with a major offensive purpose, the capture of Suez. But by then he had as enemies Great Britain, the U.S.S.R., and the United States, and it was too late. Suez was not reached and, in the west, the blunder of the French Armistice went unrepaired and Gibraltar remained open.

The problem of the French Fleet

ALTHOUGH the French Government steadily maintained that under no circumstances would it let its ships fall into the hands of the enemy, the fate of the French Fleet profoundly troubled Great Britain. On 25 June, the day after the signature of the Franco-Italian armistice, Churchill stated to the House of Commons: "The safety of Great Britain and the Empire is powerfully, though not decisively, affected by what happens to the French Fleet."

The main naval items in the Franco-German armistice were contained in Article VIII, worded as follows:

The French war fleet, with the exception of those units released to the French Government for protection of French interests in the colonial empire, is to assemble in ports to be later designated, and is there to be demobilized and disarmed under the control of Germany and Italy. Designation of these ports will follow the peacetime home port assignments of the ships.

The German Government solemnly declares to the French Government that it does not intend to use during the war for its own ends the French war fleet stationed in the harbors under German control, with the exception of units necessary for guarding the coasts and for minesweeping. It further solemnly and expressly declares that it does not intend to bring up any demands respecting the French fleet at the time of the conclusion of the Peace Treaty.

With the exception of that part of the French war fleet which will be designated for the protection of French interests in the colonial empire, all warships outside France are to be recalled to France."

Article XII of the armistice with Italy was analogous to Article VIII of the Franco-German armistice.

The French delegates had attempted to have the requirement concerning disarmament in home ports modified, observing that French ships based in the Atlantic and the Channel would be in danger of destruction from British air attacks. Keitel had then pointed out that the German text used the word *soll*, which left the question open to discussion by the Armistice Commission, and not the word *muss*, which is imperative, a distinction not apparent in the French text for both *muss* and *soll* are translated by the French word *doit*.

Certain French ships had as their home ports Brest, Lorient, and Cherbourg; sending them to these ports would have effectively placed them in the power of the Germans.

On this point, however, the discussion was largely academic, for at the time of the armistice the French Fleet was divided between unoccupied French ports and ports under British control. So far as those in the latter situation were concerned, it was quite clear that Great Britain would not permit their departure, and not only would she never have been willing to have a ship of military importance brought back from Africa to a French Atlantic or Channel port, but she also had the power to prevent such moves. No responsible officer ever thought of attempting to send *Richelieu* from Dakar back to Brest.

Nevertheless the British Admiralty saw danger in the presence of French ships not only at Toulon but also in Africa; it would only accept as a solution their disarmament in a British port or, if necessary, in America. The British Government felt that it had freed France from the obligations of the Treaty of Alliance only on condition that her ships were sent to ports under its control. Such a condition, which the Germans would never have accepted, would have prevented conclusion of the armistice which the French Government believed necessary. The positions were thus irreconcilable.

Like Churchill, the British Admiralty thought it essential to neutralize the French Fleet, and it requested the Government to authorize the desired measures. This authorization was given following a dramatic meeting of the War Cabinet at Downing Street in which the decision of the members was unanimous. Necessity knows no law, and furthermore an illustrious precedent was available: because the League of Armed Neutrality appeared to threaten British maritime supremacy, Nelson, on 2 April 1801, had destroyed the neutral Danish Fleet at Copenhagen.

While these events were taking place Admiral Darlan issued a series of orders to the French Fleet, knowledge of which is necessary to an understanding of events. On 20 June he addressed the commanders of the various naval forces in the following message:

1. The Admiral of the Fleet believes he may be able to retain command of the naval forces, and is taking the steps necessary to this end.

2. In the event that the Admiral of the Fleet is unable freely to exercise his command, the naval forces will be placed under the orders first of Admiral de Laborde, then of Admiral Estéva, then of Admiral Abrial, then of Admiral Gensoul.

3. All these flag officers or those who may succeed them will comply with the following general orders: to fight fiercely to the end so long as a French government, legal and independent of the enemy, has not given orders to the contrary; to disobey all other governments; no matter what orders are received, never to abandon a fighting ship to the enemy intact. 1330/20/6.

On 24 June Admiral Darlan sent a further message:

Armistice clauses are being sent you in plain language by other means. I use this last chance of sending enciphered communications to make known my thoughts on the subject.

1. Demobilized warships must remain French with French flags, reduced French crews, stationed in French metropolitan or colonial ports.

2. Secret preparations for sabotage will be made so that no enemy or foreigner seizing a ship by force will be able to make use of it.

3. If the Armistice Commission charged with interpreting the text decides otherwise than in Paragraph 1, at the moment of execution of this new decision and without further orders warships will either be taken to the United States or, if no other way exists of keeping them from the enemy, will be scuttled. Ships thus taking refuge abroad will not be used for war operations against Germany or Italy without orders from the Commander in Chief of French Naval Forces. 1245/24/6.

On 26 June he again addressed the fleet in the following order of the day:

I have received the clauses of the two armistices; none is dishonorable. Our Navy and our Air Force will see in the exceptional treatment accorded them tribute to their conduct and recognition of their worth. . . . You will receive from me the complete texts, and the agreements which mitigate their

severity on certain points. . . . We keep all our ships and naval
aircraft, active service personnel is not limited, and our adversaries have solemnly undertaken not to touch our navy in the
peace treaty. Being defeated, what more could we expect? The
agreements must now be carried out with dignity. To do otherwise would be finally to consummate the ruin of our country,
already gravely wounded by defeat. To answer interested ap-
peals from abroad would result in our metropolitan territory
becoming a German province.

Our former allies must not be listened to: let us think as
Frenchmen, let us act as Frenchmen. . . . The anxiety of the
Navy springs from lack of knowledge of the facts and of the
decisions that have been taken. . . . I appeal to the spirit of
discipline which was our strength during hostilities. I cannot
believe that those who faithfully obeyed me when I could ask
them to die for the country will lack the moral courage to
obey me in order to ensure its rising again, no matter how
difficult it may be.

Mers el Kébir

THE French Atlantic Squadron had been concentrated
at Mers el Kébir, where it was about to begin its demobilization. It comprised four battleships, *Dunkerque, Strasbourg, Provence*, and *Bretagne*, and six destroyers, *Volta,
Mogador, Terrible, Lynx, Tigre*, and *Kersaint*, all under
command of Admiral Gensoul. Also at Mers el Kébir were
the aircraft transport *Commandant Teste*, and a few torpedo boats and submarines attached to the Algerian-Tu-
nisian Sea Frontier.

Early in the morning of 3 July Admiral Somerville arrived off Mers el Kébir at the head of an imposing British
force which included the great battle cruiser *Hood*, the
battleships *Resolution* and *Valiant*, the aircraft carrier *Ark
Royal*, two cruisers, and nine destroyers, and sent in to
Admiral Gensoul an ultimatum requiring that he adopt
one of the following courses of action: to get underway and
continue the fight with Great Britain against the Germans
and Italians, to sail with reduced crews for a British port,
or to take the Squadron with reduced crews to a French

port in the West Indies where it would either be disarmed or placed under American supervision. The ultimatum ended as follows:

If you refuse these fair offers, I must, with profound regret, require you to sink your ships within six hours.

Finally, failing the above, I have the orders of His Majesty's Government to use whatever force may be necessary to prevent your ships from falling into German or Italian hands.

After having consulted Naval Headquarters at Vichy, Admiral Gensoul rejected the ultimatum.

It is not easy to obey foreign orders under threat of force.

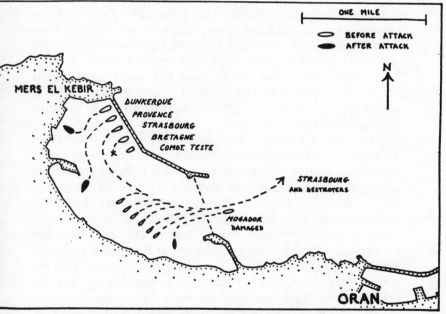

Fig. 2. The Action at Mers el Kébir, 3 July 1940

Nevertheless, in view of the interests at stake, such a consideration should have been surmounted. By accepting the ultimatum the admiral would have saved his Squadron and preserved it for the future. But he would also have violated the armistice, which might have involved disastrous consequences, perhaps even resumption of the struggle and the occupation of North Africa. It cannot be known with certainty how the Germans would have reacted, but the French command had to weigh all the consequences. Discussion with the British continued throughout the day, the time limits being extended by Admiral Somerville. Having consulted his rear admirals, the Division Commanders, who considered the ultimatum unacceptable, Admiral Gensoul offered to disarm his ships where they lay, but felt himself unable to make further concessions. At about 1750, all chances of agreement appearing to be exhausted, the British squadron opened fire.

It was not a battle but an execution. The French ships, assembled in a restricted space, had not the slightest freedom of maneuver. Admiral Gensoul had had the fleet get up steam but had been unable to get underway, having been informed at the outset that any movement would break off negotiations. The British squadron was aided by aerial spotting while no French aircraft were in position to intervene immediately.

The British bombardment lasted less than a quarter of an hour, the French ships replying while attempting to get underway. *Strasbourg* succeeded in this difficult maneuver and, although pursued and attacked by aircraft from *Ark Royal*, was able to reach Toulon accompanied by a few destroyers. *Dunkerque* was hit in the engines and immobilized. *Bretagne* received two 15-inch shells, one in a fire room, the other in the magazines, and rapidly capsized. *Provence*, leaking badly, had to be run aground. The destroyer *Mogador*, already underway, was hit by a large caliber shell which removed its stern. No losses, however, resulted from magnetic mines laid by the British aircraft.

During the following days British aviators, sent to ascertain the condition of the French fleet, reported that *Dunkerque* appeared insufficiently damaged. On 6 July three squadrons of torpedo planes returned to the attack. A trawler armed with depth charges was alongside *Dun-*

kerque and this, hit by a torpedo, blew up, causing further damage to the battleship. The losses of the French Fleet on 3 and 6 July totalled over 1,300 dead.

Nevertheless, ships sunk in a shallow port are rarely placed permanently out of action. After preliminary repairs all ships except *Bretagne* were able to reach Toulon, where work was continued and where it would have gone rapidly had the Germans only furnished the necessary materials. It may be questioned whether, from the British point of view, the disadvantages of the operation did not outweigh its benefits. It infuriated the French Navy, thus producing a state of mind which was to influence subsequent events. Furthermore, the French Government was now obliged to accept the concentration of most of the Fleet at Toulon, where it was trapped, a situation which might have been avoided if the affair at Mers el Kébir had not taken place. Following the defeat all French forces— land, sea, and air—suffered great spiritual agony, but it was the Navy which had the most painful Calvary, a Calvary marked by numerous stations not the least tragic of which was Mers el Kébir.

Alexandria

AT ALEXANDRIA things worked out with the least possible difficulty. At the time of the armistice the French Squadron under Admiral Godfroy, moored in the port alongside the British ships, contained the old battleship *Lorraine*, the cruisers *Suffren, Tourville, Duguay-Trouin,* and *Duquesne,* the three destroyers *Fortuné, Forbin,* and *Basque,* and the submarine *Protée,* which had arrived after the armistice. The British Fleet, much more powerful, was composed of the four battleships *Warspite, Ramillies, Malaya,* and *Royal Sovereign,* the aircraft carrier *Eagle,* and cruisers and destroyers. Relations between the two commanders, Admiral Godfroy and Admiral Cunningham, were on a basis of mutual friendship and trust.

Despite the superiority of the British Fleet, a battle in the center of the port might have involved serious losses.

Not only did Admiral Cunningham wish to avoid these, but the thought of such a struggle was most repugnant to him. The two commanders, equally lofty in character, brought to their discussions a notable spirit of conciliation.

Shortly after the armistice Admiral Cunningham sent Admiral Godfroy a friendly note, informing him that the British Admiralty was opposed to the sortie of the French squadron. This was followed on 3 July by a message requesting Admiral Godfroy to choose one of the following alternatives: to join forces with the British Navy, to permit his fleet to be disarmed in the port, or to scuttle the fleet.

In the course of the discussion that followed, Godfroy stated that the first two terms seemed to him to be in violation of the armistice. Like Gensoul at Mers el Kébir, he could not overlook the consequences his decisions might have for the French Government. Therefore he accepted the third solution, and resigned himself to scuttling his fleet off Alexandria. But in the evening word was received by radio of the events at Mers el Kébir, high feeling ran through the French Squadron, and Admiral Godfroy seriously considered the possibility of battle. Nevertheless, in the course of still another interview, the two admirals again agreed to temporize.

In the meantime an order had been received from Admiral Darlan: "Get underway immediately, if necessary by force." The order could not be carried out. In the crowded harbor, without the help of tugs and under the fire of the British Fleet, such a maneuver amounted to suicide. Admiral Godfroy replied: "Anchorage such as to prevent sortie even by fighting our way out."

During the night Admiral Cunningham took advantage of his freedom of maneuver to move his ships into position for battle. British destroyers took station so as to be able to torpedo the French warships at the first signal. After having consulted his commanding officers, Admiral Godfroy decided to accept the solution of disarmament on the spot, and the agreement made by the two admirals was approved by M. Pozzi, the French Minister at Cairo. Admiral Cunningham had greatly exceeded the time limits fixed by the British Admiralty, and this factor, together with the understanding and coolheadedness of both British and French commanders, enabled them to avoid the worst. But it is also fair to recognize that their situation was less difficult than that at Mers el Kébir—there if the French squadron had joined the British ships, it might have been considered by the Germans as a flagrant violation of the armistice and have had grave consequences for France. At Mers el Kébir Admirals Gensoul and Somerville found themselves in the most extraordinary and dramatic circumstances that two squadron commanders could face.

It is to the honor of the admirals who commanded the British Fleet at Alexandria that in the following years they never attempted to seize the disarmed vessels, although twice the advance of Rommel might well have induced them to do so, and this despite the fact that in 1942 the Germans attempted to seize the French ships at Toulon. In 1943 the French Alexandria Squadron voluntarily resumed the struggle against the Axis.

Meanwhile on 3 July Great Britain seized from their unsuspecting crews those French ships that had taken refuge at Portsmouth, Plymouth, and Sheerness. These were turned over to the Free French Forces of General de Gaulle. And at Dakar, on 8 July, the battleship *Richelieu* was attacked and damaged.

Following this series of events Italy modified the clauses of the armistice and authorized France to maintain her Mediterranean military ports in a state of readiness. The warships kept their crews, their provisions, and their munitions, and thus in actual fact remained in commission. Mussolini, indeed, thought this situation dangerous for the Italian Fleet, but the Germans, after Mers el Kébir, cherished hopes of drawing the French Navy into the conflict on their side. The French Government had forbidden British ships and aircraft to come within twenty miles of the coast of France under penalty of being attacked without further warning, and on 7 July, the day after the second attack on *Dunkerque*, French air units bombarded Gibraltar by way of reprisal. Fortunately these hostilities remained limited.

Other incidents of a less serious nature occurred subsequently. For two years the French Navy and Merchant Marine labored to improve the country's food supply by imports from the Empire overseas. Amid the noise of battles this essential action passed unnoticed and remains unrecognized. Owing to the contradictory requirements of the Allies and the Axis it was carried out under the greatest difficulties, difficulties which were surmounted without too serious consequences for the country as a result, in part, of the coolness of all ranks of seagoing personnel.

PART II
THE DUEL
BETWEEN GREAT BRITAIN
AND ITALY

3. Italian Strategy

The Italian war potential

MUSSOLINI used to say that Italy was an island. Cut off from the continent by the easily defensible Alpine masses, she is almost entirely surrounded by the Mediterranean. She has a very long coastline and little hinterland except in the valley of the Po; eighty per cent of her imports come by sea; she carries on an intensive inter-island and coastal trade; finally, she possessed a considerable overseas empire. Italy lives by the sea, and for her the decision to go to war with Great Britain was more serious than for any other European power.

Even assuming that the peninsula can manage to feed itself in the event of a blockade, it still lacks four important raw materials: iron, coal, petroleum, and rubber. From an economic point of view Italy is a burden to her allies, particularly so in the case of Germany, who was herself lacking in these materials with the single exception of coal. Nor had Italy had either the time or the means to accumulate stockpiles. She was short of foreign exchange which, prior to the war, Mussolini had rather childishly counted on acquiring from the Rome International Exposition in 1942. In June 1940 the Minister of Armaments estimated that all reserves would be used up within a few months; only the Navy had accumulated stocks of fuel which permitted it to hold out, although with difficulty, until the autumn of 1941.

Italian industry, although often of excellent quality, was weak; its capacity was estimated at a tenth of that of Germany and, in the course of a staff conference in 1943, Mussolini declared that this figure should be reduced to a sixteenth. In the first six months of 1943 Italy produced 900,000 tons of steel; in this same year the United States produced ninety million tons. The Duce spoke with pride of his eight million bayonets, but today God is no longer on the side of the big battalions but on that of the big factories. Despite the ability of Italian scientists, the lack of a large industrial base had kept research behind the times. Thus Italy, once cut off from the sea, was unable to sustain a major war without powerful German assistance, and we know from the declarations of General Favagrossa, the Minister of Armaments, how inadequate this help in fact proved to be.

In order to magnify German assistance Mussolini issued the following figures covering material supplied in 1940-1942: coal, 40 million tons; iron, 2.5 million tons; rubber, 22,000 tons; oil, 421,000 tons; aviation gasoline, 220,000 tons. But these figures demonstrate that the sum total of assistance was slight, especially in liquid fuels, and in no way comparable to the scale of the conflict. The result was that the wartime expansion of the Italian forces was small, and on 8 March 1943, after three years of war, Mussolini wrote to Hitler: "Our tragedy is that we are forced to fight a people's war with arms left over from the war of 1914-1918." By that time he had been forced to recognize that Italy had attempted the role of a first-class power with only a third-rate industrial base.

At the outbreak of the war the Italian Fleet contained four 23,000-ton battleships, *Cavour, Cesare, Duilio, Doria,* built in 1911 but modernized before hostilities began; two 35,000-ton battleships, *Littorio* and *Vittorio Veneto,* being completed; two 35,000-ton battleships, *Roma* and *Impero,* under construction. The Navy possessed seven 10,000-ton cruisers, *Trento, Trieste, Zara, Fiume, Gorizia, Pola, Bolzano;* six of 5,000 tons, *Barbiano, Giussano, Colleoni, Bande Nere, Diaz, Cadorna;* six of between 7,000 and 8,000 tons, *Montecuccoli, Attendolo, Duca d'Aosta, Eugenio di Savoia, Garibaldi, Duca degli Abruzzi;* twelve 3,400-ton cruisers of the *Regolo* class under construction; and two old ex-German cruisers. Italy had in service about sixty destroyers of between 1,000 and 2,000 tons and eight more building. Of her submarines, twelve ocean-going boats of over 1,300 tons were in service and six were building; forty-eight of medium range were in operation and six were building; fifty-three coastal submarines were in service, as were eight submarine mine-layers. She thus had a total of one hundred and twenty-one submarines in active service and a dozen under construction. Finally the Italian Fleet contained numerous motor torpedo boats, the famous M.A.S. (*motoscafi anti-sommergibili*) of under 20 tons, and the M.S. (*motosiluranti*).

The war effort affected both the completion of the battleships and the construction of smaller vessels. The battleships *Littorio* and *Vittorio Veneto* were commissioned in late 1940; *Roma* was completed in early 1943; *Impero* was never finished. Of the dozen cruisers under construction only three, *Regolo*, *Scipione*, and *Pompeo Magno*, were completed; the others never entered service.

Increasingly, as the war went on, the need for escort vessels became urgent. In the Italian terminology, those of between 1,000 and 3,000 tons were designated as destroyers, while those of less than 1,000 tons were classed as torpedo boats. So far as the former are concerned, eight ships of the *Soldato* class entered service during 1942, and eight of the *Commandante* class were under construction at the time of the Italian armistice. In addition to these, Italy acquired in the course of the war a few French and Yugoslav destroyers. The Italians also built several series of torpedo boats: eight of the "arms" or *Alabarda* class of 700 tons, eight escort torpedo boats of the "wind" or *Ciclone* class, and eight of the "warlike quality" or *Ardito* class. Six over-age torpedo boats were seized from the Yugoslavs, as were a few 600-tonners from the French at Bizerte.

As the need became more and more pressing, two new classes of escort vessels, especially suited for Mediterranean operations, were built. The first consisted of about sixty corvettes of 600 tons with diesel-electric propulsion; the second of about forty V.A.S. (*vedette anti-sommergibili*), wooden ships of 70 tons. Finally, the Italian Navy increased the number of its motor torpedo boats. But despite all efforts it was unable to replace its losses and, in view of the colossal production of the Allies, its relative importance steadily declined.

Of the six ocean-going submarines which the Italians had under construction in 1940, none was completed. A few 1,370-ton submarines were converted into gasoline and oil tankers, while others served as undersea transports. The Italian Navy did, however, build two cargo-carrying submersibles, *Remo* and *Romulo*, and about twenty 700-ton submarines which were considered especially suitable for war in the Mediterranean. In Yugoslavia the Italians captured a few submarines and in 1942 they seized nine old French boats at Bizerte; these they incorporated into their formations but with little profit.

Special mention must be made of what the Italians called the *mezzi navali d'assalto*, or assault machines. During the war of 1914-1918 the Italian Navy had accomplished, with the primitive devices of the day, feats of arms which have remained justly legendary, and in this respect the sailors of 1940 showed themselves worthy of their forebears.

These assault machines were of four main types. First, the pocket submarines, *sommergibili tascabili*, of about 30 tons, carrying two torpedoes and manned by two men; these were similar to those later employed by the Japanese at Pearl Harbor. The Italian and Japanese Navies had not cooperated before the war on the construction of these small vessels, and it is difficult to establish which of them deserves credit for priority of invention. The Italian pocket submarines were principally employed in the Black Sea against the Russian Fleet, and Admiral Raeder has given them deserved praise.

The second group, the piloted torpedoes or *siluri pilotati*, were long-range torpedoes piloted by two men in diving suits seated astride them. Known to the Navy as *maiali* or "hogs," these devices were intended to penetrate enemy ports and approach the target, whereupon the crew detached the warhead of the torpedo which contained the explosive charge and fastened it by special methods to

38

the hull of the target ship, often under a bilge keel. Since the warheads were provided with delayed action fuses, the crew of the torpedo had, at least in theory, time to escape the explosion. These torpedoes proved particularly effective and all navies built similar ones. In France they are often called "human torpedoes" but the Italian term "piloted torpedo" seems a better one. The Japanese were to build similar machines but here the crews were deliberately sacrificed and went up with the torpedo. In Japan these torpedoes were part of the suicide corps and the term "human torpedo" may be reserved for them.

The third class of assault machines was composed of motor boats loaded with explosives, *motoscafi esplosivi*, modern versions of the ancient fireships. The crew aimed the boat at the target, and then at a distance of about a hundred yards leaped overboard while the motorboat continued to its goal. The Japanese were to use similar machines, but here again they sacrificed the crews by sending them all the way to the end.

The last type consisted of explosive mines towed by swimmers, who attached them beneath the hull of the target ship.

These assault machines were organized as part of the Tenth M.A.S. Flotilla, based at Spezia, to which were also attached the submarines and other ships used to carry them to their targets. The Italian Navy had been preparing these methods of attack since 1935. Fortunately for the Allies, they had not been fully perfected by the time the war began but, as will be seen, after a few failures these machines provided the means of gaining great successes.

To return to orthodox methods of warfare, it may be said that in 1940 the Italian Navy was, technically speaking, excellent in respect to speed, gunnery, torpedoes, communications, and maneuvers, but that it had certain serious weaknesses. For one thing, it had no aircraft carriers. Many naval officers thought this type of ship indispensable, but the airmen believed them to be so vulnerable as to be useless in a narrow sea. This dispute had had to be decided by Mussolini, who ruled against the construction of carriers, but the absence of this type of ship was to be heavily felt. Another aspect of inferiority, perhaps most serious of all, was the lack of radar. By early 1941 British ships in the Mediterranean had been equipped with this device and thus gained a most important advantage, particularly in night actions. Italian methods of submarine detection were mediocre, but this situation was to improve somewhat in the course of the war with the adoption of German apparatus. In their cruisers, with the exception of the latest 10,000-ton type, the Italians had sacrificed protection for speed to such an extent that they themselves spoke of their "cardboard fleet." Their destroyers had poor sea-keeping qualities and had to be modified as a result of experience to reduce this defect. As in all secondary navies, auxiliary ships had been neglected. From both defensive and offensive viewpoints the mine warfare service was inadequate, as was also the organization for the protection of anchorages.

The Italian Navy placed great hopes in its strong and well-trained undersea fleet. The submarines were well designed and possessed good underwater stability and maneuverability; they were far more stoutly constructed than those used in the war of 1914-1918. But compared to the German submarines which operated in the Mediterranean, the Italian boats dove more slowly, requiring about a minute and a quarter as compared with thirty or forty seconds; they had a lesser maximum depth, which not only reduced their ability to escape by diving but also implied a lesser resistance to depth bombs. Furthermore, their periscopes were too short, with the result that at attack depth the superstructures were nearer the surface, thus increasing not only the risk of being sighted by aircraft, already great in the transparent waters of the Mediterranean, but also the danger of ramming by enemy ships. The Italian submarines had a surface speed several knots inferior to that of German boats of equal tonnage and they also carried a smaller number of torpedoes.

All navies began this war with certain technical inadequacies which were more or less rapidly corrected. This was inevitable: for example, the British and American Navies, like all others, had wholly inadequate antiaircraft batteries. But the Italian situation was complicated by the country's industrial weakness which made it impossible to remedy the original mistakes. The Italian sailors had to fight the whole war without aircraft carriers or radar. Their qualitative inferiority steadily increased.

The officers of the Navy were well-informed, well-trained, and competent. Although they had welcomed Fascism in the hope that it would renew the energies of the country, they remained devoted to the Monarchy and paid little attention to politics. Preoccupied with technical matters, the Navy had succeeded in keeping to itself; the "hierarchs" of Fascism had not penetrated the Fleet to any great extent. The Navy was accused of exclusiveness, an accusation true here as in all navies, but many confused this exclusiveness with class consciousness, forgetting that it is as noticeable in the quartermaster as in the admiral. Ciano stated that the whole Navy was anti-German. This was particularly true of the senior officers, who sadly cherished memories of their partnership with the French and British in the struggle of 1915-1918. In their relations with the French after the armistice, such officers as Admiral de Feo and Admiral di Giamberardino showed a consideration which deserves recognition despite our bitter memories of Italian aggression.

Like Great Britain, Italy had an independent Air Force. But whereas in the Fleet Air Arm the British Navy possessed its own powerful naval aviation, the Italian Navy had only a few shipborne aircraft and a handful of reconnaissance machines. The chiefs of the Air Force, supported by Mussolini, felt that their service was destined to operate both independently and in cooperation with the Army and Navy. Since missions would continually be changing, it was thought that a judicious economy of force could best be secured by assigning the greatest possible number of aircraft to the Air Force, which would employ them as seemed best in varying circumstances. This concept, which was also adopted in Germany, was theoretically sound but in practice proved disappointing, most notably in Italy but also in the Reich, where the Navy incessantly pleaded for a naval air force independent of the Luftwaffe. In the Italian Air Force certain squadrons were, at least in theory, trained in naval air tactics although not under naval command. This specialization, however, was a very relative matter, and was considered wholly inadequate by the Navy. As a result of its experience in the first operations of the war, the Italian Navy insisted that it should have at least 250 reconnaissance planes of its own, but as the production of these types amounted to only eight a month it was impossible to satisfy this demand.

During peacetime the Italian Air Force had gained spectacular successes in its conduct of mass flights and its winning of the Schneider Cup; it had also made great contributions to the conquest of Ethiopia. Proud of these accomplishments, energetic, skillful, and well-trained, the men of the Air Force were confident that they could interdict the Mediterranean to the British Fleet. *A priori*, this view was not unreasonable. In 1940 ships' antiaircraft batteries were feeble, and the British had only very limited air strength locally available. But the Italian Air Force had a mistaken tactical doctrine. Its plans were based principally on the employment of high altitude attacks with small-caliber bombs, but the aircraft lacked gyroscopic sights and the accuracy of their drops was uncertain. Little attention was given to dive bombing and there were as yet no torpedo planes.

So far as the latter are concerned, the Air Force had perhaps tried to accomplish too much. The Navy had developed an excellent aerial torpedo but the Air Force, believing its maximum dropping altitude and speed to be too small, had prior to the war refused to accept it. Instead it had continued its own experiments which in June 1940 were still unfinished. Consequently the Air Force was deficient in techniques appropriate to the attack on such small mobile targets as ships. When at the end of 1941 the Japanese gained astonishing successes over the British and American fleets, their whole procedure was based on the use of torpedo planes and dive bombers; high altitude bombardment, which they considered to be purely secondary, was used principally to distract the antiaircraft batteries and to facilitate the attacks of dive bombers and torpedo planes. It must, however, be recognized in this connection that the Japanese were able to profit from the prior experience of the belligerents, an experience which did not exist when Italy entered the war, and further, that all aviators employed by the Japanese against enemy fleets belonged to their Naval Air Arm.

As official sources do not agree, it is difficult to establish the number of aircraft which the Italians possessed in June 1940. Ciano relates in his *Diary* that in order to get accurate information he suggested to Mussolini, shortly before the start of the war, that he have the prefects make a count of the number of planes. It may be estimated that Italy had between 2,500 and 3,000 aircraft, of which about half were first-line machines. For that date this was quite an important force—in 1941-1942 the Japanese were to gain their victories using only 1,500 planes—and in any case it was vastly greater than the British Mediterranean air strength. Nor, at the start, were the Italian machines inferior to those the British could send against them. The Navy had a catapult seaplane which was better than the Swordfish and also a reasonably good trimotor bomber, the Cant Z 506. In its CR 42 fighter the Air Force had a machine superior to the enemy's Gloster Gladiator. Subsequently the situation was reversed by the British Hurricanes and Spitfires, which were superior to the G 50 and MC 200 fighters which replaced the CR 42. Still later the Italians introduced the MC 202, a remarkable plane but one which was never available in quantity.

Despite the introduction of these last-mentioned fighters, and of torpedo planes and dive bombers, the Italian situation deteriorated steadily. The war involved an appalling expenditure of aircraft, and Italy's production capacity was barely sufficient to provide replacements. Counting those which they received from the Germans, the Italians employed a total of about 7,000 planes, of which they lost 6,500. Numerically the Air Force was able to keep itself at about the level at which it started the war, but it was unable to increase its strength while its enemies were being powerfully reinforced. In 1943, the year of greatest production, the Italians were completing 250 planes a month, a quantity which the United States produced daily.

Of the three armed forces, the Army was probably the worst prepared. In June 1940, according to Marshal Badoglio, there were in Italy about twenty divisions which had received seventy per cent of their necessary equipment and training, and another twenty which were about half prepared. Few motorized elements existed; there were no heavy tanks; the ammunition supply was inadequate. "We do not even have shirts for all our soldiers," the Marshal told the Duce, and General Giacomo Zanussi, who reports this conversation, writes that "Badoglio might have added that we were equally short of shoes and socks." The strength maintained in the empire overseas was considerable: 300,000 men in East Africa, 220,000 in Libya, 10,000 in Albania; but the troops were badly equipped, badly supplied, and without reserves of fuel and materiel. Badoglio spoke categorically: "War is suicide," to which Mussolini replied in substance, "You, Marshal, see the war only from the narrow military point of view; I look upon it in its general and political aspects."

Command and organization

At the beginning of June 1940 the King entrusted command of all the armed forces to the Duce. Thus Mussolini, who was already Chief of Fascism, Chief of the Government, Minister of the Interior, Minister of War, Minister of the Navy, and Minister of the Air Force, became in addition Generalissimo of the Armies of Land,

Sea, and Air. Despite his great powers of work and his intelligence, this was a great deal for a single man already worn down by serious illness, and although he subsequently denied all responsibility for the King's decision, all that we know today shows that not only did he ask for the command but that he insisted on it. The House of Savoy had in the past always exercised nominal leadership and its members had frequently commanded troops; this was a tradition which it could only renounce at the cost of great loss of prestige. Moreover, the King had always followed military matters closely and had real competence in this field; his authority would have been exercised tactfully, with consideration for the commanders, and would have been accepted without difficulty in the often necessary arbitrations between the different forces.

During the last war the heads of government—Hitler, Stalin, Roosevelt, Churchill, and Mussolini—all directed the strategies of their countries. Hitler did this in rigorous fashion; Roosevelt and Churchill, while themselves making the principal military decisions, never restricted the initiative of their chief commanders and always listened to their advice. We do not know exactly what went on in Russia, but in the United States and Great Britain, in any event, the intervention of the chiefs of government was skillful, opportune, and successful.

Such, however, was not the case in Italy, where Mussolini subordinated strategy to policy. This subordination is, of course, proper, provided only that strategic requirements be given consideration, which here was not always the case. Too often the military leaders were forced to adapt themselves to a policy that was both uncertain and vacillating.

The Duce's principal military adviser and assistant was the Chief of Staff of the Armed Forces, originally Marshal Badoglio, who had a fairly small staff of his own, an organization known as Comando Supremo. Under Comando Supremo came the command organizations of the Army, Navy, and Air Force, known respectively as Superesercito, Supermarina, and Superaereo, and directed by Chiefs of

Staff acting also as Commanders in Chief. In the Navy and the Air Force the Chiefs of Staff were also the Under Secretaries of State for Navy and Air; in the Army these two functions were separated.

Although the reasons for the difference between the Army on the one hand, with its separated functions of Chief of Staff and minister, and the Navy and the Air Force on the other, are not clear, this organization seems on the whole a logical one. It was similar to the German organization in which the High Command, the Oberkommando der Wehrmacht or O.K.W., capped the command of the three forces. In Italy, however, it seems not to have functioned smoothly. Badoglio made the mistake of giving Comando Supremo an inadequate staff, with the result that it was sometimes overwhelmed. The heads of the Air Force and Navy were not very happy about the authority of the higher organ. Often the high commanders combined incompatible functions: thus Graziani commanded in Libya while remaining at least nominally Chief of Staff of the Army, and Cavallero, who replaced Badoglio at Comando Supremo, at the same time undertook to direct operations in Greece. Nor were these the only difficulties. The military complained of the intervention of the Minister of Foreign Affairs in the conduct of operations, an activity which went on behind the scenes; and while Mussolini thought himself highly competent, the armed forces did not share this belief. Perhaps his great abilities, worn down by age and sickness, were declining: General Armellini of Comando Supremo noted in his diary "*E un po ramollito.*"

Finally, it does not seem that complete loyalty existed in the high command. General Visconti Prasca observes in this connection, "If Badoglio succeeded in affirming some principle of coordination his subordinates would approve it in their capacity of Chiefs of Staff, but once at liberty they would suddenly change themselves into Under Secretaries of State, and hasten to have Mussolini annul that which they had already approved."

The Italian high command maintained too rigid a control over the lower echelons. For major Mediterranean operations Superaereo and Supermarina exercised direct command of their forces on the basis of plans drawn up at Rome; a Squadron Commander needing air support had to request it from Supermarina, which in turn notified Superaereo of the request. When the operation was undertaken by the Italians the inconvenience was not too serious, but when it was necessary to reply to enemy initiative the loss of time was considerable. Consequently after a few months of experience the Supreme Command authorized certain local agreements.

The extreme weakness of naval aviation was a major handicap, but the Navy soon saw that this could in some measure be repaired by placing part of the Air Force under the orders of Supermarina. The British took such a step when they placed the R.A.F. Coastal Command under Admiralty orders for the duration of hostilities; the airmen played their part perfectly and the system gave complete satisfaction. A similar organization also existed in France: the so-called Aviation of Naval Cooperation, belonging to the Air Force, was placed under the orders of the Navy. But in Italy no such measures were taken. Although participating in the same operations, air and sea forces remained under separate commands, and throughout the war the Fleet commanders complained bitterly of the lack of liaison between the Navy and the Air Force. The conflict soon demonstrated that, under the conditions of the time, a navy that did not possess a strong air arm lost much of its effectiveness. Here lay the principal fault in Italian organization for a war in which it was absolutely necessary to gain the mastery of the Mediterranean.

With the exception of light coastal defense units attached to the Naval Districts, the Italian Fleet was divided into three Squadrons. The First Squadron, containing the battleships, two divisions of light cruisers, and destroyers, was stationed at Taranto and Augusta. The Second Squadron, two divisions of heavy cruisers, two divisions of light cruisers, and destroyers, was based at Naples, Messina, and Palermo. The Third Squadron, which contained the submarines, was under an admiral whose headquarters were at Rome. No Squadron Commander was subordinate to another; all were directly responsible to Supermarina, although in the event of an operation involving elements of all three the senior officer present assumed command.

At the time of mobilization the Italians organized the Sicilian Channel Force containing minelayers, minesweepers, submarines, torpedo boats, M.A.S., and various auxiliary ships, the mission of which was to block the Strait of Sicily. The commander of this Force had his headquarters at Messina and was directly responsible to Supermarina. Shore-based naval aviation was also directly controlled by Supermarina, while ship-based aviation naturally formed a part of the Squadrons. In addition to the forces listed above, a few light vessels were stationed in the Dodecanese and in East Africa.

The Italians had naturally studied methods of interrupting British commerce in the Red Sea, an objective complementary to those assigned the Fleet in the Mediterranean. The shape of this sea, its extreme length and slight breadth, makes convoys very vulnerable. On the Red Sea coast of Eritrea the Italians had a major port at Massawa and a minor base at Assab; on the Indian Ocean they had another minor base at Kismayu in Somaliland. These bases were well located for attacks on the important commerce which Britain carried on with the Near East by way of the Cape. But the Italian bases were not strong, they had very limited repair facilities, and their supplies of fuel and materiel were small. Wisely, therefore, Supermarina had sent only old surface ships to East Africa, believing that after a few months of hostilities they would be immobilized. In this area Italy had seven old destroyers, two torpedo boats, five M.A.S., and eight submarines, under a commander who was responsible both to the Governor and to Supermarina. Only the submarines were of recent type, and they were reduced to almost complete impotence as

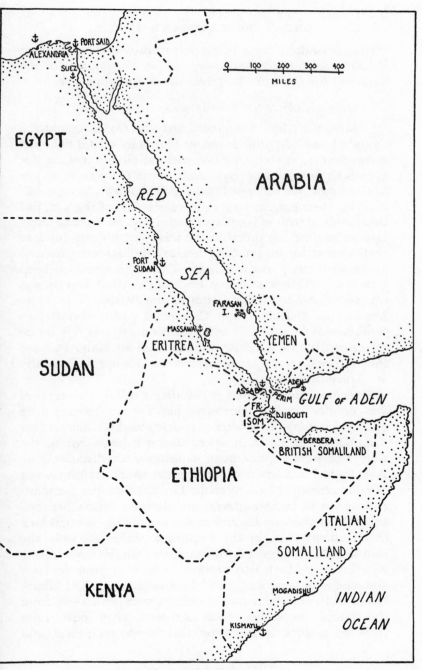

Fig. 3. The Red Sea

the result of their crews being poisoned by toxic gases from the air-conditioning machinery. All in all, the fate of the detached forces in the Red Sea was an unhappy one.

Strategic concepts: parallel war

MUSSOLINI had announced that he would conduct a "parallel war." By this he meant that Italy would fight the same enemies as Germany but without closely linking her actions to those of her ally: "*Non con la Germania, ne per la Germania, ma solo per l'Italia, a fianco della Germania.*" Nor, for their part, at least in the early days of the war, did the Germans wish to cooperate with Italy. Hitler was reluctant to meddle too much in the affairs of his ally for fear that Comando Supremo would ask indiscreet questions about German plans which the O.K.W. wanted to keep secret; the Fuehrer said that the Italian Royal Family was capable of passing information to the British. The members of the German High Command considered Italian assistance as helpful but wholly secondary, and felt themselves capable of winning with or without Italy. In 1940 they referred to the Mediterranean somewhat disdainfully as "Mussolini's theater."

Since both sides desired only indirect collaboration there was neither unified command nor even a coordinating agency. Liaison officers were of course attached to the major commands, but on both sides, during a large part of the war, these were kept as much as possible at a distance. The Axis leaders had frequent meetings at which frankness was notably absent. When, after the Greek affair, the Germans intervened in the Mediterranean theater, liaison between the staffs necessarily became closer despite the mutual lack of confidence, but in the beginning there was only the minimum exchange of views. Rear Admiral Weichold, who for more than two years held various posts in Italy and who in general was not ill-disposed toward the Italians, said that the German liaison officers were kept away from the central operations rooms and were given only uninteresting reports. In short the distrust was reciprocal, and indeed it could hardly have been otherwise, for political aims were often discordant, notably in Balkan questions, and parallel war often proved to be divergent war.

From the outset Mussolini's inconstancy was apparent. On 4 June 1940 he decided to remain on the defensive in the Alps, in accordance with Plan K set up before the war, and on the other hand to take vigorous offensive action in the air and on the sea. This offensive was, however, to be directed only against Great Britain: "*Niente contro la Francia.*" But to take the offensive is a rather vague term if the objectives are not clear. The term certainly did not have the same meaning for Comando Supremo as it did for the O.K.W. or for the Japanese Imperial General Staff. To the Italian High Command it was a matter merely of a few air raids on Malta, Gibraltar, and Alexandria, of a few sorties by light naval forces, and of scouting by submarines. But suddenly Mussolini changed his plans. On 17 June he summoned Marshal Badoglio and ordered him to take the offensive in the Alps the next day, thus forcing the Italian Army to shift immediately from a defensive to an offensive deployment. To Badoglio's objections Mussolini replied simply, "I need a few thousand dead to justify my presence at the peace table."

After the fall of France the Italian attitude at sea and in the air remained much more passive than offensive. No attempt was made to take Malta, at the time only feebly defended, because of unpreparedness, because of fear that the British Fleet might intervene, and because its potential importance was not yet fully appreciated.

As for the Italian Fleet, it was to fight if the enemy appeared but there was no thought of forcing an action. A Comando Supremo directive of mid-September sheds light on the state of mind of the High Command:

Naval actions occur for one of two reasons: first, an encounter between two enemy squadrons one of which seeks to prevent the other from fulfilling its mission; second, determined search by one squadron for the enemy fleet with the purpose of destroying it. The first situation may develop unexpectedly: in such a case the Italian Navy, if it has a chance of success, will fight with extreme resolution. The second alternative is not open to us because we are the weaker. To conceive of a battle as an end in itself is an absurdity not worth discussing.

The Italian Navy might well have been surprised by this renunciation of the initiative, for control of the sea is gained by destruction of enemy forces, that is to say by combat of whatever nature. Offensive thrusts followed by retirement might have enabled the Italian fleet to draw British units into a concentration of submarines; of these the Italians at this time had about a hundred in the Mediterranean and the British only eight, and their action could more easily have been coordinated with that of the air and surface forces in this way than if they merely awaited enemy initiative. Perhaps without fully realizing it, Comando Supremo tied down the Italian Fleet because of lack of confidence in its capabilities. It is worth noting that at this same time the British considered themselves definitely outnumbered.

Given this attitude on the part of Comando Supremo, Supermarina decided that the action of the Italian Fleet would be governed by the following principles:

1. The battle line was to be kept ready to intervene in case of an important enemy initiative.
2. Operations were to be carried out with light fast elements, torpedo boats and M.A.S., and with submarines; mines were to be laid on enemy lines of communication, especially in the Sicilian Channel.
3. The greatest emphasis was to be placed on air action in direct and indirect collaboration with the Navy.
4. The assault machines were to be developed and used in surprise attacks.

But none of this took the place of the overall plan which Comando Supremo should have established. No attempt was made to eliminate the key enemy positions at Malta and Alexandria. Three months after the outbreak of hostilities the Libyan offensive was begun; its strategy was one of pure opportunism with the result that when subsequently the enemy received reinforcements it became necessary to call for German assistance.

To sum up, then, at the beginning of the war the Italian naval and air forces, despite certain technical weaknesses, were in a respectable state of preparation and training. The Army was not ready. Strategy was uncertain. Liaison between the Navy and Air Force was poor. The Air Force's tactical doctrine for over-water operations was wrong. Finally, Italian industry was too weak to sustain effectively the effort of a long war.

The situation of Italy had much in common with that of Japan. These two overpopulated countries felt that they were being stifled by more affluent nations. They were led by dynamic statesmen who believed that circumstances favored an entry into war. The industrial strength of both countries was inferior to that of their adversaries. Although their total forces were weaker than those of their enemies, they could hope for local superiority. There the similarity ceases. Japan was ready, Italy was not. Japan had a bold plan, well thought-out and precise; Italy did not. And this country, which in the course of centuries had produced great captains, entered the war without a strategic plan and under the deceptive political belief that the conflict would be short and was already three-quarters won.

4. British Strategy

Basic concepts

THE Abyssinian War had led the British to re-examine the Mediterranean problem in the light of a possible conflict with Italy in which France remained neutral. As a result of this reconsideration there arose a new school of thought, the so-called Cape School, which felt that the progress of aviation had made the movement of ships through the Mediterranean impossible, and which advocated abandoning the Gibraltar-Suez route and replacing it, as an imperial line of communications, by the route around the Cape of Good Hope. This latter route increased the length of voyages to the Near and Far East in a way which can perhaps be appreciated from the following examples:

Distance	Via the Cape	Via the Mediterranean	Difference
London-Alexandria	11,608 miles	3,097 miles	8,511 miles
London-Abadan	11,400 miles	6,600 miles	4,800 miles
London-Bombay	10,800 miles	6,280 miles	4,520 miles
London-Singapore	11,750 miles	8,250 miles	3,500 miles

It will be seen that the distance to Alexandria is almost four times as great by way of the Cape as it is through the Mediterranean.

To Great Britain, furthermore, the Mediterranean is more than just a thoroughfare, for she has important interests in the Near East and depends upon this region for a great part of her supplies, especially of fuel. Doubtless, if the occasion had arisen, she could have supported a campaign in Asia Minor with the use of the Persian Gulf route alone, but this would have involved major difficulties. Abandoning the Mediterranean would also have meant abandoning to the enemy the control of the Balkans with all their resources in raw materials, and would have opened to the Italians the possibility of gaining supplies from Russia by way of the Dardanelles. Finally, to the British leaders, the Mediterranean was the preferred area in which

54

to counterattack a power seeking to dominate Europe. A struggle against Italy might develop into a struggle against Germany; but whether Italy were alone or allied with the Reich, it was by way of the Mediterranean that Great Britain planned to return to the Continent. British strategists have long expressed this thought in a concise phrase: "Who holds the Mediterranean holds the world." The statement is an extreme one, but it illustrates the ideas of the British political and military leaders and helps to explain their attitude in subsequent debate with the Americans on overall strategy.

So long as France remained in the war the question of abandoning the Mediterranean did not arise. Since France was responsible for control of the western basin, the British concentrated on strengthening their position in the Near East. The Egyptian Treaty of 26 August 1936 authorized Great Britain to maintain a peacetime garrison of 10,000 men and 400 airplanes for the defense of the Suez Canal, and further provided that in case of war Egypt would place her ports, her airfields, and her communications at the disposal of her ally. This treaty was faithfully carried out by the Egyptians. On 11 June they broke off diplomatic relations with Italy and the hopes that the Axis had founded on Egyptian opposition to the British fell to the ground. Even when Rommel was advancing on Alexandria, Egypt remained loyal. In the northern Near East, Great Britain was covered by the Anglo-Turkish Agreement. In the Western and Central Mediterranean, however, the defenses of Gibraltar and, more particularly, of Malta, had been insufficiently strengthened. Prior to 1937, despite the Abyssinian warning, the British Admiralty had been more preoccupied with Far Eastern questions than with those of a European naval war. When, after 1937, a European conflict seemed probable, the French alliance appeared to lessen the importance of Malta and the dangers which faced Gibraltar.

In June 1940 Great Britain suddenly found herself threatened with disaster. She had not foreseen that the fall of France would carry with it that of the whole French colonial empire. And although the British Fleet enjoyed a two-to-one superiority over the combined naval forces of both Germany and Italy, the Royal Air Force was relatively weak, and Great Britain was faced with the greatest threat of invasion since the time of Napoleon. She was forced to keep the greater part of her armies in the home island, and such sea and air strength as could be sent to the Mediterranean had to be divided into two groups, one in the western and the other in the eastern basin, subject to attack in detail by the Italian Fleet which was concentrated at the center. In the Near East the British at this time had only a very few airplanes, most of which were obsolete. The antiaircraft defenses of Malta were insignificant. In Egypt there were only about 35,000 men and no heavy tanks.

In these grave circumstances the British leaders showed both wisdom and energy. Nothing more was heard of the Cape School. Not for an instant was there thought of abandoning the Mediterranean. Not only was it decided to fight for Alexandria and Gibraltar but also to contest with Italy the mastery of the Central Mediterranean, and this was one of the great decisions of the war. Had Great Britain at this time decided to evacuate Malta and to hold merely Alexandria and Gibraltar, the whole Mediterranean war would have taken a very different course and one infinitely more favorable to the Axis. Furthermore, the British decided to push urgently needed Alexandria convoys through the Mediterranean, a decision which may today seem natural but which in June 1940 was exceedingly bold. Finally, despite the weakness of his forces in England and the imminent threat of invasion, Churchill sent two divisions to the Near East, a measure wholly deserving of the admiration it commands.

The Cape route, used as a rule by those convoys which were not urgent, would have been very dangerous where it passes through the Red Sea, had the Italians only been able sufficiently to reinforce their positions there. In this region the British had bases at Suez, Port Sudan, Aden, and on the little island of Perim which guards the Strait of Bab el Mandeb. They also built an air base in the Farasan Islands opposite Massawa. Despite the presence of Italian naval forces at Massawa, the movement of British convoys through the Red Sea was carried out almost without loss,

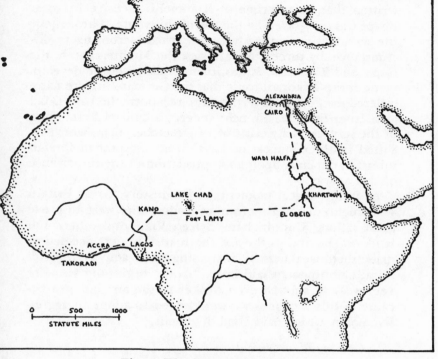

Fig. 4. The Takoradi Airway

but until the conquest of Italian East Africa, that is to say until April 1941, Great Britain was obliged to provide strong escorts for her Red Sea merchant shipping, and for this purpose to base a division of cruisers and some destroyers at Aden.

Finally, to speed up the shipment of airplanes to Egypt by a route that was safer than the Mediterranean and faster than that around the Cape, the British in the course

57

of the war developed the Takoradi airway. Planes were carried by ship to Takoradi on the Gold Coast and then flown to Alexandria by way of the airfields at Accra, Lagos, Kano, Fort Lamy, El Obeid, Khartoum, Wadi Halfa, and Cairo. The Takoradi airway thus became one of the great British imperial routes of communication, and it has been written that, at the time of Rommel's offensive in 1942, Egypt was only saved by the use of this route. Throughout the war British strategy was supported, according to circumstance, by three great arteries, the Mediterranean, the Cape, and Takoradi. It was in anticipation of the development of the Takoradi route that the Germans, in late 1940, ordered the Pétain Government to recapture the Lake Chad area from the Free French; indeed, a full understanding of the serious Vichy crisis of 13 December 1940, which resulted in the dismissal of Laval from the post of foreign minister, depends upon an appreciation of the importance of this airway.

As in all critical moments of her history, Great Britain was able to discover a group of leaders who were to prove great sailors: Cunningham, Syfret, Vian, and others. On land, on sea, and in the air, the British leaders decided to mask their weakness by increasing their activity. As Admiral Cunningham said later, "In the beginning we were very weak at sea and even weaker in the air; but just because of this weakness we were forced to adopt an aggressive policy which paid good dividends."

Command organization

IN THE NEAR EAST the Army, the Navy, and the Air Force were each placed under the orders of a commander in chief: Commander in Chief Middle East for the Army, Commander in Chief Mediterranean for the Navy, Air Officer Commanding in Chief for the R.A.F. Following a principle dear to the British, although one which was later abandoned under American influence, there was no subordination among these three general officers, who cooperated on a basis of common understanding. Close collaboration was maintained by periodic conferences presided over by the Minister of State for the Near East; by a permanent council, the Commanders in Chief Committee; by an inter-service intelligence organization; by an inter-service committee on antiaircraft defense; and finally by frequent staff conferences. Mutual understanding and liaison were thus well assured and, so far as can be told from narratives of the combatants and from official reports, collaboration was both confident and effective.

The Americans, of course, applied different principles. Admiral Nimitz, Commander in Chief Pacific Ocean Areas, had under his orders all naval, land, and air forces of the theater; similarly, in the Southwest Pacific, General MacArthur commanded all three arms. When the Americans intervened in the Mediterranean their concept prevailed, and Eisenhower was given command of all forces. But the British, having in the course of history carried out countless combined operations with separate Army-Navy commands, had always found this method satisfactory. So long as they remained alone in the Mediterranean, they employed the principle of separate commands for Navy, Army, and Air Force.

Commanding as he did a naval theater, Admiral Cunningham controlled all naval surface, submarine, and air strength, and had a general headquarters at Alexandria. However, he frequently went to sea for operations which seemed likely to lead to fleet engagements. At the Battle of Matapan he was embarked on a battleship, but he supervised the evacuations of Greece and Crete from his Alexandria headquarters. The Italian Admiral Iachino, who was in command of the Italian surface fleet for a great part of the war, felt that Cunningham had an important advantage in having not only the surface forces but also submarines and aircraft subject to his orders. In other words, Admiral Iachino felt that the fleet commander should also command the theater.

Nevertheless it is very difficult to control all the forces of a theater from a ship where space is lacking and where radio silence is often necessary. The organization of the British naval command in the Eastern Mediterranean was an unusual one. In the North Sea theater the Admiralty retained direct control of the submarine commander and of the R.A.F. Coastal Command as well as of the Commander in Chief of the Home Fleet, the latter having under his orders only surface ships and their embarked aviation. This organization was analogous to that of Supermarina. It was not here that the fault of the Italian system lay, but rather in the lack of strong naval aviation and in inadequate liaison.

In the Eastern Mediterranean, moreover, the British were faced with special circumstances: the remoteness of the theater, the relative weakness in everything but surface forces, the personality of the commander. If a great naval battle was to be fought they wanted Admiral Cunningham to fight it, but on the other hand, in view of his seniority and ability, it was impossible to subordinate him to another commander on shore at Alexandria. The British, not being dogmatic, did not everywhere adopt similar solutions. When Admiral Cunningham weighed anchor he was forced to delegate part of his powers as theater commander to one of his subordinates ashore, a minor inconvenience in view of the perfect unity of doctrine of his staff.

Forces available

IN JUNE 1940 the British Army in the Near East was very weak: 36,000 men in Egypt, 27,000 in Palestine, 9,000 in the Sudan, 8,500 in Kenya, 1,500 in Somaliland. All these forces were without much heavy equipment; no formation was completely outfitted; weakness in antiaircraft and antitank armament was very serious; the Air Force had only about a hundred machines of obsolete types.

The principal British strength was provided by the Navy. Throughout the period of diplomatic tension which had begun in March, Admiral Sir Andrew Cunningham's fleet had been progressively reinforced. It contained the old aircraft carrier *Eagle* with about thirty Swordfish biplanes and only four Gladiator fighters; three old but modernized battleships, *Warspite, Malaya,* and *Royal Sovereign;* five light cruisers, *Orion, Neptune, Sydney, Gloucester,* and *Liverpool;* two destroyer flotillas; and eight submarines. The main fleet base was at Alexandria, while Port Said, Haifa, and Cyprus were used as auxiliary bases.

At Gibraltar, commanding the passage between the Mediterranean and the Atlantic, the British had stationed a force of varying strength known as Force H, to which was given the double mission of helping to protect the ocean routes against possible German raids and of escorting through the Western Mediterranean convoys destined for Malta and Alexandria. At the end of June Force H contained the great battle cruiser *Hood,* the battleships *Resolution* and *Valiant,* two cruisers, the aircraft carrier *Ark Royal,* and a dozen destroyers. This force was commanded by Admiral Somerville, who reported directly to the Admiralty, and it was the Admiralty which gave Force H and the Alexandria Fleet general instructions for coordinating operations for the passage of convoys. In addition to Force H the British had in the Western Mediterranean a few destroyers and minor vessels which were assigned to the Admiral commanding at Gibraltar for the purpose of guarding and blocking the Strait.

In aircraft carriers and battleships the British were superior to their enemies; the Italians had no carriers and in June 1940 had but two battleships ready for action, although this number was within two months to be increased to six. On the other hand the British were notably weaker in cruisers, destroyers, and submarines. We have already seen that each of the two adversaries felt himself handicapped by material inferiority. This can perhaps be explained by the different importance which they attributed to the various elements of the armed forces.

To many naval officers in 1940 the battleship was the basic unit of strength, all other ships existing only to per-

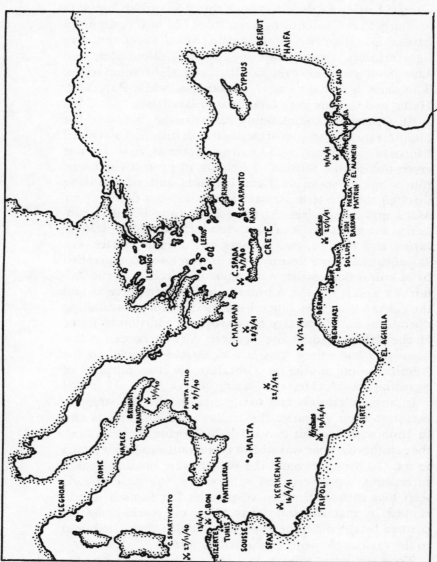

Fig. 5. The Central and Eastern Mediterranean

mit or to prevent its entry into action. The Italians, anticipating that an engagement would ultimately resolve itself
into a duel between battleships, considered themselves at
a disadvantage. The British, on the contrary, having in the
entire Mediterranean less than 200 aircraft, including their
embarked aviation, could not but be disturbed by the apparently crushing numerical superiority of the enemy air
strength. Furthermore, they did not compare the strength
of their united forces with that of the Italian Fleet but considered the Alexandria and Gibraltar groups separately,
for it seemed a task of some difficulty to effect a concentration of forces which were separated by a distance of
1,800 miles and which could only be joined by way of the
Strait of Sicily.

The Sicilian Strait is about ninety miles wide and is
guarded by the island of Pantelleria, which the Italians
had strongly fortified. Between Pantelleria and the Sicilian
coast the waters are easily mined; south of Pantelleria the
greater depths make this more difficult, but this passage,
only thirty miles wide, can be easily watched by light forces
and submarines. Throughout the war the minefields in the
Sicilian Strait were continually strengthened, the Italians
laying a total of about 11,500 mines between Sicily and
Tunisia. In the beginning these were old models which
were easily swept, but little by little the Italian Navy
adopted various German types, sweeping of which was difficult and dangerous. The hazards of the passage were further increased by the presence of Italian air strength in
Sicily and Pantelleria.

In so far as possible the British avoided sending their
battleships and carriers through the Strait of Sicily. They
expected in consequence that they would have to engage
the entire Italian battle fleet with only one of their two
Mediterranean forces, and such indeed ultimately proved
to be the case.

5. Operations During 1940

First actions at sea; the Battle of Punta Stilo

THE Italian declaration of war and the fall of France forced Great Britain hastily to reinforce the Near East, and so great was the urgency that the Cape route could not be used. The first British Mediterranean convoy subsequent to Italy's entry into the war passed the Sicilian Strait on 23 June. From the very start the British adopted a system which with minor modifications was followed throughout the war. Force H, based on Gibraltar, escorted the convoys to a point north of Bizerte. If at this time there appeared to be no danger of intervention by Italian battleships, the convoys passed the Strait of Sicily protected only by light forces while the main body of Force H, including the battleships and carriers, returned to Gibraltar and in this way avoided action in the dangerous area between Tunisia and Sicily. The Alexandria Fleet met the convoys in the Central Mediterranean and escorted them to Egypt. Thus protected, the convoy of June went through without difficulty.

On 28 June the first encounter between surface vessels took place. A division of three Italian destroyers of the *Turbine* class, en route from Taranto to Tobruk, was attacked by two enemy cruisers, one of which was the Australian *Sydney*. The Italians, greatly outgunned, did not have time to escape. The destroyer *Espero*, quickly hit and immobilized, sank with its flag flying, firing to the last. A few days later on 5 July the destroyer *Zeffiro* was sunk at Tobruk by torpedo planes of the Fleet Air Arm.

A more important event was to follow. Two convoys destined for Alexandria had been formed at Malta, to carry to Egypt supplies which had arrived from England and to evacuate civilian personnel from the island. The first convoy, proceeding at thirteen knots, contained three ships on which the evacuees were embarked; the second with a speed of nine knots contained four cargo ships. On 8 July the

64

Alexandria Fleet, which had got underway to cover the two convoys, was south of Crete on a northwesterly course; at the same time an Italian force, which had escorted five ships loaded with troops and supplies to Libya, was returning to Italy. It was this squadron which became involved in the engagement with the Alexandria Fleet known to the British as the Action off Calabria and to the Italians as the Battle of Punta Stilo.

The British force was divided into three groups: in the van the scouting force under Vice Admiral Tovey with five light cruisers; next, screened by destroyers, the *Warspite* with Admiral Cunningham embarked; and finally the battleships *Malaya* and *Royal Sovereign* and the aircraft carrier *Eagle*, accompanied by destroyers. On 8 July Italian bombers attacked the British ships off Crete; the cruiser *Gloucester* was hit on the bridge, eighteen men and the captain were killed, but the ship was not slowed down. On the 9th, British aircraft from Malta reported the Italian squadron heading towards Calabria; it included the two battleships *Cavour* and *Cesare*, six heavy cruisers, twelve light cruisers, and twenty-four destroyers, that is to say a very large portion of the Italian Fleet. Admiral Cunningham increased speed to intercept the enemy, and had *Eagle's* Swordfish deliver an attack which proved unsuccessful. In the afternoon at about 1550, after a cruiser action which on the British side was supported by *Warspite*, the battleships gained contact and a gunnery duel began between *Cavour* and *Cesare* on one side and *Warspite* on the other. *Malaya* also opened fire but the range was too great and her shots fell short. The Italian battleships were armed with ten 12.6-inch guns; the British battleships with eight 15-inch guns apiece had far heavier broadsides than the Italian ships of the line, but this was made up for by the very great Italian superiority in cruisers.

During the battleship action the cruisers reengaged. *Bolzano* was hit by three 6-inch shells, her rudder was jammed, she made a complete circle to the left, and then having succeeded in repairing the damage resumed her

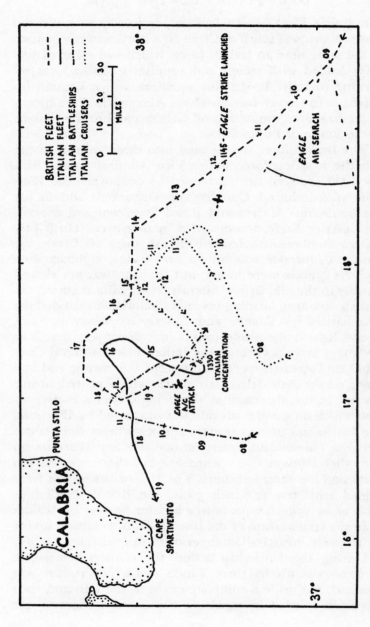

Fig. 6. The Battle of Punta Stilo (Action of Calabria), 9 July 1940

course. At 1557 *Cesare* received a 15-inch hit at a range of 26,000 yards which reduced her speed to eighteen knots. Admiral Campioni, commanding the Italian fleet, then broke off action by retiring westward under cover of smoke, and at about 1600 launched an attack with his destroyer squadrons to cover this turn away. The destroyers made a torpedo attack on the British squadron and were driven off by cruiser and battleship fire; this phase of the battle passed without loss to either side. At about 1615 torpedo planes from *Eagle* attacked the Italian cruisers but without success. The British squadron pursued the Italian ships until about 1730 but the battleships were unable to get within range. Before turning back, the British had come within twenty-five miles of the coast of Calabria.

Countless vain attacks were made by the Italian Air Force against the retiring Alexandria Fleet, including twenty-two against *Warspite* alone. But convoys and warships alike reached Egypt without damage; the only British loss was the destroyer *Escort* of Force H which was sunk off Alboran by a submarine.

In this engagement damage had been slight, but while the encounter between the two fleets had little importance from the material point of view, it had considerable consequences for morale. In Italy it led to a violent dispute between the Navy and the Air Force. The latter thought they had gained important results which the former rightly denied. The error of the aviators was understandable, for photographs of the battle show clearly that the bombings scored straddles and near misses. But there were in fact no hits, and although seriously threatened, the British ships did not suffer. Not only had high altitude bombardment showed itself ineffective but another factor embittered the argument: by mistake the Italian aviators had bombed their own ships for a period of several hours. In this the naval officers again found reasons for demanding a purely naval aviation, while the airmen replied that the errors had been committed in part by former naval personnel who had transferred to the Air Force. "The battle," wrote

Ciano, "was not a fight between British and Italians but a dispute between our sailors and our aviators." And again on 24 September he noted in his diary: "Cavagnari absolutely denies that we sank a cruiser of the *London* class; it is probably one of the usual Air Force boasts inspired by their hatred and distrust of the Navy." Thus the rift between the two services grew, at a time when close collaboration was essential in view of the hard fighting that was to come.

Even today the arguments about the Battle of Punta Stilo remain lively, although the lessons of the action are clear. Despite the proximity of the coast, the Navy and Air Force had been unable to coordinate their action in time; the Fleet needed an aircraft carrier. Furthermore, the Air Force had failed to obtain results because it had no torpedo planes or dive bombers. All felt this, but techniques could not be changed nor materiel modified overnight. As for the British, their concepts were borne out by this action in which they had brought their squadron close to the shore of the peninsula, indeed almost into the mouth of the Strait of Messina, without suffering damage.

In his action report Admiral Cunningham wrote as follows:

Our cruisers . . . were badly outnumbered and at times came under a very heavy fire. They were superbly handled by Vice-Admiral J. C. Tovey, who by his skilful maneuvering managed to maintain a position in the van and to hold the enemy cruiser squadrons. . . .

The meagre material results derived from this brief meeting with the Italian Fleet were naturally very disappointing to me and all under my command, but the action was not without value. It must have shown the Italians that their Air Force and submarines cannot stop our Fleet penetrating into the Central Mediterranean and that only their main fleet can seriously interfere with our operating there.

Thus the Italian Air Force, whose threat had weighed so heavily on British decisions at the time of the Ethiopian campaign, now in 1940 appeared unequal to its task.

The day after Punta Stilo an air attack on Augusta, which sank the destroyer *Pancaldo* (a ship which was later raised and then again sunk by the R.A.F. in 1943), led the Italians to abandon this base. They left their battleships at Taranto and placed their cruisers at Naples. At the end of August this distribution was again altered, and the Fleet was divided between the three ports of Taranto, Messina, and Brindisi. After the disaster at Taranto still further changes were made.

The Battle of Cape Spada; convoy movements

ON THE MORNING of 19 July, shortly after the action off Calabria, the British destroyers *Hyperion*, *Hero*, and *Ilex*, which were making an antisubmarine sweep off northwestern Crete, were sighted by the two Italian cruisers *Colleoni* and *Bande Nere*. These two 5,000-ton ships, which mounted eight 6-inch guns apiece and had a speed of thirty-six knots, were en route to Leros via Antikithera Channel under the command of Admiral Casardi. As soon as the contact was made, the British destroyers retired at high speed toward the cruiser *Sydney*, which in company with the destroyer *Havock*, was patrolling further to the north. At 0627 the Italian cruisers opened fire at about 22,000 yards; firing was made difficult by the necessity of aiming into the sun. At about 0645 the British disappeared behind a smoke screen, still pursued by *Colleoni* and *Bande Nere*. Then at about 0800 the Italians sighted *Sydney*, followed by *Havock*, which they took to be a second cruiser.

Now the first British destroyers turned about and, accompanied by *Sydney*, headed to engage. Their ruse had succeeded. The British now had eight 6-inch guns and twenty 5-inch guns as against sixteen 6-inch guns on the Italian side, and the Italians in their turn retired to the southwest at full speed. The engagement reopened at 0810; at 0824 *Colleoni* was hit in the engine room and stopped, and the British destroyers concentrated their fire on her. Hit by numerous shells and torpedoes, she sank at 0840, while *Bande Nere*, although damaged and pursued by *Sydney*, succeeded in escaping. At the end of the engagement *Sydney* had almost exhausted her ammunition. Italian bombers, coming to the rescue, succeeded in slightly damaging the destroyer *Havock*. Thus the first engagements between light units showed the Italians that their superiority in speed, the principal characteristic of their navy, had not enabled either *Colleoni*, or *Espero* in the earlier instance, to escape from a dangerous situation, and that it was neces-

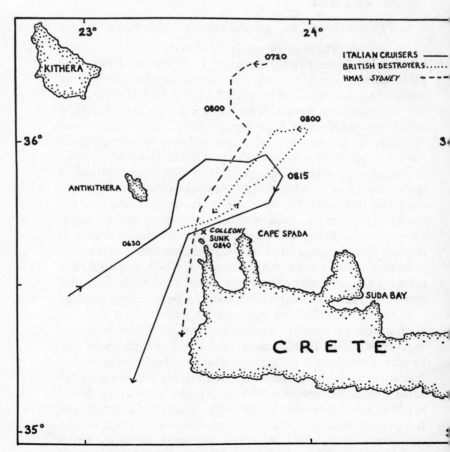

Fig. 7. The Battle of Cape Spada, 19 July 1940

sary to strengthen their light forces, especially when sending them far from the Italian coast.

Subsequent to this action the aircraft carrier *Eagle* attacked Tobruk, where *Bande Nere* had taken refuge. The Italian cruiser was not found but merchant ships and auxiliaries were hit.

At the beginning of August the British sent aerial reinforcements to Malta. Twelve Hurricanes were embarked on the old carrier *Argus*, which was escorted by Force H through the Western Mediterranean to a point from which the planes could be flown in, while at the same time aircraft from *Ark Royal* moored mines off Cagliari and bombed the airfield at Elmas in Sardinia. In the same period Swordfish from the Alexandria Fleet attacked targets in Cyrenaica, Bardia, and the seaplane base at Bomba. On 17 August the battleships *Warspite, Malaya*, and *Ramillies* bombarded Bardia at long range; hits were scored on ships and on a munitions depot, and the reply of the Italian batteries fell short.

In late August and early September another convoy was sent from Gibraltar to Malta and Alexandria. The battleship *Valiant*, the aircraft carrier *Illustrious*, the antiaircraft cruisers *Calcutta* and *Coventry* were transferred to the Alexandria Fleet, and at the same time troops and materiel were sent to Malta and Egypt. Only one cargo ship, the *Cornwall*, was hit by Italian aircraft, and although her rudder was destroyed she succeeded in reaching Malta by steering with her engines. In the course of the passage, planes from *Illustrious* and *Eagle* bombed airfields on Rhodes. The arrival at Alexandria of *Illustrious*, with her fast and heavily armed Fulmar fighters, constituted an important addition to British naval strength. While the convoy was en route Supermarina ordered out the Italian Fleet from Taranto, but recalled it before contact was gained.

In mid-August four more Italian battleships, the 35,000-ton *Littorio* and *Vittorio Veneto*, and the modernized *Cavour*-class *Duilio* and *Doria*, had entered service. As the Fleet now contained six battleships, and as the Air Force

71

had received a few torpedo planes, the Italian situation was improved, but lack of aircraft carriers and inadequate coordination between the Air Force and Navy still disposed the high command toward prudence. Until the month of September the British convoys passed without serious loss, but at the same time the Italians, opposed only by the few but active enemy submarines, were able to send reinforcements to Libya. On shore there were only scattered skirmishes. The war was soon to take a more active course.

The Italian offensive in Libya

On 28 June Marshal Balbo, governor and commander of Italian forces in Libya, was killed when the antiaircraft batteries at Tobruk shot down his plane by mistake. His place was filled on 6 July by Marshal Graziani, who had serious misgivings regarding an African offensive against the British. The valley of the Nile is protected on the west by more than 450 miles of Libyan Desert, and indeed Egypt has never been conquered from this direction; the Italian Army had only a few motorized vehicles; so small was the supply of provisions, munitions, and fuel, that as early as the third day of the war it had proved necessary to send supplies to Libya not to increase reserves but to provide for immediate consumption. In an advance on Alexandria, Graziani could not hope to be supplied by coastal shipping because of the threat from the British fleet based in that area. Although the high command had contemplated sending a force of 800 aircraft to Libya, this number had been reduced owing to various reasons, principally the lack of maintenance facilities, to a mere 300, and once the offensive was underway Graziani had the greatest difficulty in replacing his losses. In short, the threats that had been brandished about before the war of seizing Egypt by a great pincers movement, with one arm coming from the west and the other from the south, proved to be merely bluster.

Yet at this very time Mussolini suggested to the Germans that he send bombers to take part in the Battle of

Britain. This assistance, though scorned at first, was subsequently accepted, and in October 200 planes departed for Belgium. In addition the Italians sent their so-called ocean-going submarines to the Atlantic, and twenty-eight of these boats were based at Bordeaux. These were no larger than the "O" Class submarines which the British operated in the Mediterranean; not only was their employment in the ocean unnecessary but the Italians had no strength to spare in their own theater. This kind of dispersion of strength, insisted on by Mussolini throughout the war, was inspired much more by reasons of prestige than by strategic considerations. It was said that had he been able he would have sent Italian armies to the Pacific.

Graziani managed to accumulate a few supplies and to improve his lines of communication, and wasted valuable time in constructing an aqueduct. Only on 13 September, on imperative orders from Mussolini, was the attack finally launched. While the very inadequate British forces retired, their Navy and Air Force carried out incessant delaying actions and the retreat of the Army of the Nile was accomplished in good order. On 18 September the Italians reached and captured Sidi Barrani. This seemed to them to be a very exciting success, and despite his earlier pessimism Graziani sent the Duce enthusiastic reports on the way the troops had performed despite temperatures of over one hundred degrees. But in fact the gains were small. At the very least they should have reached Mersa Matruh, from which place bombers could have attacked the Suez Canal with fighter protection. Nevertheless, to the surprise of the British, Graziani now halted his advance owing to increasing logistic difficulties caused by his lack of motorized transport. For two months the Libyan front remained stabilized while the Army of the Nile gathered strength.

On 17 September British aircraft attacked Benghazi and sank the destroyer *Borea*, while *Aquilone*, escorting a convoy off the harbor, was blown up by a magnetic mine. On the 20th planes of the Fleet Air Arm torpedoed and sank the destroyers *Nembo* and *Ostro* at Tobruk. Between the

20th and the 23rd another British convoy carrying urgent reinforcements for Egypt was passed through the Mediterranean. The Italian fleet was at sea in very superior strength, with five battleships including *Vittorio Veneto* and *Littorio*, but once again Supermarina recalled it too soon. Between 9 and 14 October Admiral Cunningham successfully brought back an empty convoy from Malta to Eygpt. East of Malta on the night of 11-12 October the cruiser *Ajax* made radar contact on the destroyer *Artigliere* and two torpedo boats, *Airone* and *Ariel*; all three Italian ships were sunk after fighting bravely to the last. On 13 October aircraft from *Eagle* and *Illustrious* attacked Rhodes and Leros.

The invasion of Greece

INSTEAD of following up the Libyan offensive with all available forces, the Italians now decided to invade Greece, a decision which was to have important consequences. Wishing to exploit circumstances to the maximum, Mussolini had originally envisaged an invasion of Yugoslavia and in the summer of 1940 had concentrated some thirty divisions in Venetia. This project he abandoned, however, apparently as a result of opposition from the Germans who hoped to draw Yugoslavia into the Axis orbit by diplomatic means, and during September the Italians demobilized 600,000 men, some of whom had shortly to be recalled in view of the operation against Greece. Here again one may see how greatly the vacillations of policy complicated the tasks of the military command. In the Greek affair motives were involved that could not be avowed—personal ambitions and an unbridled lust for expansion—but there were also more honorable reasons for the decision. By moving first, Mussolini hoped to preserve the Balkans from German or perhaps from Russian influence and to keep the *barbari* away from the Mediterranean. By an irony of fate this undertaking ended with the arrival of the Germans at the Acropolis and the subjection of Mussolini's policy to that of Hitler.

On 15 October the Duce held a council of war in the Palazzo Venezia to determine the broad outlines of the invasion. Taking part were Ciano and Badoglio; Soddù, the Undersecretary of State for War; Roatta, Assistant Chief of Staff of the Army; Iacomoni, the Governor of Albania; and General Visconti Prasca, commander of the Army which had been assembled in Albania for the operation. The plan called for occupation of Epirus and the Ionian Islands of Zante, Cephalonia, and Corfu; although Badoglio urged the seizure of Crete and the Peloponnese, Mussolini decided not to extend the operation beyond Athens and Salonika. No one expected a repulse. Visconti Prasca had great confidence in his soldiers and in the weakness of the adversary. "The enthusiasm of the troops," he said, "is at its highest point. . . . The only manifestation of indiscipline that I have had to repress was the result of excessive eagerness to advance and fight." In passing it was decided to create the classic frontier incident in order to put some of the blame on the Greeks.

One surprising thing about this meeting, at which such important decisions were taken, is that though the venture could have completely changed the air and naval situations, neither the Navy nor the Air Force was directly represented. With naval and air officers absent, the question of Crete was given only hasty consideration. The record indicates that the decisions were made after only superficial study. General Graziani, commanding in Libya but also Chief of Staff of the Army, who with this double responsibility was particularly concerned, even declared after the war that he first heard the news of the invasion of Greece on the radio. Perhaps General Armellini did not exaggerate when he wrote: "They spoke of seizing Greece or Yugoslavia in the same off-hand way that they would decide to order a cup of coffee." And what they were planning with such levity was an unjust war, a badly prepared war, an inglorious war which would spread desolation into a neutral area of Europe and lead to new and fruitless hecatombs —inadequately clothed Italian soldiers freezing by thousands on the mountains of Albania, and emaciated Greek children searching the ruins for scraps of food.

The ultimatum to Greece demanded the installation of Italian forces in Crete, but no plans were made for the occupation of this island in case of refusal. The plan did, however, provide for the capture of Corfu, a position valuable not only for the Greek campaign but also for observation of the Ionian Sea; intensive air search from this base, had it been available, would have enabled the Italians to forestall the November attack on Taranto. But at the very start of the campaign it proved necessary to send the Bari Division, which had been designated for the occupation of Corfu, to Albania.

The Greek campaign placed a heavy load on the Italian Fleet. By 30 April 1940 it had transported to Albania 620,000 men, 87,000 horses, 700,000 tons of materiel, and 16,000 vehicles. Losses were very small, amounting to only one per cent of the tonnage carried, an accomplishment in which the Navy can take pride. But the effort would much better have been made in Libya. The Italians often accused the German High Command of failing to recognize the importance of the Mediterranean and, in a broader sense, of failing to understand naval matters. These criticisms are in part just, but in the Greek campaign, so badly conceived and badly begun, it was the Italians who compromised the naval situation and the Germans who reestablished it.

On 19 October Mussolini wrote Hitler to inform him of these plans. The Fuehrer was in France: on the 22nd he met with Laval, on the 23rd with Franco, and on the 24th he was at Montoire; the letter reached him late. He did not want to have the Balkan situation disturbed; he feared a British invasion of the Greek islands, particularly of Lemnos, from which bombers could reach the Rumanian oil fields. As quickly as possible he hastened to Florence to dissuade Mussolini from the enterprise; there the latter, delighted with his trick, reported that the operation had begun and could not be stopped. "We arrived," said Jodl, "a few hours too late."

The invasion of Greece began on 28 October, the eighteenth anniversary of the March on Rome, following the Greek rejection of the ultimatum. At first the Italians advanced a few miles, but in the first half of November they were counterattacked by superior forces and the Italian Army shortly found itself in a critical situation. On 30 October the British, never slow to occupy islands of strategic importance, landed at Suda Bay; on the same day the Admiralty announced that Greek waters had been mined; by early November British aircraft were in Attica and had begun bombing attacks on Brindisi, Bari, and Italian communications in the Adriatic.

The Greeks are excellent sailors but they possessed only a small fleet. This contained the old battleship *Kilkis*, which had been rebuilt as an antiaircraft vessel; an old 10,000-ton cruiser, the *Georgios Averof*; nine 1,000-ton destroyers; eight 275-ton torpedo boats; six 700-ton submarines. Previously, on 15 August 1940, the little cruiser *Helle* had been torpedoed under peculiar circumstances by an Italian submarine while anchored off Tinos during the Feast of the Miraculous Virgin, the great religious festival of Greece.

The Greek surface ships were used principally in the escort of convoys between Egypt and Greece, and their submarines in the attack on lines of communication. All fought bravely and, as will be seen, their losses were heavy. The Greeks also possessed about 200 aircraft, half of which were either useless or obsolescent, and all of which, having been purchased from different countries, were of ill-assorted types. The problem of obtaining spare parts rapidly became serious and, despite the energy of its crews, the Greek Air Force lost almost all effectiveness within a month. Great Britain sent five squadrons of Blenheim bombers and Gladiator fighters to Greece, and subsequently added a few Hurricanes. She could do no more and, in any event, the poor condition of the airfields prevented employment of large forces. Despite the wishes of the Greek Staff, which preferred direct support at the front, the British planes concentrated their attack on harbors and focal points of Italian communications, a policy which proved effective. In March half a dozen Swordfish of the Fleet Air Arm were added to the R.A.F. contingent and succeeded in damaging a number of Italian merchant ships. So long as Italy was alone, British air support was adequate. But when the Luftwaffe intervened the R.A.F., fighting under conditions of crushing inferiority, could only attempt to delay the German advance.

Although the invasion of Greece gave the Alexandria Fleet the use of valuable bases, it also greatly increased its responsibilities. In addition to protecting the Egyptian convoys and supporting the troops in Africa, it now had to protect the sea routes to Greece, which passed within range of Italian air and naval forces in the Dodecanese, and ensure the defense of the Greek coast not only against bombardment but also against attempts at landing. This was the more difficult since British air weakness prevented full use being made of Cretan bases. At this moment the Italian Navy, with its six battleships, constituted a major threat, but the thunderstroke of Taranto suddenly reversed the situation.

The attack on the Italian Fleet at Taranto

As FAR BACK as 1938 Captain Lyster, one of the leading experts of the Fleet Air Arm, had been studying the problems involved in attacking the Italian Fleet at its moorings. In August 1940 Lyster, now Rear Admiral commanding the aircraft carriers of the Alexandria Fleet, again took up his scheme. The British Navy had gained some experience from the attacks on *Richelieu* at Dakar and *Dunkerque* at Mers el Kébir, and in August the Fleet Air Arm began preparing for an attack on Taranto. This it was unable to carry out until Glenn Martin reconnaissance planes were based at Malta, success being dependent upon an accurate knowledge of the mooring plan. The attempt, originally planned for 21 October, the anniversary of the Battle of Trafalgar, was put off until November.

The plan contemplated an attack on the anchorage by two waves of twelve Swordfish each. On 6 November the Alexandria Fleet got underway with the aircraft carrier *Illustrious*; *Eagle*, being under repair, was unable to take part, but five of her Swordfish were embarked on *Illustrious*. Between 9 and 11 November three planes were lost as a result of forced landings and the striking force was thus reduced to twenty-one aircraft. Excellent photographs had been taken by the Malta R.A.F., and on the evening of the 11th a Glenn Martin was sent to make sure that the Italian Fleet had not left Taranto.

At 1800, with the Fleet in position 37° 33′ N 19° 35′ E, *Illustrious* was detached to continue towards Taranto escorted by four cruisers and four destroyers. At 2040 the first wave of planes took off from the carrier which was then forty miles WSW of Cephalonia and 170 miles from Taranto. This group contained six aircraft with torpedoes, four carrying bombs, and two carrying bombs and flares. While passing through cumulus clouds en route four planes became separated and continued independently a short distance behind the main group. Off Cape San Vito the squadron commander, leading the first eight planes, detached the two flare-droppers which at about 2300 dropped clusters of flares over the anchorage and then, after cruising around in search of an objective, dropped their bombs on the oil storage depot south of the harbor. The other Swordfish crossed San Pietro Island at 4,000 feet and then dove towards the inner breakwater. The antiaircraft defenses had already opened on the flare-dropping planes and were putting up an intense fire. Lieutenant Commander Williamson, the squadron commander, disappeared, but the other planes passed successfully between the cables of the balloon barrage and dropped their torpedoes. Arriving upon the scene the aircraft of the delayed group glide-bombed their targets.

The second wave, five torpedo planes, two flare-droppers,

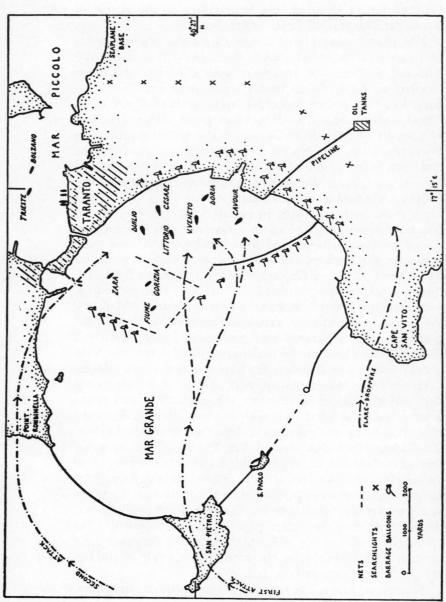

Fig. 8. The Attack on the Italian Fleet at Taranto, 11 November 1940

and one bomber, took off at 2135 with one plane twenty minutes behind. Another plane, as a result of malfunction, was forced to turn back at 2200, and returned to *Illustrious* despite some difficulties of recognition. This formation, led by Lieutenant Commander Hale, when still sixty miles from Taranto observed the flares dropped by the first group and the bursts from antiaircraft fire. At 2355 the two illuminating planes were detached over Cape San Vito; they dropped their clusters of flares to the east and southeast of the harbor, then glide-bombed their targets and retired. The five torpedo planes circled San Pietro Island, crossed over Rondinella Point, and headed for the anchorage where they attacked the two *Littorio* class battleships and the two most northerly of the *Cavours*. One plane, which was last seen over Rondinella Point, did not return. The only bomber in the group dropped on the cruisers inside the Mar Piccolo. All aircraft, except for the two that were lost, were back on board *Illustrious* before 0250, and the carrier and its escort rejoined Admiral Cunningham at 0730.

In this operation the British lost two aircraft, with one officer killed and three taken prisoner. The Italians lost three battleships. *Cavour* was hit by one torpedo abreast number two turret, her bulkheads gave way, and after some hours she sank. *Duilio* was hit by one torpedo near number two turret and sank by the bows. *Littorio* was hit by three torpedoes, two on the starboard side forward and one on the port side aft, and sank. The cruiser *Trento* and the destroyer *Libeccio* were slightly damaged by bombs which did not explode. *Littorio* and *Duilio* had to remain under repair for almost six months, and *Cavour* throughout the war.

The spirit of the British crews may be seen from the report of Captain Boyd of *Illustrious*:

This attack was carried out under somewhat difficult conditions. Owing to the heavy Fleet programme no rehearsals had been possible. Aircraft from H.M.S. *Eagle* were embarked the day before leaving harbour and had had no previous experience of landing on H.M.S. *Illustrious'* deck or of our controlled

81

landing and the use of the barrier. A third obstacle was presented by the discovery that our petrol was contaminated, three Swordfish being lost on the preceding days from this cause. In spite of this the zeal and enthusiasm of everyone to carry out this great enterprise was unabated and it is impossible to praise too highly those who in these comparatively slow machines made studied and accurate attacks in the midst of intense anti-aircraft fire.

The moorings at Taranto were inadequately protected. The planned installation of torpedo nets had been only partially completed. Furthermore, they extended to a depth of only 26 feet, which at the time was thought to be sufficient. But the torpedoes which were dropped were set for a depth of 35 feet and were armed with both percussion and magnetic fuses, of which the Italian Command had no knowledge. There was thus both tactical and technical surprise. The British were puzzled to observe no searchlights in use at Taranto, and indeed it appears that the searchlights were unsuccessful in locating their targets. Furthermore the Italians did not use smoke for concealment, a fact which led to heavy criticism. But doctrine on this point was not yet established in the Fleet, and the use of smoke in case of an attack on an anchorage was thought by many officers to be more detrimental than helpful, because by hiding the attacking planes it decreased the effectiveness of antiaircraft fire. Subsequently, however, the disappointing results and excessive ammunition expenditure of night firing led the Navy to adopt the procedure of defense by smoke.

Following the attack on Taranto and while awaiting a reorganization of the defenses of this base, the Italians moved their remaining battleships into the Tyrrhenian Sea, where they were stationed alternately at Naples and at Spezia. Spezia was made safe by distance and at Naples the breakwaters gave effective protection, a protection which could be increased by placing merchant vessels alongside the battleships. Later in the war, capital ships at Taranto were protected by very closely laid nets. Never again were major Italian ships to be damaged by aircraft torpedoes while in harbor.

While *Illustrious* was attacking Taranto, Admiral Pridham-Wippel entered the lower Adriatic with a division of cruisers, *Orion*, *Sydney*, *Ajax*, and destroyers. Shortly after midnight on the 12th this squadron sighted an Italian convoy escorted by destroyers and sank one merchant ship and damaged two others.

The victory of Taranto enabled Admiral Cunningham to send two battleships, *Ramillies* and *Malaya*, to the Atlantic; as he wrote to the Admiralty, the results permitted a judicious economy of force. Eleven months after this memorable affair the Japanese repeated the British exploit at Pearl Harbor by destroying the battle line of the American Pacific Fleet at its moorings, and it is interesting to compare the two actions. The Japanese operation was particularly audacious for the point of departure was four thousand miles from the target; the means employed were much more powerful—360 aircraft—but only some forty torpedo planes were used and they were what did the most damage. The two operations were equally difficult; surprise was complete in both cases. But the Japanese feat is sullied by the fact that they attacked before war had been declared, while the British attack, in no way immoral, was one of the most brilliant victories of the war. As often happens at sea, the action of a few skillful and brave men had reversed the balance of strength. At the end of 1941 a similarly audacious enterprise, although carried out by different means, again profoundly altered the Mediterranean situation, this time in favor of the Italians.

The action off Cape Spartivento

ON 25 November, after having bombarded ports in Libya and airfields in the Dodecanese, Admiral Cunningham detached a group composed of the battleship *Ramillies*, the cruisers *Berwick* and *Newcastle*, and five destroyers to rejoin Force H. The latter, which was advancing through the Western Mediterranean to cover a Malta convoy, contained the battleship *Renown*, the carrier *Ark Royal*, cruisers *Sheffield, Southampton, Manchester,* and five destroyers. The Italian Fleet, which had come down through the Tyrrhenian Sea and was standing off southern Sardinia, once again had an opportunity to throw its considerably superior strength against a single group of the enemy's divided forces. Under the command of Admiral Campioni it contained the battleships *Vittorio Veneto* and *Cesare,* six heavy cruisers, and fourteen destroyers. Wishing to profit from the support of shore-based aviation, Campioni was unwilling to move too far from Sardinia, and as he was poorly informed of enemy movements by his air search, he was unable to make contact with the *Ramillies* group before its meeting with Force H at 1220.

At this very moment the opposing cruiser forces sighted each other. Believing his force to be inferior to that of the enemy, Campioni ordered a withdrawal to the northward, thus committing the Italians to a retiring action. A mistaken maneuver caused by a signalling error had separated the Italian cruiser squadron under Admiral Iachino into two groups about four miles apart, with the division containing *Pola, Fiume,* and *Zara* to the eastward and that containing *Trieste, Trento,* and *Bolzano* to the west. The British first concentrated their fire on this latter group, hitting the destroyer *Lanciere.* Shortly afterward the battleships *Ramillies* and *Renown* were able to engage the *Trieste* group which was retiring northward at high speed, while a gunnery action took place between the British cruisers and the *Pola* division in the course of which *Berwick* was damaged.

At 1230 the *Vittorio* group came to the southwest to support the cruisers; the Italian battleships were then attacked by two waves of torpedo planes from *Ark Royal* which dropped at short range, and although no hits were scored the Italian squadron was forced to take evasive action. At 1300 the Italian battleships were on a course of 050, paralleling that of their cruisers. Unable to maintain speed, *Fiume* fell astern under the concentrated fire of the British

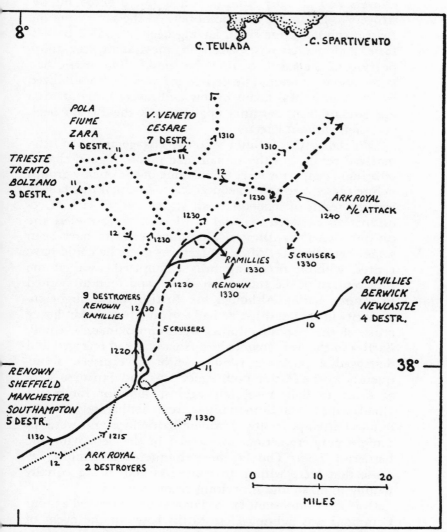

8°

C. TEULADA   .C. SPARTIVENTO

POLA
FIUME
ZARA
4 DESTR.   V. VENETO
                  CESARE
                  7 DESTR.   1310
                                      1310

TRIESTE
TRENTO
BOLZANO
3 DESTR.   12   ARK ROYAL
                                                                            A/c ATTACK
                                          1230   1240

                                          1230   5 CRUISERS
                                                                  1330

                          12   1230
                                                    RAMILLIES
                                                      1330   RAMILLIES
                                  1230   RENOWN   BERWICK
                                                 1330   NEWCASTLE
                9 DESTROYERS   4 DESTR.
                RENOWN   12 30
                RAMILLIES   10
                                   5 CRUISERS

                          1220   38°

RENOWN
SHEFFIELD
MANCHESTER   11
SOUTHAMPTON
5 DESTR.   1330

      1130   1215

              12   ARK ROYAL
                        2 DESTROYERS   0   10   20

                                                            MILES

Fig. 9. The Action off Cape Spartivento (Battle of Cape
Teulada), 27 November 1940

85

cruisers and at 1307 Admiral Campioni ordered his destroyers to lay smoke to conceal her. At the same time the British column came right, having been straddled by *Vittorio*, and combat was broken off, the Italian fleet disappearing to the north behind the smoke. The battle had lasted about an hour. The destroyer *Lanciere*, immobilized by its damage, was taken in tow and saved. Only at 1530 did aircraft from Sardinia finally attack the British fleet, and then without effect.

Like the battle of Punta Stilo this engagement had little material result, but the Italians had missed a good chance of bringing superior force against one of the enemy groups before these were able to concentrate. As usual this failure was the result of inadequate air search and of lack of coordination between sea and air forces. Nevertheless the caution shown by Admiral Campioni seems to have been somewhat excessive. After contact was made he could have retired without becoming fully committed, awaited the intervention of the Italian Air Force, and then attempted to resume battle. Although the British had a slight superiority in capital ships, he had a great advantage in heavy cruisers; the opposing forces were approximately equal. Earlier in the war Commodore Harwood had engaged and destroyed a pocket battleship with his cruisers; subsequently in the Pacific both Americans and Japanese were at times to fight resolutely against superior forces. At Guadalcanal, American cruisers were deliberately to seek out and attempt to stop Japanese battleships and were, in a night gunnery action, to succeed in the destroying the battleship *Hiei*. The Japanese conquered an empire because they were willing to take risks and, being equally willing to do so, the Americans reconquered it.

One other important factor favored a determined action: Campioni was fighting close to his base. In the event of damage his ships could easily have reached Cagliari, only fifty miles distant, while British ships in trouble would have had either to cover the 700 miles to Gibraltar or the 300 to Malta, and in the latter case pass the Sicilian Strait within close range of Italian air strength based in Sicily. It does not therefore appear that the Italian admiral's situation was such as to oblige him to retire and break off the action. But Taranto had further increased the caution of the High Command which, having three battleships under repair, hesitated to risk the others. This factor had weight but it would not have stopped some men. During World War II the Italian Fleet was led by commanders of ability, but Italy was not to find the great captain, the *Andrea Doria*, which she so badly needed at this critical moment of her history.

The British offensive in Egypt

ON THE NIGHT of 7-8 December the Army of the Nile, under the command of General Wavell, attacked Sidi Barrani. Its strength amounted to only 31,000 men but it had 225 tanks, including some Matildas which were greatly superior to anything possessed by the Italians. Sidi Barrani was taken on the 10th, and by the 15th all Egypt was free of Italian troops. Continuing their advance into Cyrenaica, the British captured Bardia on 4 January 1941, Tobruk on the 22nd, Derna on the 30th, Benghazi on 1 February, and on the 9th the Army of the Nile stood before El Agheila. It had advanced almost 600 miles and had taken 130,000 prisoners, 400 tanks, and 1,290 guns. It had lost only 2,000 men, killed, wounded, and missing.

The Alexandria Fleet supported these operations all along the coast. On 2 January the battleships and *Illustrious* bombarded Bardia, thus assisting the capture of this town. The monitor *Terror* and the gunboats *Ladybird*, *Aphis*, and *Gnat* were continuously in action, often supported by destroyers. At Tobruk the old Italian cruiser *San Giorgio* was being used as a floating battery. With the advance of the British armies Supermarina requested its withdrawal but Comando Supremo, hoping to halt the enemy, refused. But Tobruk was unable to hold out, and on 2 January *San Giorgio* had to be scuttled.

The Libyan disaster resulted in the removal of Marshal

Graziani, who had been completely demoralized by the defeat, and events in Greece brought the fall of Marshal Badoglio, who was sacrificed as a scapegoat. In Libya Graziani was succeeded by General Gariboldi, while Badoglio was replaced at Comando Supremo by General Cavallero, who retained the position until the fall of Mussolini.

Despite its activity in support of operations in Libya, the Alexandria Fleet was also busy elsewhere. On 18 December battleships *Warspite* and *Valiant* bombarded Valona. On 20 December Cunningham detached the battleship *Malaya* to the Atlantic; its passage through the Mediterranean was unopposed, although the destroyer *Hyperion* was blown up by a mine off Pantelleria.

The reorganization of the Italian naval command

On 8 December Admiral Riccardi replaced Admiral Cavagnari as Chief of the Naval General Staff and Undersecretary of State, while Admiral Campioni became Assistant Chief of Staff. Admiral Angelo Iachino became Commander in Chief of the Italian Fleet, in which capacity he commanded the united surface squadrons which previously had been separately responsible to Supermarina. But the submarine force was not put under his command, and continued to be directed by the Naval General Staff through the Admiral Commanding Submarines, whose headquarters remained at Rome. The surface fleet was organized as follows: *Vittorio Veneto*, flagship of the Commander in Chief, V Battleship Division, *Cesare, Doria*; I Cruiser Division, *Zara, Pola, Gorizia, Fiume*; III Cruiser Division, *Trieste, Trento, Bolzano*; VII Cruiser Division, *Eugenio di Savoia, Duca d'Aoste, Montecuccoli*; VIII Cruiser Division, *Abruzzi, Garibaldi, Attendolo*.

Fleet destroyers were distributed among the various divisions of heavy ships. Ships assigned to escort duty were controlled by Supermarina through the admirals commanding the Naval Districts. Three battleships, *Littorio, Duilio*, and *Cavour*, were still under repair. During an air attack on Naples on 14 December the cruiser *Pola* was heavily damaged by two bombs, but repairs were completed prior to the Battle of Matapan.

Admiral Iachino, who was to retain command of the surface fleet until 5 April 1943, was at this time fifty-one years old. He had held numerous sea commands. From 1931 to 1934 he had been Naval Attaché at London, and had thoroughly studied the British Navy for which he had great admiration. When the war began he had been in command of the Naval Academy at Leghorn but had requested immediate sea duty; the request was granted and he was given command of a division of *Cavour*-type battleships. Shortly afterward Admiral Paladini, Commander of the Second Squadron, fell ill at Spezia; Iachino replaced him in time to command this Squadron in the action off Cape Spartivento. Highly cultivated, an excellent technician and a good sailor, he enjoyed a splendid service reputation and his advancement to the position of Commander in Chief was welcomed enthusiastically. But the course of events affected his popularity. Little by little the conviction spread that the Admiral was unlucky. This reputation, very different from one of incompetence, was nevertheless discouraging to the crews. After the war Admiral Iachino published an account of the Battle of Matapan and a number of articles in *Rivista Marittima* which give important information not only on the course of events but also on the organization, the methods, and the morale of the Italian Fleet; all these writings are notably calm, objective, and precise.

At the end of 1940, despite the defeat at Taranto, the Italian Fleet remained strong. It still disputed the control of the Central Mediterranean with the British Fleet and, despite losses, was able to supply the Italian forces in Libya. But the repulse in Greece and the retreat in Africa had seriously compromised Italian prestige. The Germans were about to intervene; a new phase in the Mediterranean was about to begin. Hitler now took Mussolini in tow.

PART III
GERMANY TO THE RESCUE OF ITALY

6. The Beginnings of German Intervention

The concept of intervention

AT an early date the Germans had made an offer, although with certain conditions attached, to send forces to the Mediterranean theater. In War Instruction 18, dated 12 November 1940, Hitler had written as follows regarding the Egyptian campaign:

> Intervention of German forces is not envisaged until after the Italians reach Mersa Matruh. Even then the Luftwaffe will be employed only if the Italians place the necessary bases at our disposal. In anticipation of German action the following preparations will be made: the Army will keep one armored division available; the Navy will fit out German merchant ships in Italian ports; the Air Force will prepare for air attacks on Alexandria and the Suez Canal.

Mussolini would have preferred to restrict German assistance to the shipment of supplies. "If the Germans ever get here," he said, "they will never go home." He had begun to realize that he was no longer an equal partner in this alliance, and on his instructions Badoglio had refused Keitel's offer to send self-contained German units to Africa. But Wavell's victorious offensive and the Greek advance in Albania now forced the Italians not only to accept but actually to beg for help at a time when assistance would look like rescue.

If the invasion of Greece had displeased the Germans, the defeats which followed infuriated them. The O.K.W. now lost all illusions regarding the effectiveness of the Italian Army. Not only did they feel that Italy would be unable to capture Suez and defeat the Greeks, but also that she would be hard put to it to resist British blows. But Hitler, for both ideological and strategic reasons, wished above all to prevent Italy from deserting the Axis. Thus the Germans found themselves forced to intervene on a large scale. And since it was impossible to take effective action in the

Balkans before the end of winter, they found themselves handicapped in their preparations for war against the U.S.S.R. On 13 December Hitler issued the directives for Operation MARITA against Greece: "The Battle of Albania has not yet had decisive results. Owing to the dangerous situation in Albania the British must be prevented from establishing air bases in Greece from which they could attack both the Rumanian oil wells and Italy."

In January the Germans also decided to intervene in Tripolitania, where the Italian situation was very serious and where a retreat to Tripoli was feared. The Luftwaffe was consequently no longer concerned with an immediate attack on Suez, but with the more modest problem of assisting the Italians in the Central Mediterranean. Thus German intervention took three forms: an invasion of Greece in the spring of 1941, Rommel's counter-offensive in Libya to reestablish the Italian situation there, and operations by the Luftwaffe in the Central Mediterranean. As a matter of overall strategy these were defensive operations; the Germans did not attempt to eliminate the British by driving them from the Mediterranean. They wished to prevent an Italian collapse, to protect their Rumanian oil supply, and to secure their southern flank for the invasion of Russia. And so as not to compromise the main objective, the elimination of the U.S.S.R., they attempted to gain these ends by only limited commitments of force.

The intervention of the Luftwaffe

IN DECEMBER and January the Tenth German Air Fleet, known to the Italians as X Cat (*Corpo aereo tedesco*), moved into the airfields of Reggio Calabria, and the Sicilian fields at Catania, Comiso, Trapani, and Palermo. This force had a total of between four and five hundred planes: Junker 87's, single motored Stukas with fixed streamlined landing gear; fast and heavily armed two-engined Junker 88's and Heinkel 111's; ME 110 fighter-bombers, and a few scouting planes. In March a few more Messerschmidt 110's were added. X Cat, however, had no torpedo planes. The German personnel was skilled in overseas operations, was of high quality, and possessed of great self-confidence.

The Germans insisted on being placed directly under the orders of Goering, the Commander in Chief of the Luftwaffe, this under the pretext that he wished to keep in close touch with operations and that he could not permit others to come between him and his forces. Superaereo was offended; it insisted that it had to coordinate the German and Italian air forces and, in theory, won its point. But the subordination was purely a formal one and General Geissler, commander of X Cat, operated almost entirely at his own discretion. The missions assigned the Germans were to protect communications with Libya, to prevent the passage of British convoys, and to take part in the attack on Malta. With their arrival the Mediterranean war took a wholly new turn.

On 6 January a convoy of four fast cargo ships got underway from Gibraltar for Malta and Egypt, escorted by Force H with battleships *Renown* and *Malaya*, the carrier *Ark Royal*, four cruisers and a destroyer flotilla. On 8 January, in coordination with this operation, Malta-based bombers attacked the Italian Fleet at Naples; the battleship *Cesare* was damaged by three near misses and put out of action. On the 9th Italian aircraft from Sardinia bombed the convoy; with evening the battleships of Force H turned back towards Gibraltar, leaving the convoy to continue escorted by cruisers *Southampton, Gloucester, Bonaventure*, and destroyers, under Rear Admiral Renouf.

Off Pantelleria, on the night of January 9-10, the convoy was attacked by the Italian destroyers *Vega* and *Circe*, and the former was sunk by *Bonaventure*. But the Italians had strengthened their minefields in the Strait of Sicily; the destroyer *Gallant* ran upon a mine, her bow was blown off, and she had to be towed into Malta by *Mohawk*.

On the morning of the 10th the Alexandria Fleet took over protection of the merchant ships. About noon a strong formation of Stukas with fighter escort appeared and attacked with skill and determination, concentrating on *Illustrious*. The carrier was quickly and heavily hit, and one 500-kilo bomb penetrated the armored deck aft and exploded, damaging the steering gear. Steering with her engines, *Illustrious* headed for Malta. In the afternoon the Stukas returned and scored several more hits. The after part of the ship was a furnace, the hull had been holed in many places by bomb bursts, and much of the antiaircraft armament had been destroyed; but although slowed, the great ship succeeded in reaching Malta under cover of darkness.

On the 11th the cruiser *Southampton* was also attacked by Stukas and Italian bombers, the latter scoring two hits. As she had a list of thirty degrees and was unable to make headway, Admiral Cunningham in the evening ordered her sunk by gunfire. The convoy had been pushed through, but losses had been heavy.

What was the Italian battle fleet doing while all these events were taking place? On the 8th, after the damage to *Cesare*, Supermarina had ordered the battleships to retire to Spezia; only on the 11th, by which time Force H was well on its way back to Gibraltar, were they sent out on a rather pointless search for the enemy in the Western Mediterranean. After a short cruise the Italian battleships again retired to Spezia. Changes in personnel had not increased the audacity of the Italian High Command.

Illustrious had to be repaired at Malta. The great floating dock had been sunk by the Italians early in the war and no drydock was large enough to take her. The carrier was moored in French Creek and lightened as much as possible so that damage could be discovered and repaired. More air attacks were made on the 16th and 18th, but the island's defenses had been heavily reinforced and the Luftwaffe was unable to finish *Illustrious* off. On the 23rd, temporarily patched up, she made her escape and reached Alexandria safely although still in need of major repairs. For these it was necessary to send her to the United States, so that for several months the Alexandria Fleet was without a carrier.

Throughout the winter Malta underwent incessant attacks, both from the Luftwaffe and from the Italian Air Force, which reduced the effectiveness of the R.A.F. detachment there. Not until May did another convoy go through from Gibraltar to Egypt, but Rommel's armored force reached Libya with insignificant losses.

The attacks on Genoa and Leghorn by Force H, and on Suda Bay by the Italian assault machines

HARD PRESSED by the Luftwaffe, the British Fleet reacted by counterattacking. On 31 January the battleships *Warspite, Barham, Valiant*, the monitor *Terror*, and light units bombarded Bardia, where an Italian battery, although several times silenced, stubbornly resumed fire. At this time also the Admiralty decided to undertake a more important diversionary operation in the Western Mediterranean in order to destroy Italian battleships or cruisers, lower enemy morale, force the Italians to shift some of their Central Mediterranean forces northward, and damage war industries, shipping, and supplies. This decision on the part of the Admiralty was strengthened by intelligence which raised fears of an Italian occupation of the Balearic Islands.

Force H at this time was composed of the battleships *Renown* and *Malaya*, the aircraft carrier *Ark Royal*, the cruiser *Sheffield*, and ten destroyers of the 13th Destroyer Flotilla. In the first attempt, which took place between 31 January and 4 February, aircraft from *Ark Royal* attacked the dam at Lake Tirso in Sardinia, but poor weather forced Admiral Somerville to retire to Gibraltar without striking the ports of the Upper Tyrrhenian. On 6 February Force H again got underway and on the night of 8th-9th separated into two groups, one centered around *Ark Royal*, which, escorted by three destroyers, was to bomb Leghorn, and the other comprising the rest of the Force, whose mission was to shell Genoa. In the early morning fighter-escorted bombers from *Ark Royal* attacked Leghorn and dropped mines off Spezia. Shortly before 0900 the battleships appeared off Genoa and bombarded the port from a range of about 20,000 yards, their fire being spotted by their own and *Sheffield's* planes. On shore damage was heavy but the battleship *Duilio*, then at Genoa for repairs, was not hit.

The British lost only a single plane. The only reaction was from shore batteries and antiaircraft. The ponderous Italian organization was unable to mount an air attack. After having rejoined according to plan, both groups of Force H retired by a northerly route.

Having had advance intelligence of the operation, Supermarina had sent out the Italian Fleet. At 0800 on the 9th three battleships, *Vittorio Veneto, Cèsare,* and *Doria,* three heavy cruisers, and ten destroyers were concentrated forty miles west of Cape Testa at the northern tip of Sardinia, where they were awaiting information from the Air Force. But the information that Admiral Iachino received from Supermarina was vague and contradictory, and his own shipboard planes failed to locate the enemy. After their attack the British ships were sighted only by a single naval reconnaissance plane, which was shot down before being able to transmit a report. Iachino headed north on varying courses and the two fleets crossed without sighting each other.

Although visibility was limited, the weather was not so bad as to justify such a complete failure of air search. In his action report Admiral Iachino pointed out that in view of the incompetence of the Air Force it would in the future be necessary to employ 5,000-ton cruisers for scouting, and that while perhaps he should have deployed his cruisers and destroyers in a scouting line to seek out the enemy, an encounter without aerial support might have developed into a defeat. In any event, a British squadron had reached as far as Genoa and had withdrawn without being attacked either by a surface ship or by a submarine or by a single plane. It was very clear that more flexible methods were needed by the High Command, but with every failure the rivalry between Superaereo and Supermarina increased in bitterness, preventing the establishment of a rational and efficient organization. The lessons were lost upon the Italians. Shortly after this event Comando Supremo was to undertake an important operation without having effected any genuine improvement of coordination between Navy and Air Force; the result was the disaster of Matapan.

But before this took place the Italians gained a very notable success at Suda Bay by the use of their assault machines. On the night of 26 March the destroyers *Crispi* and *Sella* carried five motor boats loaded with explosives, under the command of Lieutenant Faggioni, to the harbor entrance. Suda Bay is long and narrow and was defended by three rows of obstructions. Handled with great skill, the motor boats succeeded in passing the barriers and in penetrating deep into the anchorage. There they awaited the first light of dawn when, taking the enemy completely by surprise, they hit and sank a large tanker and a transport and heavily damaged the stern of the 8,000-ton cruiser *York*. The cruiser was run aground, after which it served first as a floating antiaircraft battery and then, during the evacuation of Greece, as general headquarters. Unable to get underway, it was finished off by aircraft on 21 May 1941 during the invasion of Crete. This attack on Suda Bay, a very fine feat of arms on the part of the assault machines, was to be only the first of an important series.

7. The Battle of Matapan

The Italian plan

IN early February Admiral Iachino suggested a raid against enemy shipping between Benghazi and Crete, but the project was disapproved by Supermarina. On the 15th Admiral Raeder and Rear Admiral Fricke, representing the German Navy, and Admirals Riccardi, the Chief of Staff, and Courten, Brenta, and Giartoso, representing the Italians, met at Merano. The accomplishments of the two navies were described; the Italians heartily congratulated their allies on their successes in Norway; the Germans hinted indirectly that the activity of the Italian Navy might be increased and suggested, first in the conference and subsequently in individual conversations, an attack on Allied communications in the Aegean. The Italians shied away, pleading the distance of the objective and the uncertainty of air support, and on this point the conference had no immediate results. On the other hand it was decided to strengthen the mine fields in the Strait of Sicily, and the Germans offered to provide mines suitable for deep water and of a type difficult to sweep, an offer which was accepted by the Italians.

Nevertheless Raeder continued to exert pressure by way of the German Naval Mission for action by the Italian Fleet in the Aegean. On 15 March Iachino was called to Rome. Riccardi informed him that his plan of a raid between Cyrenaica and Crete had been revived with some modifications. Supermarina envisaged a double *puntata offensiva*, a thrust south of Crete as far as the little island of Gavdo, accompanied by another to the northward as far as Avgo Rocks, while at the same time motor boats were to attack the anchorage at Suda Bay.

As the operation would take the Italian Fleet far from its bases, both the success of the effort and the safety of the force depended upon excellent scouting. Supermarina had planned a rather inadequate submarine deployment in which one submarine was stationed in Kaxo Strait between Scarpanto and Crete and four others in a square in the Eastern Mediterranean. The Air Force was to reconnoiter Alexandria and Suda Bay during the two days preceding the operation and was subsequently to carry out searches from Sicily, Taranto, and the Dodecanese. Direct cover for the fleet as far as longitude 21°E was to be provided by X Cat, and beyond that line by aircraft from the Dodecanese. Finally, on D-Day Italian planes were to bomb the airfields on Crete and the Luftwaffe those on Malta.

Admiral Iachino was not satisfied by these arrangements. Beyond the 21st meridian he was to be covered only by Dodecanese-based aviation, which he considered inadequate; furthermore the operation plan which was sent him following the discussions at Rome spoke of "aerial protection or armed reconnaissance," an ambiguity which disturbed him. He rightly felt that it was necessary to have continuous fighter cover over the Fleet, and twice he telephoned to Rome for fuller information, only to be put off with vague words. Furthermore, the Fleet had never operated in concert with the Germans. In the two days preceding the sortie, which was scheduled for 27 March, the staffs endeavored to reach an understanding and to establish liaison, but operating experience was lacking. For their first operation they would have done better to have restricted themselves to a sortie in the Central Mediterranean.

None of this was very reassuring. At the moment of getting underway the Fleet Commander once again attempted to telephone Supermarina to secure, at this eleventh hour, improved methods of aerial support. But he was told that the cables had already been slipped and the shore telephone line cut off. The operation was under way; he had to take his chances and trust to luck.

The day action

BY NOON of the 27th the Italian force, which had sortied from Naples, Taranto, Messina, and Brindisi, was advancing in two groups about sixty miles off Cape Murro di Porco. The Cattaneo group, which was to operate north of Crete, contained the I Cruiser Division, *Zara, Pola*, and *Fiume*, and the 4th Destroyer Squadron, under the direct command of Admiral Cattaneo, and also the VIII Division, cruisers *Abruzzi* and *Garibaldi* and two destroyers, under Admiral Legnani. The second group, under Admiral Iachino, contained *Vittorio Veneto* escorted by the 13th Destroyer Squadron, and Admiral Sansonetti's III Cruiser Division, *Trieste, Trento, Bolzano*, with the 12th Destroyer Squadron. The two groups were to separate at 2000. The sea was rough, the weather overcast. During the day only scattered Italian and German aircraft appeared; doubtless the Air Force was hindered by the visibility, which was limited to seven or eight miles. A joint training exercise which had been planned with the Germans failed to come off, a fact which did not augur well for collaboration with the air forces.

At 1225 *Trieste* reported that a British Sunderland aircraft was in sight. A few minutes later a most urgent message from the enemy plane, reporting the position of three Italian cruisers and some destroyers, was deciphered on board *Vittorio Veneto*. Fifteen minutes later a second signal gave the course and speed of the cruisers: course 120 degrees, speed 15 knots. In actual fact the Italians were on course 134 degrees and were making 20 knots, but in any case the Italian squadron had been sighted and it was certain that if the Alexandria Fleet was not already at sea it soon would be. Admiral Iachino turned to course 150 from 1400 to 1600 in the hope of misleading the enemy, but the effort was wasted. Despite incessant requests from Alexandria the Sunderland sent no further reports.

At 2200 Supermarina sent a dispatch which ordered the Cattaneo Group to rejoin the Iachino Group at dawn, while leaving the mission of the latter unchanged. Thus the offensive thrust north of Crete was cancelled. During the day Iachino had received reports from Italian aircraft indicating that at 1445 three battleships, two carriers, and cruisers had been observed at Alexandria. From this time on no further information regarding the British forces was received.

At Alexandria Admiral Cunningham, with remarkable prescience, had already made a whole series of arrangements, apparently on the assumption that a battle would take place on the 28th. He ordered Admiral Pridham-Wippell, commanding the four cruisers and four destroyers of Force B, to get underway from the Piraeus so as to be southwest of Gavdo Island at daylight 28 March where he would be joined by five destroyers from Alexandria. He decided to get underway on the evening of the 27th with his battleline and most of the Fleet. Finally, he ordered Convoy AG-9, which on the 27th was en route to the Piraeus, to hold its course until nightfall and then to turn back, thus using this convoy as bait. All these steps had been taken before the signals from the Sunderland were received. In his report the British Commander in Chief explains that he had been alerted by the unusual activity of enemy aviation. In Admiral Iachino's opinion, Cunningham had been forewarned by the espionage network which Great Britain maintained inside Italy.

Following receipt of the signals from the Sunderland, the British admiral made only minor changes in his plan. He retained in company the five destroyers which had been designated to join Pridham-Wippell, and he requested R.A.F. reconnaissance for the next day, 28 March, over the southern Ionian Sea, the southwest Aegean, and the area south of Crete. At dusk, as the Italian Fleet advanced towards Gavdo at 23 knots, the Alexandria Squadron sortied and took a course of 300 degrees, speed 20 knots.

At dawn on the 28th the Italian Fleet was approaching Gavdo in the following order: Admiral Sansonetti's cruiser division was in the van; seven miles astern came the *Vittorio Veneto* group; while the Cattaneo Group was about ten miles north of the battleship. Shortly before 0600 Admiral Iachino had catapulted his battleship's seaplanes, and at 0643 one of these planes reported the presence of British cruisers and destroyers about fifty miles to the east-

ward of *Vittorio Veneto*. These were Pridham-Wippell's
cruisers. The Italian squadron increased speed, and at
about 0740 the *Trieste* cruisers sighted the British division,
which, on a course of 120 degrees, appeared to be retiring
toward Alexandria. Although he had been ordered to wait
for *Vittorio Veneto*, Sansonetti pursued the British at full
speed, and at 0812 his three cruisers, *Trento*, *Trieste*, and
Bolzano, opened fire.

Outgunned by the Italian force, Admiral Pridham-Wippell retired at top speed, hoping to draw it into contact
with Cunningham's battle fleet. For about forty minutes
the Italians fired on the enemy cruisers: the range was
great, between 25,000 and 29,500 yards; visibility was re-

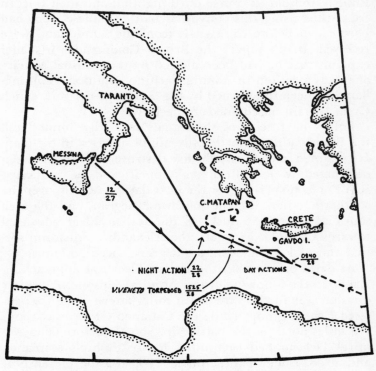

Fig. 10. The Battle of Matapan, 28-29 March 1941

duced by a light mist which hung over the sea; the obsolescent Italian range-finders did not give accurate readings. As for the British, they found their 6-inch splashes hard to see, and the few salvos that they fired fell short. The gunnery action had no result. Admiral Iachino, although ignorant of the fact that Cunningham was at sea, feared a trap. At about 0840, deciding that they were unable to close, the Italians turned about to a course of 300 degrees. At this moment they were distant 60 miles bearing 162 from Gavdo, and had thus gone somewhat beyond the limit that Supermarina had laid down for the raid.

As soon as Pridham-Wippell observed the Italian movement he too turned about and began to pursue the enemy. He maintained contact with Sansonetti's division, but did not notice *Vittorio Veneto*, which, ahead and to starboard of the *Trieste* cruisers, was also steering a course of 300 degrees. At ten o'clock Admiral Iachino turned about with *Vittorio Veneto*, so as to close the British cruisers from the north. This maneuver succeeded and the Italian battleship soon surprised the enemy cruisers, which hastily retired behind a smoke screen. *Vittorio Veneto's* fire was accurate, and salvos straddled the cruiser *Orion*, which suffered light damage from a near-miss. But the smokescreen soon became opaque, and *Vittorio Veneto* fired more than ninety 15-inch shells without scoring a hit. At about 1115 the battleship was unsuccessfully attacked by torpedo planes from *Formidable*, and at 1130 Iachino broke off his pursuit and turned back to 300 degrees.

As for Pridham-Wippell, realizing that he had had a narrow escape, he retired on Cunningham's force, with which he made contact at 1230. By this time the whole Italian squadron was retiring to the northwest; they knew they were being followed but were ignorant of the precise position and strength of the British, while the latter had themselves only an uncertain knowledge of their enemy. Cunningham now attempted to slow the Italians by air attack, planning to destroy with his surface ships any units that fell astern.

These attacks were carried out not only by the aircraft from *Formidable*, but also by R.A.F. planes from Greece and by Swordfish from *Illustrious'* squadron which had been sent to Crete while the carrier was being repaired. The attacks began in early afternoon, and at 1520 a torpedo from a *Formidable* plane hit *Vittorio Veneto* astern near her port outboard propeller. Four thousand tons of water entered the ship, steering control was lost, and at 1530 the engines stopped. But the crew succeeded in regaining steering control and in starting the starboard engine, and the battleship was able to continue her course, first at 16 knots and then, after 1700, at 19 knots.

Anticipating further attacks, the Italian admiral assumed a concentrated formation in order to protect the damaged battleship: I and VIII Cruiser Divisions were stationed 1000 meters to starboard and III Cruiser Division to port, while the destroyers ringed the heavy ships. At about 1930, as twilight was falling, British air attacks began again. The Italians zigzagged, laid down clouds of smoke, trained their searchlights on their attackers, and fired off everything they had. When the attack ceased at about 1950, Iachino and his staff thought that the squadron had escaped undamaged. Night had come; all seemed well; but then a signal was received from *Zara*: "*Pola* reports being hit aft by a torpedo; the ship has stopped."

Iachino then dispatched cruisers *Zara* and *Fiume* and destroyers *Alfieri, Carducci, Oriani,* and *Gioberti* to assist *Pola*, an unfortunate decision and one which subsequently was to be heavily criticized. On the basis of available information, Iachino could not be sure that Cattaneo would not encounter greatly superior enemy forces; on the contrary he knew that an aircraft carrier was at sea in his pursuit, and that the British always accompanied this type with battleships. Cattaneo's mission might take a long time and the British had excellent chances of overtaking him. For these reasons some think that Iachino unwisely exposed a very important part of his squadron to destruction, and that he would have done better to have detached only two destroyers to help *Pola*, as Cattaneo himself had originally intended. But Iachino felt that destroyers alone would be unable to tow the damaged cruiser, and that by sending only small ships he would lose all chance of saving her; he believed that his enemy was much further to the east; he thought that Cattaneo's group, being composed of fast units, could avoid battle in the event that it met the enemy by day, and he felt a night contact improbable.

These are strong reasons, and it seems unjust to blame the Italian Commander in Chief for having taken risks to save one of his best ships. Had he not done so, he would have been condemned for inactivity.

The night action

AT ABOUT 2100, after an exchange of signals which indicated, at least on Cattaneo's part, certain doubts regarding the wisdom of his mission, *Zara*, *Fiume*, and the four destroyers turned eastward in column in search of *Pola*. At 2225 they suddenly ran upon the British battleships. All were surprised, the British as well as the Italians, but the former were ready for a night engagement. By contrast, on board the Italian cruisers the crews were busy preparing the tow lines and only the secondary batteries were manned. The British destroyer *Greyhound* illuminated the enemy ships with her searchlights, and first *Warspite* and *Valiant*, and then *Barham* opened fire. Within a few minutes both Italian cruisers were burning and two destroyers had been sunk. Not a single shot had been fired by Cattaneo's division; only the destroyer *Alfieri*, on the initiative of an ensign, fired three torpedoes which missed their target since the ship was turning at full rudder at the moment of firing. Very quickly the British battleships turned away to starboard, leaving the destroyers to finish up the work of destruction. *Fiume* capsized at 2315, and at 0230 of the 29th *Zara* was sunk by the destroyer *Jervis*.

A few miles away lay *Pola*, without a list but very low in the water. She had been hit in the stern by a torpedo. The port engines were flooded as were most of the boilers, the

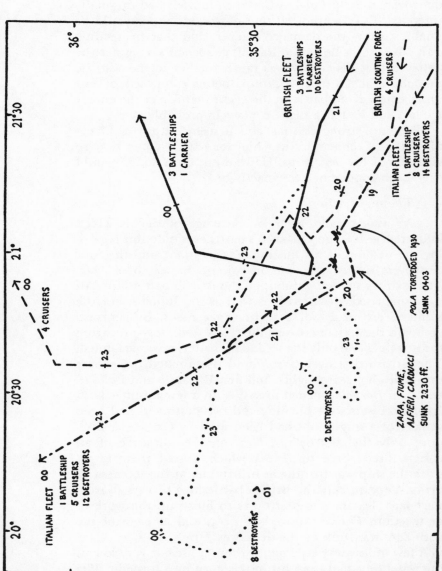

Fig. 11. Matapan: the Night Action

condensers had been disabled, and the ship was unable to get underway. Ready ammunition had been thrown overboard for fear of fire. The generators had broken down, there was no light, and it was impossible to load either by using the ammunition hoists or by hand. The ship could neither maneuver nor fight. From the bridge, the dark masses of the enemy heavy ships had been seen passing in the night. These indeed had detected *Pola* by radar but, uncertain of her identity, had continued in pursuit of the Italian main body. Shortly after they had passed, *Pola* saw firing to the westward and observed ships burning. As the situation continued to deteriorate the commanding officer, Captain de Pisa, gave the order to abandon ship. This command was being carried out when a shape loomed up out of the darkness; it was the British destroyer *Havock* which had become separated from its squadron. Recognizing an Italian cruiser, *Havock* opened fire; surprised by the enemy's inaction, she came closer and, observing that *Pola* was disabled, alerted the British squadron. The 14th Destroyer Flotilla now arrived upon the scene, and its commander, Captain Mack in *Jervis*, went alongside and recovered 236 prisoners including Captain de Pisa. *Jervis* and *Nubian* finished off the damaged ship and at 0320 *Pola* disappeared beneath the surface.

The Italian hospital ship *Gradisca*, sent to the scene at Admiral Cunningham's request, recovered and brought back to Messina about 160 men, some of whom had remained five days on rafts; the British and Greek ships had succeeded in saving a total of about 900 men but had been forced to break off rescue operations in the morning of the 29th as a result of air attacks by the Luftwaffe. The British squadron had lost only one man, Lieutenant Commander Dalzell Stead, who was lost with his plane at the time of the torpedoing of *Vittorio Veneto*. Although the disproportion of these losses had no precedent in naval history, Admiral Cunningham was not entirely satisfied. *Vittorio Veneto* had succeeded in escaping and, with complete objectivity, the British commander set down the reasons: mistakes made during the search phase by Pridham-Wippell's cruisers and Mack's destroyers, and his own mistake in having steered too long to the eastward after the night engagement. During the return to Alexandria, the Fleet was at long last attacked by aircraft of the Luftwaffe, but without effect.

Only on arriving at Taranto with his diminished force did Iachino learn of the disaster that had overtaken the Cattaneo Division. Radio London had announced that the cruisers *Zara*, *Fiume*, and *Pola*, and the destroyers *Gioberti* and *Maestrale* (actually *Carducci* and *Alfieri*) had been sunk by His Majesty's forces during the night of 28-29 March.

Consequences of the battle

SUMMONED to Rome, Iachino was received by Mussolini in the famous Sala del Mappamondo. After asking a few questions the Duce declared:

Throughout the operation you had neither a single Italian nor a single German plane overhead. You were in the position of a blind man fighting men with open eyes. This is a serious matter; this state of things cannot be permitted to last. It is inconceivable that naval operations should take place in enemy-controlled waters without the necessary air search and without essential fighter cover. I have ordered my Chief of the General Staff to have construction of an aircraft carrier begun at once, and I am sure that we will have it soon, probably within a year. In the meantime, in order to avoid useless losses of ships and men, the Fleet must not operate beyond maximum fighter range.

"I admired Mussolini's understanding," said the Admiral, "but it occurred to me that if we had no carriers the fault was very largely his."

In actual fact, Axis aviation had been more active than Iachino thought, and several planes had flown unobserved over both friendly and enemy fleets. But they had succeeded neither in protecting the Italian ships, nor in providing them with information, nor in effectively striking the enemy. It was very clear that an aircraft carrier would have been of the greatest help to the Italians. They decided to convert the liner *Roma*, which they renamed *Aquila*, but neither this ship nor *Sparviero*, on which work was subsequently undertaken, was ready in time to take part in the war. To build a carrier and put it into operation takes a great deal of time. The Germans were no more experienced at this than the Italians, and the Japanese, who could have instructed them, showed no eagerness to disclose their secrets to their allies.

One further question greatly concerned the Italian Command. Deciphered signals seemed to indicate that the British had discovered and reported Cattaneo's cruisers before arriving within visual range of these ships. Supermarina therefore decided hastily to resume the research on radar which had been begun before the war but which had been abandoned at the start of hostilities. General Matteini, who was in charge of the armament program, undertook to provide a satisfactory apparatus in three months, but it was not until the end of 1941 that the first set was installed on *Littorio*. And even then the tests of this model proved disappointing, and interminable adjustments were necessary.

Throughout the war the Italian Navy had to fight without radar and without aircraft carriers; the grave technical inferiorities with which they began the war were never rectified, but on the contrary became more serious owing to the great strides made by the enemy. On the tactical level, the lessons of the battle were also very disturbing. The Italian Navy had emphasized the study of night destroyer attacks, but it had considered night contacts between heavy ships unlikely, and attempted to avoid them because here again it labored under numerous technical weaknesses: it lacked flashless powder except for small-caliber guns; searchlights were of relatively short range and their control mechanism was poor; the central fire control system was ill-suited to the requirements of night vision. After dark, therefore, only the locally controlled guns of the secondary battery were kept manned and ready for action to drive off attacking destroyers. Tactical doctrine assumed that heavy units would always be protected at night by a screen of destroyers ahead; they would receive warning of the approach of an enemy, and could turn away so as to avoid night melees which were rightly considered risky. In the event, however, Admiral Cattaneo, for reasons which are still unknown, headed towards *Pola* with his ships in column and his destroyers in the rear.

Nevertheless, even if it seemed necessary to avoid nocturnal encounters between heavy ships, there was no assurance that this would be possible, and it would have been only prudent to prepare for such engagements as, indeed, the British Navy had long taken great care to do. The Italians afterwards changed their doctrine and prepared their heavy units for night action, but the lack of radar remained a handicap which was particularly serious during darkness.

The battle was in no way decisive—the Italian Fleet remained powerful—but Matapan had clearly indicated the existence of serious technical and tactical inadequacies. The result was increased caution on the part of the High Command. During the British evacuation of Greece and Crete the Italian heavy ships did not intervene, and this perhaps was for Italy the most unfortunate consequence of the engagement of 28 March.

8. The Axis Offensive in the Eastern Mediterranean

The Libyan offensive

THE pounding of Malta continued without let-up. Port installations were destroyed; surface ships could make only furtive and precarious stays in harbor; submarines were often forced to submerge during the day and to carry out their repair work at night; the offensive capacity of the base was reduced. During the month of April the rate of loss of Axis supplies en route to Libya fell to less than two per cent and Rommel's Corps crossed over into Africa unhindered.

The Axis advance in Libya in 1941 is often called Rommel's First Offensive. Rommel, who commanded the German-Italian fighting forces at the front, was under the orders of the Italian General Gariboldi, who in turn was responsible to Comando Supremo. According to a written agreement Rommel could appeal to O.K.W., the German High Command, in the event that the instructions received from the Italians seemed unacceptable. Although such escape clauses are customary in coalition warfare, existing in fact even when not put in writing, a discreet commander will employ them only in the most serious situations, such as when he feels that the orders he has received place his forces in danger of disaster or threaten the success of a campaign. But in Libya Rommel's personality was dominant. He rapidly gained overriding influence in Axis councils and frequently bypassed his Italian commanders by dealing directly with O.K.W. After his first successes nothing could stand against his influence. All this in part justifies the term of Rommel's Offensive, but the Italians still continued to supply the majority of forces—and also of losses.

At this time the Italians had about four hundred aircraft in Libya. X Cat had about two hundred excellent planes manned by first-class personnel who, however, at first lacked experience of desert war, particularly in aircraft maintenance and preservation. Axis air strength was generally used in cooperation with the ground forces, but it also took part in the attack on British shipping, and later attempted to block the Suez Canal.

On 31 March, three days after the battle of Matapan, Rommel attacked Cyrenaica. The Army of the Nile had been weakened by the dispatch of reinforcements to Greece; it had very few fighter planes and very little anti-aircraft artillery; its lines of communication were greatly extended. Indeed, as early as the third week of February the port of Benghazi had become untenable for shipping as the result of attacks by the Luftwaffe; supplies consequently had to be unloaded at Tobruk and brought forward by land. The progress of the German-Italian forces was rapid: Benghazi, Derna, Bardia were taken; on 11 April Tobruk was invested; and on the 14th Axis troops once again stood upon the Egyptian frontier. The British Inshore Squadron supported the retreating forces and mined evacuated ports, but was able to effect only a slight delaying action. The loss of the bulge of Cyrenaica, which complicated the movement of supplies to Malta, was a great disadvantage to the Alexandria Fleet.

Despite Axis air strength, the few destroyers based at Malta displayed the greatest activity. On the night of 15-16 April, the 14th Destroyer Flotilla (*Jervis, Nubian, Janus, Mohawk*) was patrolling off the Tunisian coast when its commander, Captain Mack, was informed by Malta of the passage of an important enemy convoy containing five cargo ships escorted by three destroyers. The 14th Flotilla caught up with the convoy near the Kerkenah Light buoy. The cargo ships were in column, speed eight knots, course south, with one destroyer ahead, one astern, and the third on the port beam of the convoy. Having increased to twenty-seven knots, Mack used his superior speed to place the enemy up-moon and then attacked by gunfire at a range of 2400 yards. Within a few minutes the Italian destroyers *Baleno* and *Lampo* were on fire and sinking; the third, *Tarigo*, although burning and disabled, managed to fire three torpedoes at *Mohawk*, which was hit and sunk. The five cargo ships defended themselves with machine-guns but were rapidly set on fire; their cargoes of munitions exploded, and the whole convoy was destroyed.[1] Following this engagement the Italians decided to escort their important convoys with cruisers.

Other British successes followed. During the night of 21-22 April the battleships of the Alexandria Fleet violently bombarded Tripoli; a ship loaded with munitions and bombs was sunk and the torpedo boat *Partenope* damaged. On the night of the 24th the Italian auxiliary cruiser *Egeo* was destroyed. But these accomplishments at sea did not make up for Rommel's advance. And soon the Alexandria Fleet was to find itself beset by fearful difficulties. The hour of its most terrible trial had struck.

The German offensive in the Balkans

ON 26 NOVEMBER 1940 Rumania joined the Tripartite Pact and almost immediately the country was "peacefully" occupied by German forces. Bulgaria signed the Vienna Pact on 1 March 1941, whereupon the Germans passed through the country and established themselves on the frontier of Thrace. Aware of the impending menace, the Greeks in January attempted to drive the Italians out of Albania so as to be able to face eastward with all their forces, but their offensive had only limited success. Fearing to provoke the Germans, the Greek government had as late as February been unwilling to accept a British expeditionary force, and when in early March General Maitland Wilson made a visit to Athens, he was compelled to travel under an assumed name.

Nevertheless facts had to be recognized and German troop movements left no possible doubt about the imminence of the offensive. Between 4 March and 24 April, 58,000 troops, including two New Zealand divisions, one Australian division, and a Polish brigade, were landed at

[1] The destroyer *Lampo* was later raised by the Italians only to be sunk again by Allied aircraft on 30 April 1943.

the Piraeus. This movement was carried out with few casualties, but six ships were lost to aircraft or submarines, four more were damaged, and on 31 March the cruiser *Bonaventure*, escorting a convoy, was hit by two torpedoes from a submarine and sank in ten minutes.

Prior to the attack of the Wehrmacht the British had urged the Greeks to disengage from the Italian Army and to withdraw into Epirus so as to shorten the front and place forces opposite the Germans; this proposal was rejected by the Greek General Staff both because of its danger to morale and because of material difficulties. On 27 March a coup d'état took place in Yugoslavia, where the pro-German government was replaced by one favorable to Great Britain. But this hardly improved the situation. A meeting of Allied commanders was held on 3 April at Florina. The Yugoslavs, who had greatly overestimated the strength of the British Expeditionary Force, were astonished at its weakness; the Greeks and the British in turn perceived that their new allies were unprepared and had no plans of any sort. Once again the Allies entered the fray in a state of disorganization and unpreparedness.

One person, however, was fully prepared, and that was Marshal List, who commanded the German armies. Above all else, he possessed a thousand planes, a force of overwhelming superiority. On 6 April the blitzkrieg began with a savage bombardment of Belgrade. The opposition of a handful of Yugoslav aircraft was rapidly overcome. The German armies streamed down the valleys of the Strumitza and the Vardar; Salonika fell on the 9th; a column drove back the Yugoslavs and outflanked the Greeks, forcing them to withdraw towards Albania. Further to the north, German forces from Hungary, Bulgaria, and Rumania rapidly penetrated into Yugoslavia. Belgrade was captured on the 13th and the Yugoslav army, liquidated in eight days, capitulated on the 17th. Greek resistance lasted three weeks in all. While the German troops were coming down through Thessaly, the Italians invaded Epirus. Driven back by greatly superior mechanized forces, the

Greek and British armies were forced to withdraw. On the 24th the Bulgarians entered Thrace. On the 27th the Germans were in Athens. The capture of Corinth by parachutists enabled Marshal List to prevent a retreat into the Peloponnese.

Churchill had decided that no British troops would be evacuated without the consent of the Greeks. On 18 April the Greek prime minister committed suicide. On the 19th the King, who had taken over direction of the government, recognized that evacuation was necessary, and the Greeks, with all hope gone, sacrificed themselves in the common cause by assisting to the last the British reembarkation.

The British evacuation of Greece

A HEAVY TASK now fell upon the British Navy, heavier perhaps than at Dunkirk, for although the forces to be embarked were relatively small, air cover was wholly lacking. On 23 April a dozen Hurricanes, the best fighter planes available, were destroyed by German bombers on the airfield at Argos which was undefended by antiaircraft guns. The Piraeus, the only well-equipped port, had been destroyed by the explosion of an ammunition ship following a bombing attack, so that embarkation had to be carried out from the beaches.

Admiral Baillie-Grohman had been ordered to Athens and given a combined Army-Navy staff with which to organize the evacuation. This had originally been planned to begin on 28 April, but on the 21st the Greek army in the Epirus capitulated and the date was advanced to the 24th. The British staff had prepared a highly flexible plan for embarkation over a wide front. Taking into account approach roads and embarkation facilities, six beaches were chosen: Raphina, Raphtis, Megara, Nauplia, Monemvasia, and Kalamata, three in Attica and three in the Peloponnese. A rear guard was left at Thermopylae to hold back the Germans, while from Alexandria any type of ship that could carry troops was sent to Suda Bay and thence to the embarkation points.

117

During daylight the few fighter planes available in Crete provided protection as far north as the 37th parallel, where the ships arrived at dark. Two circumstances favored the operation: the Luftwaffe did not attack the beaches at night, and the British had available both landing-craft and

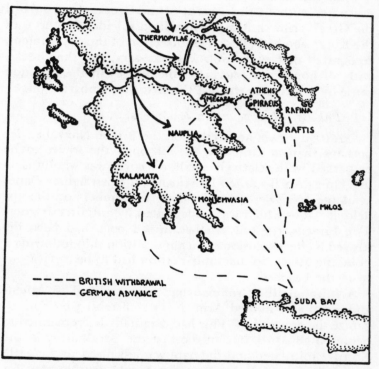

Fig. 12. The Evacuation of Greece, 24-30 April 1941

numerous Greek caïques. Evacuation was begun during the night of 24-25 April at Raphtis, Megara, and Nauplia. At Raphtis the cruiser *Calcutta*, the corvette *Salvia*, and the transport *Glengyle* took off 5,700 men. At Megara the S.S. *Thurland Castle*, although attacked by German aircraft and slightly damaged, was able to embark 3,500 men. At Nauplia the cruiser *Phoebe* and the Australian destroyers *Stuart* and *Voyager*, the corvette *Hyacinth*, and the transport *Glenearn* took 6,685 men, but the transport *Ulster Prince* ran aground and could not be towed off.

Early on the 26th German parachutists took up positions along the Corinth canal, and it therefore became necessary to re-route troops towards the beaches in Attica. Under these difficult circumstances the British troops showed admirable fortitude, and despite the succession of untoward events they retained their equanimity. On the 25th the steamship *Pennland*, en route to Megara, was sunk by enemy bombers, but during the night of the 25th-26th the cruiser *Coventry*, eight destroyers, and a transport took off 6,000 more men from this beach. On the night of the 26th-27th 22,000 men were embarked: 8,200 at Raphina and Raphtis, 4,500 at Nauplia, 9,000 at Kalamata.

The evacuation from Nauplia proved to be costly. While en route to the beaches *Glenearn* was bombed and had to be towed back to port. The plan was for ships to arrive off the beaches about 2300 and to get underway again before 0300 in the morning. But the Nauplia convoy, unable to get away before 0600, was attacked at dawn by about thirty Stukas. The Dutch steamer *Slamat*, hit and on fire, had to be abandoned and sunk by torpedo; subsequently the destroyer *Diamond* was lost, followed in turn by *Wryneck*. Also in the afternoon of the 27th the Kalamata convoy was attacked and the steamer *Costa Rica* sunk.

During the following night (27-28 April) the cruiser *Ajax* and destroyers *Kingston, Kimberley,* and *Havock* took off the 5,000 men remaining in Attica from Raphina and Raphtis. In the Peloponnese, *Ajax* and destroyers took off another 4,320 men from Monemvasia on the night of the 28th-29th. There remained 7,000 men waiting at Kalamata. Cruisers *Perth* and *Phoebe* and six destroyers had been sent to take them aboard but were forced to withdraw when the Germans, succeeding in entering the town, reached the quays just as the ships arrived off the harbor entrance. A counterattack by British troops freed the port, but the commander of the naval force, believing it in the hands of the enemy, had departed, and a large number of troops were taken prisoner. Nevertheless British destroyers searching the nearby beaches were able to recover 500 men who had escaped from Kalamata, and on 30 April the destroyers *Hotspur* and *Havock* discovered and rescued 700 fugitives who had reached the island of Milos.

The number of British troops sent to Greece totalled 57,660 men of which about 47,000 were saved, but although these brought off their own weapons, all guns, vehicles, and supplies were lost. The evacuation had taken place under very difficult circumstances: the troops had been embarked from unprotected beaches, often during bad weather, under air attack, and under pressure of the German forces which closely pursued the expeditionary corps. Part of the troops remained in Crete to help in the defense of that island, while the rest continued to Egypt under the protection of the Fleet.

During the night of the 26th-27th Radio Athens, before being occupied by the enemy, had sent the following message to Alexandria: "Last night with you. Happy days with victory and liberty. God with you and for you. Good luck."

Dispatch of British reinforcements to Egypt

SINCE January no British convoy had passed through the Mediterranean, all reinforcements having gone by way of the Cape. But in May Wavell and Cunningham were badly in need of assistance, and the Admiralty decided to attempt the Gibraltar-Alexandria passage. As the Luftwaffe was busy in Greece, circumstances were fairly favorable. During the night of 6-7 May an important convoy, containing five large cargo ships loaded with tanks, guns, vehicles, and planes, passed the Strait of Gibraltar. At the same time the battleship *Queen Elizabeth*, fresh from overhaul, the two modern cruisers *Naiad* and *Fiji*, and a flotilla of six new destroyers commanded by Captain Lord Louis Mountbatten sailed to reinforce the Alexandria Fleet.

The convoy was escorted to a point south of Sardinia by

Force H. The Alexandria Fleet had got underway to provide protection in the Central Mediterranean and also to send supplies to Malta. En route a detachment of this Fleet bombarded Benghazi and sank two Italian merchant ships at sea. The Gibraltar convoy was attacked by aircraft, M.A.S., and Italian submarines; one cargo ship was blown up by a mine, but all other ships reached their destination. Despite the importance to the Axis of preventing this reinforcement, the Italian battle fleet did not intervene. Lord Mountbatten's destroyers remained temporarily at Malta and carried out a bombardment of Benghazi, on the return from which the destroyer *Jersey* was blown up by a magnetic mine off Valetta on 26 May.

The invasion of Crete

FOLLOWING the conquest of Greece, the Germans seized several of the islands of the Aegean and garrisoned Thasos, Samothrace, and Lemnos, from which they could watch the Dardanelles. But they wisely saw that to secure their position in the Balkans and to prevent a possible British counterattack it was necessary to seize Crete, even though its conquest presented serious difficulties in the absence of command of the sea.

The island of Crete is about 160 miles long and about 40 miles wide; its mountainous surface makes movement difficult. A road runs along the north coast, but from north to south the island is crossed only by barely passable mule tracks. The British had occupied the island at the end of October but shortage of supplies had prevented thorough preparations for its defense. At the time of the German attack 28,000 Allied troops, some of whom lacked arms, were in Crete in the process of reorganization. In anticipation of an invasion which all believed certain, attempts were made to reinforce the island: nine tanks and a number of guns captured from the Italians in Libya were shipped, but half of this inadequate amount of materiel was lost en route as a result of enemy air attacks, which now extended to about fifty miles south of the island.

The points which the British particularly planned to defend were Suda Bay and the airfields at Maleme, Retimo, and Heraklion. The only two usable ports were Suda Bay and Heraklion, and these had only the most embryonic facilities as in peacetime they handled only a few hundred tons monthly. To move in reinforcements during an attack could only be a very slow process. Greek fixed defenses were practically nonexistent, consisting of a few antiaircraft guns at Heraklion, Suda Bay, and Canea. Air strength had been reduced to a handful of planes. The defense of Crete depended on the Navy.

The German plan was based on the employment of their enormous air superiority to overcome Allied resistance on shore and to drive off the British warships. The Fourth Luftflotte, deployed in the Balkans, had at this time about 800 planes. The invasion was to begin with the dropping of parachutists who were to seize the airfields on the first day; they were to be followed on the second day by airborne troops in gliders and transport planes, and by troops carried in small motor boats and protected by aircraft and Italian destroyers. The Italian Navy had placed the Dodecanese naval forces, two destroyers, four torpedo boats, nine submarines, and fourteen M.A.S., at the disposition of the German command. The German troops, which were gathered at the Piraeus, were to move first to Milos, which was to be used as a staging base, and thence to Crete. A few Italian formations from the Dodecanese were to land at Sitia at the eastern end of the island.

The imminence of the attack had not escaped the notice of the British commanders. Admiral Cunningham had divided his forces into several groups whose composition was to vary in the course of the operation owing to losses and the need of reliefs. Force A, containing battleships, was to keep station to the west of Crete to protect the other groups against a possible intervention of the Italian Fleet. The other forces, made up of cruisers and destroyers, were to sweep close to the Greek coast during the night, and to withdraw by day towards Crete so as to keep as far as possible from enemy airfields. In addition a flotilla of motor torpedo boats based at Suda Bay patrolled the coastal waters north of Crete, and the mine-layer *Abdiel* laid a mine field between Cephalonia and Levkas to interrupt enemy communications through the Corinth Canal. Arrangements for scouting by submarines completed the preparations.

While collecting shipping the Germans restored the Greek airfields and built new runways. During the first half of May German bombing attacks were directed against the port at Suda Bay; after the 15th the airfields on Crete were also continually attacked and, as it became clear that the few planes in possession of the defenders would inevitably be destroyed, they were therefore withdrawn. Nevertheless on the 23rd, at the height of the battle, two Hurricanes returned to the island. The carrier *Formidable*, the only one available to the Alexandria Fleet, had only four serviceable fighters at the beginning of the operation, and thus could not be risked in areas where enemy aircraft were numerous. Fighter planes based in Egypt, few in number and at a great distance, gave only slight assistance. The Allies therefore had to fight with clear inferiority in the air.

The attack began at 0800 on 20 May with bombing of airfields followed by parachute landings in the morning at Maleme and in the afternoon at Retimo and Heraklion. The defending forces resisted bravely and only at Maleme were the Germans able to approach the airfield. General Student, the German commander of airborne troops, had set up a precise and detailed plan which, in the event, could not be followed out in any respect. On the 21st the German aerial invasion continued against furious resistance.

Invasion by sea was speedily undertaken in accordance with plan, but ran into heavy difficulties. On the night of 20-21 May a convoy of eighteen small ships carrying about 1,500 men departed Milos for Maleme escorted by the Italian torpedo boat *Lupo*. There was a fairly high sea from the southeast, the speed of the convoy fell to two knots, and in the morning it was still about fifty miles from Crete.

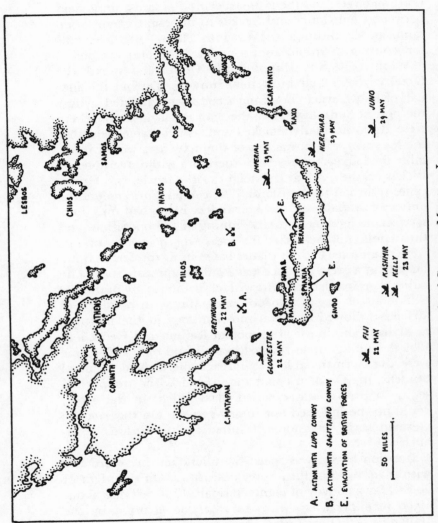

Fig. 13. The Battle of Crete, 20 May to 1 June 1941

On the following night it was sighted by a British force under Admiral Glennie comprising cruisers *Orion, Dido, Ajax,* and five destroyers: *Lupo* attempted to conceal the convoy with smoke screens but most of the ships were destroyed. Although hit nineteen times, the Italian torpedo boat succeeded in escaping.

Following the repulse of this first convoy, a second one, intended for Heraklion and containing thirty-eight ships and 4,000 men, was diverted by the German command to Maleme. It departed Milos during the night of the 22nd escorted by the torpedo boat *Sagittario.* Engaged during the morning by British ships, this convoy was saved by the skillful maneuvers of *Sagittario* and by the intervention of the Luftwaffe, but was forced to turn back. These failures led the German command to hold back the passage of reinforcements by sea. And as the airborne troops had failed to gain a decision at Heraklion and Retimo, the main German effort was made in the west.

At sea a furious battle went on between the British Fleet and the German Air Force. On the 21st the destroyer *Juno* was hit by two bombs which ripped open a fire room; a third hit a magazine and *Juno* sank in two minutes. Throughout the 22nd the German attacks continued uninterruptedly. The cruiser *Naiad* was damaged and her speed reduced; *Carlisle* was set afire and only with difficulty succeeded in controlling the flames. Resolved to prevent at all costs the movement of enemy troops by sea, the British brought up the battle squadron to join in the antiaircraft action; *Warspite* was hit by a bomb and shortly afterward the destroyer *Greyhound* was sunk by Stukas. The situation of the Fleet was becoming increasingly serious, and the light ships were running out of ammunition. At 1550 the cruiser *Gloucester* was hit and immobilized, sinking after further damage. During the evening *Fiji* was also hit, sinking during the night. At dawn of the 23rd Admiral Cunningham recalled the Fleet to Alexandria to refuel and replenish ammunition.

The Fleet had been joined by the 5th Destroyer Flotilla

from Malta. En route to Alexandria the destroyer *Kashmir* of this Flotilla, after having avoided a dozen bombs, was hit, and sank in two minutes. Then *Kelly*, of the same formation, was sunk, going under with her guns still firing. During the night of the 23rd the Fleet reached Alexandria, exhausted by the unceasing struggle and having suffered terrible losses. During the previous night the King of Greece and his suite, who had miraculously escaped the Germans, had embarked from the south coast of Crete on the destroyers *Decoy* and *Hero*.

On the 24th and 25th, while continuing reinforcement by air, the Germans succeeded in throwing troops into Crete by sea. The British also succeeded in sending a few troops in on warships which reached Suda Bay during the night, but the capacity of these ships was small and they could transport only personnel. The forces thus brought in were unable to retrieve the situation.

It was clear that without air cover the Fleet could not long continue the fight, and that it was in danger of complete destruction. Admiral Cunningham therefore decided to commit the carrier *Formidable*, whose fighter strength had now been built up to twelve Fulmars. Accompanied by the battleships *Queen Elizabeth* and *Barham* and destroyers, the carrier steamed towards Scarpanto, the German advanced base, and at dawn on the 26th British fighters and bombers destroyed a number of enemy planes on the ground. But during the afternoon German planes attacked and seriously damaged the carrier and the destroyer *Nubian*, and although *Formidable* continued to operate aircraft until darkness, she had to be withdrawn to Alexandria. On the 26th *Abdiel*, *Hero*, and *Nizam* took the last reinforcements to Suda Bay and retired to Alexandria along with the battleships. En route *Barham* received a bomb hit on one of her turrets.

Following an exchange of messages on the situation, the British Chiefs of Staff cabled from London that

The Fleet and Royal Air Force were to accept whatever risk was entailed in preventing any considerable enemy reinforcement reaching Crete. If enemy convoys were reported north of Crete the Fleet would have to operate in that area by day although considerable losses might be expected. Experience would show for how long that situation could be maintained.

Cunningham replied on the evening of 26 May that the determining factor was not the fear of sustaining losses but the need to avoid crippling the Fleet without commensurate advantage.

Events had already outstripped this discussion. On shore the Germans were making progress. The 26th was the crucial day: the Germans, whose strength then totalled about 30,000 men, pierced the British lines west of Canea and advanced rapidly. Early on the morning of the 27th General Freyberg, commanding the Allied troops, was forced to recognize that evacuation was necessary. The defense of Crete had cost the Alexandria Fleet two cruisers and four destroyers sunk; two battleships, a carrier, and a destroyer heavily damaged and out of action; five cruisers and four destroyers with minor damage.

It would be very interesting to determine precisely what part in the German victory was played by the airborne troops and what by the forces sent by sea, but the evidence is conflicting. According to the British reports, troops brought in by sea had no importance and the Navy, despite its losses, fulfilled its function by preventing such movement. Contrariwise, General Rielkhoff of the Fourth Luftflotte states explicitly that it was the Fifth Alpine Division, brought in by ship, which gave the parachute and airborne troops assistance without which they would have been overcome within a few days by the island's valiant defenders, and that it was this division that carried the day.

The British evacuation of Crete

No MATTER what the risks may be, the British Navy never abandons an expeditionary force. Now once again it found itself faced with the problem of evacuating troops hard pressed by an enemy who enjoyed almost complete command of the air. *Formidable* was out of action, and aircraft could be operated only from distant bases in Egypt. Since the harbor at Suda Bay could not be used, the troops in the region of Suda Bay, Canea, and Maleme withdrew across the mountains towards Sphakia on the south coast. The forces at Retimo were surrounded. Unable to break out, they were annihilated with the exception of a few isolated groups which escaped and reached Egypt on Greek boats. The port at Heraklion was still free and usable, but to reach it ships had to make the dangerous passage of Kaxo Strait under the nose of Scarpanto-based aviation. Once again the Alexandria Fleet took up its *via dolorosa*.

On the afternoon of the 28th a squadron under Admiral Rawlings, which contained cruisers *Orion, Ajax, Dido*, and six destroyers, entered the Strait en route to Heraklion. *Ajax* was hit and lost speed and Rawlings, who could not slow his force, sent her back to Alexandria. Shortly before midnight the squadron arrived off Heraklion; four destroyers went alongside the jetties of the little harbor and embarked troops which they then transferred to the cruisers. The position was surrounded by the Germans who had brought up tanks and were preparing an attack, but before it could be delivered the destroyers *Kimberley* and *Imperial* succeeded in taking off the British rear guard. Three quarters of an hour after departure the destroyer *Imperial* broke down. Time was pressing, Kaxo Strait had to be passed before daylight. Rawlings ordered *Hotspur* to take off *Imperial's* personnel and sink her. This order was carried out and *Hotspur* rejoined at top speed.

Enemy air attacks began at 0600 and lasted for seven hours. At 0625 *Hereward* was hit by a bomb in the boiler room and set on fire. Unable to lose a moment, Rawlings abandoned the destroyer which, five miles from Crete, was struggling towards shore. She was later scuttled by her crew and the survivors rescued by an Italian torpedo boat. Next the destroyer *Decoy* and the cruisers *Orion* and *Dido* were hit by bombs; fires broke out on *Dido* but were brought under control and the formation continued at the reduced speed of twenty-one knots. Shortly before 1100 another bomb passed through *Orion's* bridge and exploded on the mess decks causing terrible losses among the tightly packed troops. On the bridge the compasses, steering gear, and communications were destroyed. Burning and giving off clouds of smoke, *Orion* fell behind but was able to continue her course. In the evening the ships reached Alexandria; of the 4,000 troops taken off at Heraklion 800 had been lost, and the squadron had suffered terribly. On shore the British command debated the question of whether or not to continue the operation. After long and anxious consideration of the situation, Wavell and Cunningham decided to continue the evacuation of the troops.

In the meantime the British forces in northwestern Crete, worn out by six days of struggle, were retiring on Sphakia. The pursuing Germans, themselves very tired, were successfully held up in the difficult terrain by British rear guards. The beach at Sphakia is a narrow band of shingle at the foot of an almost vertical escarpment. On the plateau and on the beach between twelve and fourteen thousand men were crowded, calmly and stoically awaiting the time of embarkation. Only among a few exhausted elements was there any lack of discipline. During the night of the 28th-29th four destroyers, *Napier, Nizam, Kelvin,* and *Kandahar,* brought in provisions and took off some of the forces. On the night of the 29th-30th the cruisers *Perth, Phoebe, Calcutta, Coventry,* the transport *Glengyle,* and three destroyers embarked 7,000 men, *Perth* being hit by a bomb on the return trip. During the day of the 30th a few enemy elements attacked the plateau at Sphakia but were driven off. In the night the destroyers *Napier* and *Nizam* continued the embarkation. *Kandahar* and *Kelvin* which had accompanied them had been forced to turn back, the former as a result of mechanical breakdown, the latter after being hit by a bomb.

On 31 May there remained 6,500 men to be evacuated. During the night the cruiser *Phoebe,* the destroyers *Jackal, Kimberley, Hotspur,* and the minelayer *Abdiel* returned to Sphakia. At this moment these, with the cruisers *Cal-*

cutta and *Coventry*, were the only ships available in the whole Alexandria Fleet, and *Calcutta*, heading towards Sphakia, was hit by two bombs and sank in a few minutes. On 1 June at 0300 the squadron departed carrying another 4,000 men. Those who remained were taken prisoner.

Thus ended this dramatic evacuation. Of 24,000 troops in Crete at the time of the invasion, about 17,000 were saved. As in Greece, the Luftwaffe had not attacked the anchorages at night. Despite their small number and the great distance, the aviators of the R.A.F. had given the Fleet all the assistance that was humanly possible, but the credit for the operation belongs principally to the sailors. "The work of the Royal Navy," wrote General Wavell, "in preventing the enemy attempts at invasion by sea and in evacuation of the troops in spite of extremely heavy losses in ships and in men, was beyond all praise. To Admiral Sir Andrew Cunningham himself, who took the responsibility of ordering the evacuation to proceed in spite of the losses, the Army owes a deep debt of gratitude."

For his part, the Commander of the Alexandria Fleet wrote: "Under incessant air attack and suffering heavy losses, the Fleet and the merchant ships carried out their tasks to the end. Greece and Crete were defeats, but I have never been as proud of anything as of having commanded these men in this period of adversity."

The Greek Navy had also fought bravely and suffered heavily. In the course of the Greek campaign and the battle of Crete the following ships had been sunk by Axis aircraft: the destroyers *Psara, Vasileus Georgios, Ydra, Thyella, Kyzikos, Kidonia, Kios, Prousa, Pergamos, Alkyone, Arethousa, Doris*; the old battleship *Kilkis*; and ten small torpedo boats. Only the old cruiser *Averof*, two destroyers, eight old torpedo boats, and the submarines escaped disaster. The Greek merchant marine also suffered heavily; in the course of the war its losses reached seventy-five per cent of its tonnage, giving it, with the French merchant marine, the record of highest percentage of loss. Almost all units of the Yugoslav Navy, which was composed of a few destroyers and submarines and some small craft, were captured by the Italians in the course of the campaign; only one submarine and two motor torpedo boats reached Alexandria.

Throughout the operations in Crete the Italian battle fleet made no appearance. We have seen that following the Battle of Matapan it had been ordered to remain in the Central Mediterranean, but it thus lost a chance of fighting under highly favorable conditions, for the sky was completely dominated by the Luftwaffe. The whole campaign bore out the British axiom: "A naval force with air cover can do anything; without this protection it is destined to failure." Nevertheless the Luftwaffe had no torpedo planes and the Italians themselves had only very few. If the Axis had had an appreciable quantity of these it seems probable that Cunningham's fleet would have either been forced to retire much sooner or have been annihilated, and would have been unable to evacuate the troops.

In other respects the Battle of Crete had served as a warning to the Germans. The airborne troops had suffered heavily and a large number of gliders and transport planes had been lost. From this the command concluded that aerial invasions offered only limited prospects.

Following Crete the British command feared an attack directed against Cyprus and Syria, but the Germans, having attained the goal of their offensive, now stopped. They had reestablished the Italian situation, placed the Rumanian oil fields out of reach, strengthened their prestige in the Balkans and in Turkey, and secured their southern flank against a British attack. They did not consider following up their success at the expense of the preparations they were making against Russia. In short they put off until later a solution of the whole Mediterranean problem.

In the Balkans the Germans had used only a small part of the forces destined for the Russian front. Considering the success they gained, it seems unquestionable that if, instead of attacking Russia, they had followed up and reinforced their Mediterranean offensive, they would have driven Great Britain from this sea. But to Hitler in the spring of 1941 the Mediterranean question was a secondary one. He planned to defeat Russia in four or five months and only subsequently to undertake the conquest of Asia Minor, an operation which was to include an offensive through the Caucasus, an offensive in Libya toward Suez, and perhaps a drive from the Balkans through Turkey. At the beginning of June half of the Fourth Luftflotte was withdrawn from Greece for deployment on the Russian front; List's armored divisions were already on their way.

The campaign in Crete had strengthened Hitler's intention of attacking Russia. On 21 June he wrote to Mussolini:

... The experience in Crete showed how necessary it would be to use every plane in the much greater attack on England. It might well be that in this decisive battle we should win with a margin of only a few squadrons . . . [and that] Russia would then begin her strategy of extortion . . . to which I would have to yield in silence. . . . [The dangers] must naturally increase with the progress in preparedness of the Russian armed forces. . . .

Whether or not America enters the war is a matter of indifference, inasmuch as she is already helping our enemy with all the power she can muster.

... The elimination of Russia will also greatly alleviate the situation of Japan in the Far East, and thereby create the possibility of a much stronger threat to American activities through Japanese intervention.

... Even should I be forced to leave 60 or 70 divisions in Russia at the end of this year, that would be only a fraction of the forces that I am now maintaining on the eastern front. Should England still refuse to face the facts . . . we can then apply our increased strength to the destruction of our enemy. . . .

... Since taking this decision I feel that my spirit is once more free. . . . It has always been very painful for me to march at the side of Russia, for in a way it always seemed to me to be a denial of my whole past. . . .

I am happy now to have freed myself from this torment.

The consequences which Hitler foresaw would result from a victory over the U.S.S.R. were logical, but perhaps amounted to selling the skin of the Russian bear before having killed it. On 22 June, German troops crossed the Russian frontier and on that day, for the first time since June 1940, Great Britain was able to breathe freely.

Events in Iraq and Syria

ALTHOUGH the Germans did not intend to settle the problem of Asia Minor until after they had destroyed Russia, they were nonetheless desirous of making trouble for their enemies in that region. In April their intrigues in Iraq led to the so-called Rashid Ali coup d'état. In May the latter, having gained power, invested the air field at Habbaniyah, where there were then only a few British training planes. Rashid Ali counted on prompt assistance from the Germans, whose prestige in this area had been considerably increased by the victories in Greece. But the Germans did not intend to commit strong forces, and sent only a few planes to Mosul by way of Rhodes and Syria. Great Britain reacted vigorously: troops and aircraft were sent to Habbaniyah, an operation which was supported by a naval force made up of cruisers *Emerald, Leander, Enterprise,* and the carrier *Hermes.* The Iraqi airfields which the Germans held had few facilities for dispersal and no antiaircraft artillery; most of the German planes were destroyed on the ground, and the Luftwaffe's strength was reduced to almost nothing. At the end of May Rashid Ali fled to Iran and the British situation was reestablished. In August the British and the Russians moved into Iran in order to forestall any German attempt at intrigue.

On 8 June several columns of British and Free French troops entered Syria, one force from Palestine moving northwards along the coast. French naval strength in Syria consisted principally of the destroyers *Guépard* and *Valmy* (2,400 tons, five 5.5-inch guns, 40 knots). In the face of British numerical superiority these ships adopted the tactics of rapid attack and speedy retirement. One of these attacks brought them into action with British destroyers, and *Janus* was heavily damaged in a brief and violent engagement in which the French ships, very skilfully handled by

Captain de Lafond, demonstrated their excellent state of training. In the course of the campaign the destroyer *Chevalier Paul*, en route to Syria, was sunk by Swordfish of the Fleet Air Arm. The advance along the coast was constantly supported by a British squadron containing cruisers *Phoebe*, *Ajax*, *Coventry*, *Perth*, and *Carlisle*, and destroyers. Hostilities were terminated by an armistice which was signed on 11 July.

The conquest of Syria strengthened the Turkish will to resist Axis intimidation, and also provided the British with advanced naval and air bases north of the Suez Canal. The British command had decided in the event of an evacuation of the Canal to continue the fight in the Near East, and had planned a line of communications through the Persian Gulf, Basra, Bagdad, and Haifa. With the occupation of Syria this line was paralleled by the line Iraq-Syria-Lebanon.

Had Egypt been lost it seems probable that the British would have left submarines and light forces at Beirut and Haifa, and it is certain that Great Britain would not have given up in the Near East without a bitter fight. In July 1941 the Germans attached only slight importance to Syria; their plans were on a much vaster scale. We know that they intended to reach Asia Minor by way of the Caucasus. Their hopes were to be frustrated first by Russian resistance and subsequently by Russian victories. But for a period of two years the British command kept a strong army in Asia Minor to confront this German threat. Nevertheless, compared to the danger that Great Britain had narrowly avoided, this was but a minor inconvenience. In May 1941, when the German command halted its offensive, victory in the Mediterranean was within its grasp.

9. War of Attrition

The struggle for communications

FROM April to November the Libyan front remained stabilized. Having halted at the Egyptian frontier, the Germans now attempted to capture Tobruk, which threatened their lines of communication. The onerous task of supplying the garrison and of bringing in reliefs fell upon the British Navy. This responsibility was principally assumed by the Inshore Squadron, which, after the loss of the monitor *Terror* in February, was composed of old gunboats, armed merchant ships, a few cutters captured from the Italians, and a remarkable assortment of small craft. But as air attacks became more intense, particularly in May and June, it became necessary to support the garrison with fast ships, and the destroyers of the Alexandria Fleet were called in. Tobruk was only relieved on 9 December, after a 242-day siege which placed very heavy responsibilities on the Navy.

At sea the unceasing struggle over lines of communication continued, with submarines, aircraft, and light vessels attacking Italian convoys en route to Libya. For their own communications the British principally employed the Cape route, by which, during the first six months of 1941, more than 330,000 troops were sent to either the Near or Far East.

In the Red Sea all danger from Italian action had ended by April 1941. In August of the previous year troops under the Duke of Aosta had seized British Somaliland, but their control of the region did not last long. In early January 1941 British forces from Kenya and the Sudan undertook the conquest of Italian East Africa. The Italians evacuated the port of Kismayu between 5 and 8 February, and Mogadishu at the end of the month. They were rapidly expelled first from Italian and then from British Somaliland; on 10 March the British landed unopposed at Berbera; in Eritrea Italian resistance collapsed at the end of the month.

In February, foreseeing the loss of the port of Massawa, the Italians sent about ten surface ships, including the gunboat *Eritrea* and two auxiliary cruisers, to the Far East and Japan; all reached their destination with the exception of the auxiliary cruiser *Ramb I* which was sunk in the Indian Ocean by the cruiser *Leander*. Four ocean-going submarines succeeded in making Bordeaux. The remaining destroyers and torpedo boats lacked sufficient range to reach a neutral port and had to be scuttled. The Italians had hoped to strike one final blow against Suez or Port Sudan but were thwarted by British air attack. Their only success was scored by *M.A.S. 213*, which succeeded in torpedoing the cruiser *Capetown* before being scuttled at Massawa. The elimination of Italian naval strength enabled the Admiralty greatly to reduce its Red Sea escort forces.

Urgent convoys for Egypt and the problem of keeping Malta supplied still made it necessary to move in strength through the Mediterranean. After the departure of the Fourth Luftflotte for the Russian front, German air strength in Greece and Libya was provided by the Tenth Air Fleet (X Cat), which had about four hundred planes. By agreement with the Italians, operations of German aircraft based in Greece were as a rule restricted to the region east of the meridian of Cape Matapan, so that the responsibility of defending the Central Mediterranean fell upon the Italian Air Force and Navy. In late July a British convoy containing six troop transports and a cargo ship departed Gibraltar for Malta and Alexandria. South of Sardinia on the morning of 23 July it was attacked by Italian aircraft; the cruiser *Manchester* was heavily damaged and the destroyer *Fearless* sunk. Continuing on its course after Force H had turned back to Gibraltar, the convoy was attacked again in the Sicilian Channel and, although one merchant vessel was damaged, all ships reached Malta.

During the night of the 25th-26th the Italians attempted to attack Malta with assault machines in an operation similar to that which had succeeded at Suda Bay in March, but of greater magnitude. Shortly before midnight on the 25th the fast transport *Diana* launched six explosive-laden motorboats north of Valetta while two M.A.S. towed piloted torpedoes to within three miles of the entrance. As the obstructions which blocked the channel were exceptionally strong, the following plan had been devised: one of the piloted torpedoes was to lead the way and blow up the boom near Point St. Elmo breakwater, whereupon the motor boats, waiting nearby, were immediately to penetrate the breach and proceed to attack their targets inside the harbor; the second piloted torpedo was to attack the submarines in the Marsamuscetto basin.

The operation began well. Piloted by Tesei, an engineering officer who had been one of the founders and movers of the assault machine program, the first torpedo succeeded in approaching the obstructions unobserved while the motor boats lay waiting 900 yards away. But the explosion was delayed and day began to break. Thinking that Tesei had failed, Commander Giobbe, who was in charge of the motor boats, ordered two of them to blow up the obstacles. By an extraordinary coincidence the piloted torpedo exploded at the same time as the motor boats, and not only did the obstructions disappear but the swinging bridge above them was also destroyed and its wreckage blocked the passageway. As they advanced to the attack the remaining motor boats were illuminated by searchlights and taken under fire by the harbor defenses. All were destroyed without being able to penetrate the harbor, as were also the M.A.S. which, waiting off shore, were attacked by fighter planes flying close to the water. The heroic expedition was a complete failure, and at dawn the drifting motor boats were brought into Malta, their crews dead at their posts. But this setback did not discourage the remarkable men who manned the assault machines, and at Spezia other crews methodically and tenaciously prepared for new attempts.

At the end of September a convoy of nine transports departed Gibraltar for Malta. Force H which escorted it was particularly strong at this time, containing the battleships

Nelson, Prince of Wales, and *Rodney,* the five cruisers *Kenya, Edinburgh, Sheffield, Hermione,* and *Euryalus,* and eighteen destroyers. On the morning of the 27th the fleet was attacked by large groups of planes; at 1345 *Nelson* was hit by a torpedo but was able to continue her course. Shortly afterwards the battleships turned back and the convoy continued with the cruisers and nine destroyers. Another air attack sank the transport *Imperial Star,* but the convoy reached Malta without further loss.

This convoy, the last to pass from Gibraltar to Malta in 1941, had been escorted by Force H which, although strong, lacked aircraft carriers. Admiral Iachino's fleet (battleships *Littorio* and *Vittorio Veneto,* five cruisers, and destroyers) had gotten underway in order to be off southern Sardinia by midday of the 27th. In accordance with standing instructions from Supermarina it was to engage only when enjoying the advantage of air support in Italian waters, and then only if the enemy was inferior in strength. But the information received regarding the composition of the British squadron was contradictory, Supermarina issued orders and counterorders, and once again the chance was missed. Lack of carriers cannot be pleaded as the reason this time, for the Admiralty had sent a squadron all the way from Gibraltar to south of Sardinia without them, and had exposed battleships without fighter protection to the attacks of Italian aircraft. Within the British Fleet the intrepidity of the crews of the assault machines was compared with amazement to the extreme prudence shown by the High Command in its employment of the Italian battle squadron, a prudence amounting almost to pusillanimity.

Although the losses of the Greek and Cretan campaigns had not yet been replaced, the Alexandria Fleet displayed great activity. Cunningham had organized his light forces into three attack groups. The first of these, composed of cruisers *Aurora* and *Penelope* and destroyers, under Commodore Agnew, was based at Malta; the second, under Admiral Rawlings, based at Alexandria, contained the cruisers *Ajax* and *Neptune* and destroyers; the third, commanded by Rear Admiral Vian and also based at Alexandria, contained cruisers *Naiad, Euryalus, Dido*, and *Galatea.*

During the night of 8-9 November the Malta group, known as Force K, attacked a strong enemy convoy distant about 130 miles bearing 120 degrees from Cape Spartivento. This convoy, which was proceeding from Messina to Tripoli at eight knots under the command of Admiral Bruto Brivonesi, contained seven German ships escorted by cruisers *Trento* and *Trieste* and six destroyers. Visibility was uneven. Commodore Agnew steered so as to get the convoy up-moon; this introductory maneuver lasted over a quarter of an hour without arousing the attention of the escort. At 0100 the British ships opened fire on the destroyer *Fulmine* which was rapidly sunk. Then, dividing up the targets, within a few minutes they burned and destroyed all seven ships. The Italian cruiser division, which had been stationed astern of the convoy, arrived only tardily upon the scene as Force K was retiring at high speed towards a horizon obscured by the smoke of burning ships. Next morning the destroyer *Libeccio*, engaged in picking up survivors, was sunk by the submarine *Upholder.*

The loss of the whole of the important convoy of 9 November, coming as it did only ten days before the Army of the Nile launched its great offensive, was a bitter blow to the Italian and German armies in Libya. At Rome the maneuvers of Brivonesi's squadron were severely criticized. It was felt that the cruisers had increased speed too slowly and had blundered in their choice of a pursuit course, that the destroyers should have been able to fire their torpedoes, that the merchant ships had had time to turn away, and so on. After the event, and after having reconstructed the enemy's maneuvers on paper, it was easy enough to decide what should have been done, and Mussolini, who had little understanding of the hazards of night battle, was greatly enraged.

On 20 November, therefore, the High Command committed a division of 10,000-ton cruisers and a division of 8,000-ton cruisers, as well as destroyers, to protect a convoy of merchant ships going from Messina to Tripoli. During the evening of the 21st the Italians intercepted a message indicating that Force K was at sea in search of the convoy. At 2300 the cruiser *Trieste* was hit by a submarine torpedo. Shortly after midnight the escort was attacked by torpedo planes from Malta, and despite the use of smoke screens the cruiser *Duca degli Abruzzi* was torpedoed. Discouraged by these events, Supermarina ordered the convoy to return to Italy, thus again admitting defeat. On 24 November Force K attacked another convoy south of Navarino, sinking two merchant ships and driving off the escorting torpedo boats. On 1 December it destroyed an ammunition ship, a tanker, and the destroyer *Da Mosto* in an action sixty miles northwest of Tripoli. At this time the supply situation of the Axis armies in Libya was very critical; seventy per cent of the material shipped during November had been destroyed.

The second British Libyan offensive

As THE BRITISH prepared to launch their second Libyan offensive, the Near Eastern situation appeared as follows. The Germans, who were advancing rapidly in Russia, hoped shortly to clear the way through the Caucasus so that they would be able not only to invade Persia and Iraq but also to attack Turkey from north, east, and west. Nevertheless, as it seemed improbable that this state of affairs would develop before spring of 1942, Great Britain still had a few months in which to prepare. In Egypt her ground forces were superior to those of the Axis; in the air the British had local superiority; at sea the Fleet, although reduced, maintained by its activity its control of the Eastern Mediterranean.

The intent of the British command was to conquer not only Cyrenaica but also Tripolitania. By so doing it would be able to free troops and reinforce its northern front in Asia Minor, while holding a good jumping-off place for an ultimate offensive against the Italian peninsula. This was in accordance with the ideas of the planners in London, for these envisaged a return to the continent by way of the Mediterranean as soon as the balance of forces would permit. The scheme of maneuver for the conquest of Libya was to be executed in two phases: first the encirclement and destruction of enemy forces in Cyrenaica, and then an invasion of Tripolitania. The attack was originally planned for 1 November, but had to be postponed until the 18th owing to the delayed arrival of an armored brigade from the United Kingdom.

The offensive was a success, although less rapid and complete than had been hoped. On 10 December Tobruk was relieved. In the course of this siege the Navy had lost twenty-five warships sunk and nine seriously damaged, and five merchant ships sunk and four seriously damaged; a total of forty-three ships. Derna was taken on 19 December and Barce the 23rd. On Christmas Eve armored forces entered Benghazi to find it evacuated by the Axis troops. On 6 January the Allies reached Agedabia. General Auchinleck, commanding in the Near East, still contemplated a continuation of the attack towards Tripolitania despite the fact that Rommel's forces had not, as originally anticipated, been destroyed during the advance in Cyrenaica. But his plans were to be frustrated by the momentous events that were taking place in the Far East.

On 7 December the Japanese attacked the American Pacific Fleet and put the entire battleship squadron out of action; on the 10th the two British capital ships, *Prince of Wales* and *Repulse*, were sunk in the Gulf of Siam by Japanese aircraft; in Malaya and in the Philippines Japanese landing operations made startling progress. Hastily Great Britain reinforced her Far Eastern Fleet. As early as 12 December Auchinleck was informed by Churchill that reinforcements scheduled for the Near East were being diverted to Malaya. General Auchinleck, Air Marshal Tedder who commanded the Air Force, and Admiral Cunningham wholly understood the necessity of these steps, but at the same time they felt that the entire Near Eastern position

141

was imperiled. The German threat from the north had not been dispelled, and Rommel had not been conquered.

Reorganization and reinforcement of the German Mediterranean Command

IN EARLY DECEMBER Marshal Kesselring was sent to Rome with the title of Commander in Chief of the Southern Zone (*Oberbefehlshaber Sud* or O.B.S.), and given control of all German air strength in the theater. In theory he was responsible to Comando Supremo, but this subordination was largely one of form. Kesselring, Bavarian by birth and a former artillery officer, had transferred at an early date to the Air Force and had commanded the Second Luftflotte during the Battle of Britain and in Russia. He was, without a doubt, one of the best of the Axis generals. Alexander, at a later date his opponent in Italy, considered him greatly superior to Rommel, and this view was shared by the Italians. Indeed Mussolini, whom Rommel treated without excessive deference, described the desert Marshal as "a good battalion commander."

In his Directive 38 of 2 December 1941, Hitler defined Kesselring's mission as follows:

To gain control of the air and sea between southern Italy and North Africa, and thus ensure safe lines of communication with Libya and Cyrenaica; in this connection the neutralization of Malta is especially important.

To cooperate with German and Italian forces operating in North Africa.

To interdict enemy traffic through the Mediterranean, and prevent the resupply of Tobruk and Malta; this is to be accomplished in close cooperation with available German and Italian naval forces.

The directive placed all German air and antiaircraft forces in the theater under Kesselring's orders, and these were now reinforced by the Second Air Fleet, which was dispatched to Sicily with about 500 planes.

Although the Germans had sent air and land forces to the Mediterranean in early 1941, the decision to send naval strength was belated. On this question Hitler and Raeder had been unable to agree. Prior to Italy's entry into the war the Grand Admiral had urged sending a small number of submarines to the Mediterranean for diversionary purposes, but Hitler had not concurred for he had felt that results would be slight and that the action of these submarines might complicate the political situation. By 1941, however, their positions were reversed. Raeder now thought that nothing should distract from the main object, the attack on British communications in the Atlantic, while Hitler, giving in to arguments advanced by the liaison officers in Italy, embraced the idea of reinforcing the Italian Fleet with German elements. These could only consist of submarines and of such surface units as were of sufficiently light draft to use the inland waterways.

On 25 July, in the course of a Naval Conference, Hitler asked Raeder if he could send submarines to the Mediterranean. Raeder replied that this would prejudice Atlantic operations and, furthermore, that the British were attacking Axis transports with submarines and planes against which U-boats were useless. On 26 August, Hitler tried again, and once more the Grand Admiral raised objections: since enemy convoys in the Atlantic were being strongly escorted he needed his submarines more than ever in that ocean, both for attack and for tracking; only by concentration of effort in the main theater could one gain a decision; submarines ought not to be employed in secondary theaters except when absolutely necessary and in critical circumstances. In conclusion, Raeder felt that no submarines should be transferred to the Mediterranean so long as there were not at least forty continually on station in the Atlantic. Hitler did not let himself be checked by this argument, and ordered a first contingent of six submarines to the Mediterranean. It is curious to note that in this argument it was Raeder, who had always emphasized the importance of the Mediterranean, who now opposed the dispatch of reinforcements to this area.

In September the first echelon of six U-boats passed

Gibraltar. It was planned to increase this number, first to thirty-six and then to fifty; in fact no more than twenty-five were ever sent. They were divided into two flotillas, one in the Eastern Mediterranean based at Salamis, the other in the Western Mediterranean with its main base at Genoa and secondary bases at Palermo and at Maddalena in Sardinia. At the same time the Germans moved minelayers and motor torpedo boats into the Mediterranean by way of the Rhône waterway. German naval forces in the Mediterranean were commanded by Admiral Weichold, who was responsible to the German Naval General Staff, that is to say to Raeder, but the latter never issued orders to Weichold without consulting Kesselring.

To pass the Strait of Gibraltar while submerged is relatively easy from the navigational point of view: the depths are great, the underwater gradients steep, and the current runs from west to east thus facilitating entry into the Mediterranean. But the British kept an effective watch, and before the end of the year five German submarines had been lost while passing the Strait. This was not, however, too great a price to pay for the advantage gained from the presence of these units in the Mediterranean, for they were to strike heavy blows against the British Fleet and justify Hitler's insistence in the argument which had divided the Fuehrer and his Grand Admiral.

British success at sea; the First Battle of Sirte

THE pressing needs of the Axis armies now forced the Italians to employ warships as transports. On the night of 13 December the two cruisers *Barbiano* and *Guissano* departed Palermo for Tripoli loaded with gasoline. They were sighted by a division of destroyers, *Sikh*, *Legion*, *Maori*, and *Issac Sweers*, the last a Dutch ship. Steaming close to shore where they were invisible against the darkened coast, the destroyers succeeded in approaching within 1,000 yards without being detected. *Sikh* fired two torpedoes at *Barbiano*, which, transformed into a flaming torch, was finished off by a torpedo from *Maori*. *Giussano* managed to open fire but, struck by a torpedo from *Legion* and by shells from the whole division, she in turn burst into flames and sank shortly afterwards.

The need for protecting communications with Libya now led Supermarina to send the fast battleships to Taranto, where harbor defenses had been improved, and *Littorio* and *Vittorio Veneto* were sailed from Naples for that port. On 14 December, while emerging from the Strait of Messina en route to Taranto, *Vittorio Veneto* was hit under the forward turret by a submarine torpedo. Although the ship was able to continue at twenty knots and succeeded in reaching port, major repairs were necessary.

On the 16th the Italians sailed a convoy of four ships from Taranto for Tripoli and Benghazi. The convoy was escorted by the battleship *Duilio*, three cruisers and ten destroyers, and was protected by a covering group containing battleships *Littorio, Doria, Cesare*, cruisers *Gorizia* and *Trento*, and ten destroyers. The importance that the Italian High Command attributed to these operations can be seen from the strength of the forces committed. At the same time the British dispatched the supply ship *Breconshire* to Malta escorted by the 15th Cruiser Division and destroyers. Force K from Malta was to relieve this escort in mid-passage.

During the 17th a German aircraft signalled the presence of a British force at sea but erroneously reported it as containing one battleship, two cruisers, and destroyers. Admiral Iachino at once headed for the enemy with the *Littorio* group at a speed of twenty-four knots. During the afternoon the British convoy underwent violent attacks from Axis planes without suffering loss. Shortly before 1700 Iachino reduced speed to twenty knots; he did not wish to get too far from his own convoy and, furthermore, he estimated from the information available that he would be unable to gain contact with the enemy before nightfall. But at 1723, while the *Littorio* group was heading southward, antiaircraft bursts were seen in the east: these came from the British squadron which was firing on Axis aircraft. Iachino then bore around to the eastward and increased speed to twenty-four knots.

The opposing forces were soon in contact, and *Littorio* opened fire at 1753 at a range of 35,000 yards. At this moment Force K had just joined the Alexandria group. Nevertheless Admiral Vian, who was in command of the British forces, was in a state of serious inferiority. He sent *Breconshire* back to the southward escorted by two destroyers and then, by a series of feints and by making smoke, succeeded in frustrating the maneuvers of his enemy. In this the British formation was aided by uneven visibility which complicated the aim of the Italians and prevented them from observing their enemy's movements. Nevertheless the fire of the battleships was sufficiently accurate to worry the British. Vian's destroyers carried out attacks against the Italian ships which, although scoring no hits, gained time. Twilight was falling when, shortly after 1800, Iachino broke off the action. He had been firing for about ten minutes. Under cover of darkness *Breconshire* resumed course for Malta, where she arrived without damage. Similarly the Italian convoy, after temporarily retiring to the northward, succeeded in reaching Libya. No losses had been suffered on either side.

Admiral Iachino had received inaccurate information from the reconnaissance aircraft; his catapult planes had provided better intelligence but, even so, contact had been made too late for success. In all, this affair, called with some overemphasis the First Battle of Sirte, was a drawn game, each side succeeding in getting through supplies that were greatly needed. But given the disproportion of the two forces, the British performance constituted a success. In 1942 Admiral Vian was to repeat this performance in the face of even more difficult conditions.

In order to insure the passage of their transports, the Italians had sent very considerable forces to sea. In this connection Mussolini wrote to Hitler:

The last convoy of 4 merchant ships got through, but to protect 20 thousand tons of merchant shipping it was necessary to employ 100 thousand tons of warships. *This involves such consumption of fuel that the cost of supplying our forces in Tripolitania will become prohibitive if we do not open the Tunisian route, which from this point of view is infinitely more economical.*

. . . Free use of the Tunisian bases can be gained in two ways: by agreement, or by force.

. . . I tell you, Fuehrer, that I would rather take my armored divisions into Tunisia than watch them disappear into the depths en route to Tripoli. . . .

As a matter of fact, declining fuel reserves were to become one of the principal concerns of the Italian Navy. Rome continually pestered Berlin regarding the supply of fuel for ships, and this led to ceaseless and irritating discussions. As for transit through Tunisia, Germans and Italians in turn attempted to secure permission, but the French Government made only minor concessions.

British disasters

THESE British successes were accompanied by a series of heavy disasters which, combined with defeats in the Far East, seriously threatened British naval supremacy.

On 13 November, ninety miles east of Gibraltar, a German submarine torpedoed and seriously damaged the carrier *Ark Royal*. Although taken in tow, the ship sank when still twenty-five miles from port. On 25 November, the *U-335* encountered the Alexandria Fleet off the Libyan coast. The three battleships, *Queen Elizabeth*, *Barham*, and *Valiant*, were zigzagging in line of bearing protected by a screen of nine destroyers. *U-335* passed under the destroyers and fired four torpedoes at *Barham* at a range of only a few hundred meters: three torpedoes hit the target aft of the second stack, an enormous explosion took place, clouds of smoke covered the sky, and the battleship sank in ten minutes taking 860 men down with her. The submarine had been forced to dive deep after firing to avoid the escorting destroyers, and its commander, von Tiesenhausen, had been unable to observe the results of the attack. For over

147

a month the British Admiralty was able to conceal the disaster, but in late January 1942 admission of the loss produced an outburst of joy among German submariners.

In December losses were again very serious. On the 21st, Force K was steaming off Tripoli in search of a convoy. Under Commodore Agnew in *Aurora* it contained cruisers *Aurora, Neptune,* and *Penelope,* and destroyers *Kandahar, Lance, Lively,* and *Havock.* Twenty miles northwest of Tripoli the Force happened upon a field of German mines laid by the Italian VII Cruiser Division. *Neptune,* at the head of the column, hit a mine and was disabled. *Aurora,* following astern, turned away to port to avoid a collision and while turning also struck a mine. Two minutes later *Penelope* suffered the same fate. *Penelope* and *Aurora,* although seriously damaged, were able to extricate themselves. The destroyer *Kandahar* headed for *Neptune* to take her in tow but also hit a mine and was crippled. The captain of *Neptune* signalled to the other ships to leave him and retire, and shortly afterward the cruiser hit a second mine, blew up, and sank. *Lively* attempted to go to the rescue of the survivors but was called back by Commodore Agnew. During the following night the wind drifted *Kandahar* free of the minefield so that part of her crew was saved before she sank, but the entire complement of *Neptune* went down with the ship.

The forcing of Alexandria

THE Alexandria Fleet was now to suffer an even more serious disaster at the hands of the assault machines. We have observed their repulse at Malta in July 1941, a repulse which followed the success gained by explosive-laden motor boats in March at Suda Bay. The Italians had made several other attempts which, although unsuccessful, should nevertheless be noted, for they prepared the way for subsequent victories.

In August 1940 the submarine *Iride,* carrying piloted torpedoes for a first attempt against the harbor of Alexandria, was sighted and torpedoed in the Gulf of Bomba

148

by Swordfish from the carrier *Eagle*. In September 1940 submarines *Gondar* and *Scire* repeated the attempt, carrying piloted torpedoes to the neighborhood of Alexandria and Gibraltar respectively, but the British squadrons were not in these ports and the two submarines were ordered back to base. While returning, *Gondar* was sunk off Alexandria on 30 September by the Australian destroyer *Stuart* and a Sunderland flying boat. At the end of October 1940 *Scire* returned to Gibraltar, penetrated deep into the anchorage, and launched three piloted torpedoes. After extraordinary exertions the crew of one reached to within twenty yards of the battleship *Barham* but finally came to grief. On 20 September 1941 *Scire* returned to Gibraltar for the third time and launched her *maiali* which, although unable to enter the port, sank merchant ships in the roadstead.

This persistence on the part of the Italians was at last rewarded by dazzling success. On the night of 19-20 December the submarine *Scire* approached the harbor of Alexandria and, when less than a mile from the entrance, launched three piloted torpedoes, each carrying two men. The three commanders were Lieutenent Luigi Durante de la Penne, Lieutenent Antonio Marceglia, a naval constructor, and Lieutenent Vincenzo Martellota, a naval ordnance officer.

The harbor of Alexandria was heavily defended and well watched. It was closed by numerous obstructions and, as a preventive measure, the British exploded depth charges in the approach channels at frequent intervals. But a few destroyers were entering port and the three *maiali*, following close behind and barely submerged, were able to enter unobserved. Durante de la Penne placed his mine under the battleship *Valiant*; Marceglia his under the *Queen Elizabeth*; and the third crew attacked a tanker. Both battleships and the tanker were sunk, and although shallow water prevented complete destruction, the ships required a long period under repair. Six determined men had completely changed the balance of naval power in the

Mediterranean, and it is hard to say whether their ingenuity, their skill, or their bravery is most to be admired. Great as were the material results of this action the consequences for morale were even greater, for in the dark hours of defeat, when Italy came close to giving way to despair, the memory of such an exploit gave her faith and confidence in her destiny.

After having placed the delayed action charges under the ships' hulls the Italians emerged from the water and gave themselves up as prisoners. They warned the British captains that their ships were mined and would blow up in a set time, and advised them to put their crews in safety. On board *Valiant* the reaction seems to have been rather unsportsmanlike, for, according to the Italians, De la Penne and his fellow-crewman were locked in one of the lowest compartments of the ship. Nevertheless they survived the explosion unharmed. As the two battleships had settled vertically in shallow water they appeared to be still afloat and, having taken the six Italians prisoner, the British attempted to conceal the catastrophe which had reduced them to a state of inferiority.

In the Eastern Mediterranean Great Britain now had only destroyers and the three 5,500-ton cruisers, *Naiad*, *Dido*, and *Euryalus*. The Japanese threat made it impossible to send new battleships to Alexandria. For the greater part of 1942, therefore, the British had to fight in the Eastern Mediterranean with only light ships, submarines, and aircraft. Despite all precautions, news of the disaster which had overtaken the Alexandria battleships became known abroad, reaching the enemy in early 1942, but the Axis High Command was unable to profit from this exceptionally favorable situation.

In December the Germans sent their Second Air Fleet to Sicily with the primary mission of neutralizing Malta. At the end of 1941 the Axis possessed both naval and air supremacy in the Central Mediterranean and the British situation was seriously threatened. In the Far East, following their victories at sea, the Japanese advanced with astonishing speed and the Allied future looked very dark. Fortunately for the Allies, the German armies were held up before Moscow in early December, and a terrible winter descended upon the Russian front. The Germans, who had hoped to finish off Russia in a campaign of a few months and then settle the Mediterranean problem, saw their hopes frustrated. Russian resistance saved Suez.

10. The Axis Threatens Suez

The Libyan convoy problem

THE work of the British Navy in supplying Malta and in moving convoys over the difficult course from Gibraltar to Alexandria has been rightly admired, but it should also be recognized that the Italians were faced with a very heavy task in supplying their own army. The forces that were distributed among the Italian islands, the Balkans, and North Africa totalled about 1,200,000 men, and twice in succession the Libyan armies lost all their equipment.

The Libyan supply line began with a long journey either through the Tyrrhenian Sea to Naples or down the Adriatic to Taranto. Although the ports of embarkation on the west coast of Italy were well-equipped, Taranto and Brindisi, which were used for the eastern routes, were of indifferent capacity. At Tobruk, Benghazi, and Tripoli facilities were improvised and harbor areas limited. Equipment for clearing away sunken hulks was inadequate, with the result that blockage of the ports often made it necessary to unload in the open roadsteads. The merchant marine, which had been reduced by a third at the start of the war when ships that could not regain the peninsula were sent into neutral ports, shrank steadily as the result of continual losses. At first the fastest ships were used, but as one by one they disappeared it become necessary to fall back on slow vessels which added to the difficulties of the problem. It was impossible to rely on new construction, for this had to be sacrificed to the more important manufacture of armaments. In emergencies it was often necessary to use warships to carry cargo; but their capacity was small, the cargo made it difficult to go into action quickly in the event of an encounter, and when fuel was being carried they were exposed to the danger of quick destruction, as in the case of *Barbiano* and *Giussano*.

So far as logistic support of the Libyan armies was concerned, the area of operations seemed *a priori* highly favorable. The distance to be covered was small compared to the size of the area of departure from the Italian coast and of arrival in Africa. The voyage from Palermo to Tripoli is five or six times shorter than that from Gibraltar to Alexandria, and a glance at the map will show that geo-

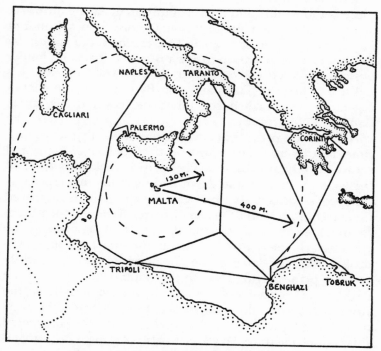

Fig. 14. Italian Convoy Routes to Libya

graphical difficulties were far greater for the British than for the Italians. But then there was Malta, whose effectiveness surpassed all expectation, and radar, which changed everything.

The great activity of the air and sea forces based at Malta obliged the Italians continually to vary their choice of route so as to confuse their adversary. For example, a convoy leaving Taranto for the Libyan coast would depart at night heading for a point midway between Benghazi and Tripoli, and only subsequently steer directly for its destination. But when Malta-based aircraft were equipped with radar such ruses became ineffective, and the British often possessed photographic knowledge of the situation.

With the improvement of torpedo planes the choice of route became more and more complicated. At the outbreak of the conflict their range was not more than a hundred miles; by the end of 1940 it had reached 130 miles; by the end of 1941 it was up to 160 miles and it was no longer possible to keep convoys clear to the westward for this radius reached the Tunisian coast. By late 1942 the operating range had reached 400 miles and covered the entire Central Mediterranean.

Axis fighters provided convoy protection only during daytime. Not flying at night, they retired before twilight and returned only after dawn. The British took advantage of these circumstances, and dawn and dusk became especially dangerous periods. As time went by the British improved their techniques, and the use of better flares enabled them to attack at any time during the night. A scouting plane would track the convoy, summon the attackers, and then drop a cluster of flares on the side opposite the attack while torpedo planes, flying close to the water, came in from the dark sector. For defense the Italians turned away from the illuminated area and made smoke, but this had to be done quickly and precisely, and surprise sometimes prevented this countermeasure. Day attacks also became more dangerous as bombsights were improved.

Since zigzagging was wholly inadequate to frustrate radar search, the Italians were forced to subdivide their convoys and to make wide detours, but subdivision of convoys required a greater number of escort ships. And even in 1942, when the British had only light cruisers available for their attacks, their superiority in night fighting forced the Italians to employ capital ships to protect transports of minor importance. The Italian Fleet Command complained bitterly at being thus compelled to risk its battleships on secondary missions, missions which involved heavy consumption of scarce fuel.

We know from Admiral Weichold, a German witness whose testimony is therefore not suspect, that the lack of fuel was not, as has too often been suggested, a pretext, but rather a very real cause of the inactivity of the Italian Fleet. Such it was, especially after the autumn of 1941, for the Germans supplied only a third of the fuel which they had promised the Italians. The Italian Navy still had fairly large quantities of diesel oil, but the supply of bunker fuel was very low and the High Command was continually faced with the problem of maintaining adequate reserves for a possible major operation. Thus its every action was complicated by the fuel problem. Finally, in comparing the accomplishments of the Italians with those of the British, it must not be forgotten that traffic to Libya was continuous, while both the Malta convoys and those sent through the Mediterranean from Gibraltar to Alexandria were sporadic. The British not only possessed an alternate route around the Cape but also the Takoradi airway.

Up to 1 November 1942 Italian vessels made 1,785 trips to Libya in 883 convoys, a very small average of two ships per convoy. In addition to attacks from surface ships these received 253 air attacks and 202 submarine attacks, the latter figure emphasizing the extreme activity of British submarines. The Axis transported 2,105,815 tons of materiel and 54,282 vehicles to Libya, losing 15.7 per cent of the tonnage shipped. This percentage is not very high, and is a credit to the Italian Navy. But the losses were not evenly distributed: while Malta was being pounded by Axis planes they were small, but when the aerial blockade was relaxed they rose. We have seen that on 9 November 1941 the loss of a whole convoy struck a deadly blow at the Libyan armies. Subsequently the destruction of tankers in the summer of 1942 was greatly to hamper Rommel. Malta controlled the passage to Libya, and Malta should have been captured.

Plans for the conquest of Malta

AERIAL bombardment of Malta had only palliative effect; whenever it stopped the island recovered its offensive capacity with extraordinary speed. In early 1942 Supermarina recommended the seizure of Malta. Kesselring and Weichold supported the idea, Raeder had long urged it on the Fuehrer, and both Comando Supremo and the O.K.W. approved. But lengthy preparations were required. The Italians needed several months to collect the necessary materiel and train their troops. The date of the operation was first set for June and then for July 1942, more than two years after Italy entered the war. On 21 April Kesselring announced that the requirements of the Russian front forced the O.K.W. to withdraw a large portion of the Luftwaffe units based in Sicily, but he promised to bring in part of Rommel's Libyan air strength when the time came for the attack on Malta.

The Malta operation was a difficult one. The island is mountainous, the shores are steep, and ever since June 1940 its defenses had been steadily strengthened. The plan included an invasion by parachutists and airborne troops followed by a landing on the south coast and capture of Marsa Scirocco, through which port heavy materiel was to be landed; at the same time the small island of Gozo was to be occupied. The attack, planned by a mixed German-Italian group, was the first operation of the war to be studied by a combined staff; the Axis had waited for two years before adopting this very elementary organizational step.

By June all was ready and the troops had undergone intensive training. But in January, as will be described below, Rommel had conquered almost all of Cyrenaica. At the end of April he reported that the British were preparing a counterattack and that he felt it desirable to forestall them. He was consequently authorized to undertake a limited offensive which was to be followed up only in case of marked success. The general plan was then as follows: first complete the conquest of Libya, next seize Malta, and then march upon Suez. But the Libyan offensive obtained astonishing results, whereupon Rommel persuaded Hitler and the O.K.W. that all hopes were justified and that Alexandria was within his grasp. Hitler in turn convinced Mussolini. In June a conference at Derna, presided over by the Duce, decided to let Rommel keep all the Libyan air strength for the continuation of his offensive, and to postpone the attack on Malta until after the capture of Alexandria. Kesselring and Weichold were opposed to this decision, which was later held against Rommel and used as further evidence that the Germans did not understand naval warfare.

But it did not require a great specialist in naval affairs to see how much Malta hampered communication with Libya and, after eighteen months of experience, Rommel was as well aware of this as anyone. He simply felt that the British Eighth Army was in a state of complete dissolution and, without ignoring his own difficulties, considered them smaller than those of his adversary. Events were to show that he was wrong and that he had been too bold.

It is perhaps wrong to make Rommel the principal scapegoat, for recent revelations such as the disclosures of General Carboni, who commanded one of the assault divisions assigned to the attack on Malta, have placed the question in a new light. Carboni thought the operation an adventure that would end up in a general drowning. He arranged that a note, in which he explained his fears, should reach the Prince of Piedmont, and it was this report, he writes, which changed the ideas of Comando Supremo. It therefore seems quite likely that, in view of the great risks involved in the operation, Rommel's opinions were welcomed as providing an excuse for cancelling it.

In any event July 1942 was rather late for an attack on Malta. The operation would have been costly in ships, planes, and troops, all of which were needed in Libya, and there was no assurance that at this time it would have succeeded. The attempt should have been made in 1940 or 1941 before the Luftwaffe was absorbed by the requirements of the Russian front. It seems probable that the British Fleet would have done everything to save the island, but to do so it would have had to operate for several days close to the Sicilian coast, thus affording the Axis air forces a magnificent opportunity to destroy its ships. But in any event it would have been necessary to send a major portion of the Luftwaffe to Sicily; and that, after all, implied a Mediterranean strategy and indeed an overall strategy wholly different from those which were adopted by the Axis.

Rommel's second offensive

ON 22 JANUARY, only nine days after Auchinleck's offensive had been checked, Rommel's counterattack began the movement which in two phases would lead him to the gates of Alexandria. On the 23rd he took Agedabia, on the 28th Benghazi, on 2 February he entered Barce, and on the 7th he was at Gazala, thus recapturing most of Cyrenaica in fifteen days. At the same time the air attacks on Malta, which had begun at the end of December with the arrival of the German Second Air Fleet, increased in intensity. In accordance with Axis plans, which contemplated a heavy pounding of Malta prior to its seizure, then scheduled for July, these intense bombardments were continued through June. In April the island received 6,000 tons of bombs. Throughout the first half of the year its situation was critical, indeed at times desperate. Food, munitions, and fuel all ran short. The submarines, which from the beginning of the war had always been able to remain at Malta, were forced to move to Alexandria at the end of April. The garrison held on, but its calls for reinforcement and supplies were often anguished. The offensive strength of the island was greatly reduced and Axis communications with Libya were maintained with small losses.

The loss of the bulge of Cyrenaica once again increased the tasks of the Alexandria Fleet. So long as the British held Benghazi, their convoys could follow the coast as far as Barce and then by day head towards Malta under fighter cover, timing their advance so as to pass the midpoint between Malta and Cyrenaica at night; at dawn aircraft from Malta took charge of the convoys and provided air cover until their arrival. But the advance of Axis forces made this impossible and forced the ships to keep clear of the African coast. In January four cargo ships succeeded in reaching Malta. In mid-February the British attempted to push through a convoy from Alexandria by using a very northerly route, but all three supply ships were destroyed by Axis aircraft while south of Crete. On 18 February Lieutenant General Sir William Dobbie, governor of the island, sent an alarming message to Alexandria reporting that he had been obliged to put the island on very short rations and that his fuel supplies were dangerously low. On 7 March a few planes arrived from Gibraltar but this reinforcement, although valuable, did not ease the supply problem.

The second battle of Sirte

On 11 March the weakened Alexandria Fleet suffered another painful loss when Italian torpedo planes sank the cruiser *Naiad* south of Crete. But in late March, despite the weakness of their forces, the British attempted to push through another convoy, thus setting the stage for one of their most brilliant naval actions. At 0700 on 20 March the supply ships *Breconshire, Clan Campbell, Pampas*, and the Norwegian *Talabot* departed Alexandria escorted by the cruiser *Carlisle* and six destroyers. The covering force was provided by the 15th Cruiser Squadron, *Cleopatra, Dido*, and *Euryalus*, and four destroyers. En route this force was joined by *Penelope* and one destroyer from Malta, and by the Fifth Destroyer Flotilla from Tobruk. The whole disposition was under the command of Rear Admiral Vian.

To help this essential operation the Eighth Army launched a limited offensive designed to draw off enemy aviation and the R.A.F. vigorously attacked airfields in Cyrenaica, Crete, Rhodes, and Greece.

On the afternoon of the 21st the convoy was reported off Tobruk by an Axis submarine and during the night an

Italian force under Admiral Iachino got underway to intercept it. This force contained the battleship *Littorio* with
six destroyers, and a group of three cruisers, *Gorizia,
Trento,* and *Bande Nere,* and four destroyers under Admiral Parona. Admiral Vian was advised by a British submarine of the presence of this Italian fleet at sea, while Axis
aircraft kept Iachino informed of the convoy's movements.
At 1030 on the 22nd Iachino ordered the Parona group to
increase speed, to gain contact with the convoy, and to
engage, but without becoming completely committed before the arrival of *Littorio.* During the morning the convoy was intermittently attacked by German-Italian aviation.

Shortly after 1400 Parona gained contact and, in accordance with his instructions, engaged at long range. Vian
intended to lay smoke screens between the attackers and
his cargo ships and to make a torpedo attack on the Italian
cruisers as soon as they came within range. A strong southeasterly wind blew the smoke toward the Italians who were
approaching from the northward. The combination of
smoke and a range of about 22,000 yards made firing ineffective, and at about 1500 Parona retired northward with
the intention of drawing the British cruisers towards *Littorio.* At 1530 the two Italian groups joined, and at about
1630 Iachino with his whole force was in contact with
Vian's squadron.

From 1630 to 1855 the Italian admiral attempted to pass
to westward of the British cruisers and destroyers so as to
reach the merchant ships. The distance between the two
squadrons fell to 11,000 yards and, in the course of the
action, the cruiser *Cleopatra* and the destroyers *Havock* and
Lively were damaged. A series of offensive maneuvers and
the use of smoke screens enabled Vian to gain time. But
between 1800 and 1900 his situation was very critical for,
thinking that an Italian detachment was maneuvering to
attack downwind, he had moved to the eastward with
cruisers *Cleopatra* and *Euryalus.* At this time Iachino was
about 11,000 yards from the rest of the British squadron,
which was only saved by a determined destroyer attack

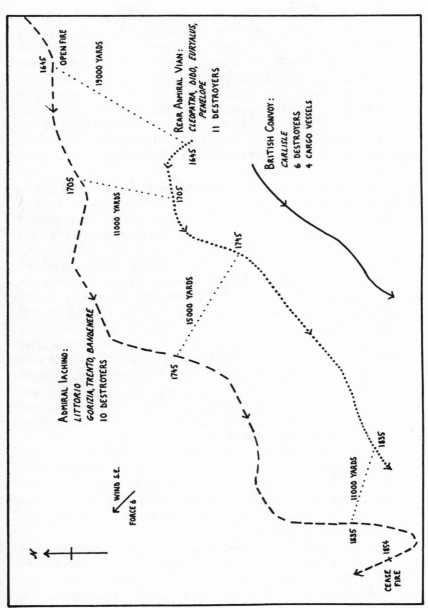

ADMIRAL IACHINO:
LITTORIO
GORIZIA, TRENTO, BANDENERE
10 DESTROYERS

WIND S.E.
FORCE 6

REAR ADMIRAL VIAN:
CLEOPATRA, DIDO, EURYALUS,
PENELOPE
11 DESTROYERS

BRITISH CONVOY:
CARLISLE
6 DESTROYERS
4 CARGO VESSELS

1645
OPEN FIRE

19000 YARDS

1705

1705

11000 YARDS

1645

1705

1745

15000 YARDS

1745

1745

1835

11000 YARDS

1835

CEASE
FIRE × 1854

Fig. 15. The Second Battle of Sirte, 22 March 1942

which temporarily slowed the Italians. Night was coming on and, at about 1900, *Littorio* was sighted for the last time headed northward. Iachino preferred not to become involved in a night action and was giving up the fight. For several hours, and in the face of very superior enemy force, Vian had succeeded in protecting his convoy by a series of maneuvers which required determination and judgement of the highest order. As the Commander in Chief of the British Mediterranean Fleet reported, "Had the roles been reversed, it is unthinkable that the convoy, or much of its escort, could have survived."

It may seem surprising that Admiral Iachino had not at the start attempted to get to windward of the enemy; had he done this the force six wind would have made smoke screens useless. Alternatively, while heading to windward with *Littorio* the Italian admiral could have detached his cruisers to attack from another bearing. He justified his maneuvers by the following reasons: by approaching the convoy from the westward, he kept between it and Malta; furthermore, to get to the eastward required heading into the wind and, as the sea was very high, he would have had to reduce speed and lose time. The state of the sea may indeed be appreciated by the fact that while returning homeward the Italian squadron lost two destroyers, *Scirocco* and *Lanciere*, as a result of flooding. Nevertheless the maneuvers of the Italian Commander in Chief were criticized and, as a result of this engagement in which seamanship played so great a part, Vian's reputation was greatly enhanced while Iachino's suffered. The German aviators were unfavorably impressed, far more so than they had been by the defeats of Taranto and Matapan: they had never been very anxious to cooperate wholeheartedly with the Italian Navy, but following this battle they showed a real aversion to combined operations.

Although it had escaped the Italian fleet the convoy had not reached the end of its troubles. It had been delayed for several hours by evasive maneuvers during the battle, a delay which must be credited to Iachino's actions, and it could no longer reach Malta by dawn as had been planned. Furthermore, the cruisers from Alexandria had had to leave the convoy during the night and return to Egypt so as to avoid having to take on fuel from the limited supply at Malta. On the morning of the 23rd the merchant ships, sailing with reduced escort, were subjected to violent attacks from Axis aircraft. The *Breconshire*, which in the course of numerous trips to Malta had hitherto escaped all dangers, was hit by a bomb and sank within sight of the harbor with her priceless cargo of fuel. *Clan Campbell* was also sunk off Malta. The destroyer *Legion* was damaged and had to be run aground, and the *Southwold* blew up on a mine. The two remaining ships, *Pampas* and *Talabot*, which had succeeded in reaching the island, were attacked at their moorings and destroyed while unloading. Out of a cargo of 25,900 tons which the convoy carried, only 5,000 tons were saved.

So violent were the attacks on Malta that all ships of Force K had to be sent either to Alexandria or Gibraltar. In April, Spitfires sent in from Gibraltar on *Eagle* and on the American carrier *Wasp* were all destroyed within a few days. Necessary supplies of fuel and ammunition then had to be sent in on the submarines *Parthian, Regent, Porpoise, Rorqual,* and *Cachalot*. In May the carriers *Eagle* and *Wasp* succeeded in sending more Spitfires to the island, and the minelayer *Welshman* ran the blockade with a load of ammunition. Malta still stood, but its offensive strength was greatly reduced.

On 1 April the Italians suffered a painful loss. The cruiser *Bande Nere*, which was being moved from Messina to Spezia for repairs, was attacked off Stromboli in the Tyrrhenian by the British submarine *Urge*. Hit by three torpedoes, *Bande Nere* sank rapidly.

In April Admiral Cunningham was summoned to London and turned over his command temporarily to Admiral Pridham-Wippell. On his departure Cunningham addressed an order of the day to the Fleet:

The enemy knows we are his master on the sea, and we must

strain every nerve to keep our standard of fighting so high that the lesson never fails to be borne in at him. We have not at times as large forces as we would like to carry the war to the enemy's front door. This will not always be so, and I look forward to the day when the Mediterranean Fleet will sweep the sea clear and re-establish our age-old control of this waterway so vital to the British Empire. I am confident that that day is not far distant. . . .

But in the meantime the situation was serious. Despite the fact that part of its Mediterranean strength had been sent to Russia, the Luftwaffe remained dangerous. On 11 and 12 May the destroyers *Kipling, Lively,* and *Jackal,* three out of four that were patrolling between Sollum and Crete, were sunk by German aircraft from the Aegean.

In mid-May the Italian assault machines renewed their efforts against Alexandria. The submarine *Ambra* brought three *maiali* close to the port but, having been forced to remain long submerged, it drifted out of position and the torpedoes were launched too far from the harbor. Two of these machines were unable to find the entrance and had to abandon the attempt owing to exhaustion of fuel. The third penetrated the roadstead, but was damaged by one of the depth charges which the British continually exploded in the approach channels as a preventive measure.

Two months later the submarine *Scire* made a similar attempt against the harbor at Haifa. Discovered by an enemy destroyer, she was sunk before carrying out her mission. These operations became increasingly difficult as the enemy steadily strengthened his defensive measures.

Rommel resumes the offensive

ON 26 MAY Rommel attacked again with a success which surpassed all his hopes. After overcoming fierce Allied resistance, notably at Bir-Hakeim where General Koenig's French troops distinguished themselves, the Axis forces arrived on 20 June before Tobruk. On the 21st this fortress, which had held out for eight months during Rommel's earlier offensive, fell to a violent tank attack. Captain

Smith, the Senior Naval Officer, Tobruk, and Captain Walter, Senior Officer of the Inshore Squadron, had to organize a hasty evacuation of wounded and get all their ships and harbor craft underway. The last ships departed protected by smoke screens and under the fire of German tanks, but on shore 25,000 prisoners and vast amounts of supplies remained in the hands of the German-Italian troops.

So great was his success that Rommel now hoped to reach Alexandria, and saw no purpose in attacking Malta before having conquered the great British naval base. At the end of June, after having taken Mersa Matruh, his forces were before the lines of El Alamein, less than sixty miles from Alexandria. Early in July a vain attempt was made to break the British lines between the sea and the Qattara Depression; despite some local successes the Axis forces were obliged to make what Rommel expected would be only a short halt. During his advance he had been supported by Axis submarines and light forces including destroyers and motor boats; the Italian heavy ships had not appeared.

As the Luftwaffe had been principally employed against the Eighth Army, these Libyan operations had to some extent eased the pressure on Malta. Nevertheless the situation of the island remained critical. In May the British Minister of State for the Middle East had returned from a visit to Malta feeling that it might be starved into surrender. It was therefore decided in London to make another attempt to relieve the island.

The Malta convoys of June 1942

In mid-June the Admiralty decided to supply Malta by sending in two large convoys, one from the east and the other from the west. The convoy from the east, under command of Admiral Vian, contained ten cargo ships protected by seven cruisers and about twenty destroyers. The western convoy, under Admiral Curteis, contained six merchant ships escorted by cruisers and destroyers and covered by Force H. On being informed of the movement of these convoys, the Italian staff estimated that the one from Alexandria had the better chance of getting through, and to prevent this sent out Admiral Iachino with a sizeable force: battleships *Vittorio Veneto* and *Littorio*, the four cruisers *Gorizia, Trento, Garibaldi,* and *Duca d'Aosta,* and three destroyer squadrons. In the west the task of blocking the approach to Malta was left to aircraft, submarines, fast motor boats, and a relatively weak squadron under Admiral da Zara which contained the VII Cruiser Division, *Eugenio di Savoia* and *Montecuccoli,* and five destroyers.

On 14 June the Alexandria convoy was attacked by ninety planes which sank one cargo ship and damaged a second. On the 15th the cruiser *Hermione* was crippled by a motor torpedo boat, the destroyer *Hasty* was sunk by a submarine, and a few hours later the cruiser *Birmingham* was damaged by aircraft. Vian had been informed of the presence of a strong Italian force across his route, and he retired in order to gain time while aircraft from Malta and Egypt attacked this squadron. *Littorio* was damaged by these British air attacks, but continued with the operation; the cruiser *Trento,* however, was stopped, and was subsequently sunk by the submarine *P-35*. But in its turn the convoy was again attacked by Axis planes; the destroyer *Avon Vale* was lost and *Nubian,* heavily damaged, had to be sunk the next day. Although Vian's retirement had prevented an encounter with Iachino's squadron, the latter was still at sea across the route to Malta. Moreover, the ammunition supply of the British ships had been reduced by antiaircraft actions and the destroyers were running low on fuel. Vian therefore abandoned the operation and returned to Alexandria.

The western convoy had passed Gibraltar on 12 June. The escort contained the battleship *Malaya,* the carriers *Eagle* and *Argus,* four cruisers, and seventeen destroyers. On the 13th the convoy was attacked by Axis planes without result. On the morning of the 14th attacks were made by fighter-escorted bombers and Savoia torpedo planes; the cruiser *Liverpool* was hit by a torpedo, its speed was reduced to three knots, and it was forced to retire to Gibraltar.

Further heavy raids came in at twilight but no damage was done. At nightfall Force H turned back towards Gibraltar, leaving the convoy to continue towards Malta under the protection of the light cruiser *Cairo* and nine destroyers. During the night Admiral Curteis was informed that Admiral da Zara's Italian squadron was headed for the convoy, but it was then too late to reinforce the escort.

At dawn of the 15th the Italian force made contact with the convoy about twenty-five miles southwest of Pantelleria. The Italians were approaching from the northeast, and *Cairo* headed towards them with five destroyers while the merchant ships retired to the southwest. Admiral da Zara's squadron was superior in strength, it was handled resolutely and it fired well. In the course of the engagement the British destroyers *Partridge* and *Bedouin* were seriously damaged, the latter so heavily that she sank. Although the action of *Cairo* and the destroyers had prevented the Italians from reaching the merchant vessels, these with their weakened escort were attacked by aircraft which succeeded in sinking three of the cargo ships.

Delayed by these events, the convoy reached Malta at night. The island was of course blacked out, and navigation was difficult. The Polish destroyer *Kujawiak* hit a mine and sank; two other destroyers, a minesweeper, and a cargo ship also hit mines but succeeded in making port. Thus this great operation, which the British had mounted in such strength, ended with the arrival of only two supply ships. But so great was Malta's need that the advent of their cargoes constituted a success, acting on the island as oxygen on a dying man.

The withdrawal of that part of the German air strength which had been sent to the Russian front in April now began to be felt. At the beginning of July, to the joyful surprise of the garrison and people of Malta, attacks on the island diminished in intensity. Not only had the Axis abandoned the attempt at seizure but the Luftwaffe was concentrating its efforts in support of Rommel's Libyan armies. But in Libya the lengthening lines of communication and the lack of air bases made the task of the German-Italian air forces increasingly difficult. The American Army Air Force had come to the aid of the R.A.F., and as British and Americans continued to send reinforcements to Egypt the Allies began to gain command of the air. The struggle in Africa was about to reach its decisive phase, Malta had to be able to play its part, and the Admiralty decided once again to attempt to supply the island.

The convoy of August 1942

THE JUNE convoy operation had shown that the conquest of Cyrenaica on the one hand and the weakness of the Alexandria Fleet on the other made the sending of reinforcements to Malta from the east exceedingly risky. The Admiralty therefore decided to send an important and heavily escorted convoy by way of Gibraltar. On 9 August a group of eleven cargo ships entered the Mediterranean, escorted by the battleships *Nelson* and *Rodney*, the carriers *Indomitable, Victorious, Eagle*, and *Furious*, seven cruisers and twenty-five destroyers, under command of Admiral Syfret. Never before had the British deployed such a concentration of aircraft carriers in the Mediterranean.

The fuel shortage at this time prevented the Italian High Command from sending forth its battleships. So low were supplies that when a ship was unavailable, even if only for a short time, its fuel was transferred to another. Nevertheless Supermarina sent forth the III and VII Cruiser Divisions, and then recalled them because it was impossible to provide adequate air cover. This mistaken action proved expensive to the Italians, for on the 13th *Bolzano* and *Attendolo* were torpedoed off the Lipari Islands by the submarine *P-42*. The two cruisers were able to make port but were seriously damaged. Consequently the Italians and Germans, lacking the help of ships of the surface squadron, had to oppose the British effort with only submarines, motor torpedo boats, and aircraft.

Five Italian and two German submarines were on station between the Balearic Islands and Algeria. Early on the

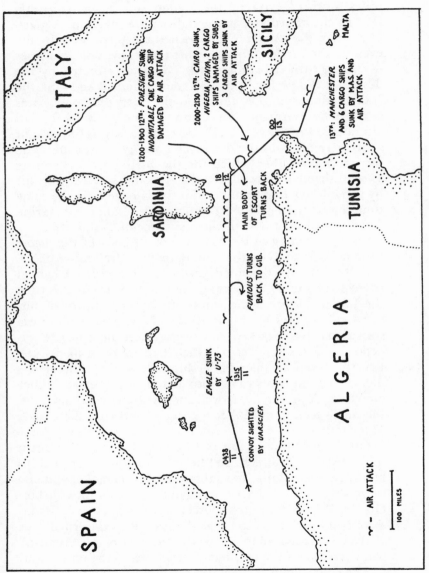

Fig. 16. The Malta Convoy of August 1942

morning of 11 August the convoy was reported about sixty miles south of Iviza by the Italian submarine *Uarsceik*. During the afternoon, about eighty miles north of Algiers, *U-73* sank the carrier *Eagle* with three torpedoes. In the evening the carrier *Furious*, which had flown off its planes to Malta, turned back towards Gibraltar escorted by the destroyer *Wolverine*, which en route rammed and sank the Italian submarine *Dagabur*. On the 11th the convoy was assailed by German planes and on the 12th by Italian aircraft. Many heavy attacks were made, several merchant ships were hit, and the destroyer *Foresight* was sunk. The carrier *Indomitable*, which the the British were planning to send through to reinforce the Alexandria Fleet, was hit by three heavy bombs and seriously damaged. At the same time the destroyer *Ithuriel* rammed the Italian submarine *Cobalto* and sank it with the assistance of *Pathfinder*.

On the evening of the 12th the main body of the escort turned back to Gibraltar, accompanied by *Indomitable*, and the convoy continued through the Sicilian Channel protected by three cruisers and ten destroyers. At this time the Italian Navy was beginning to employ groups of surfaced submarines for night attacks. Northwest of Tunisia six submarines attacked, and using these new tactics torpedoed the cruiser *Cairo*, which had to be sunk by the British, and four merchant ships. Near Pantelleria the motor torpedo boats came into action: a tanker and other merchant ships were destroyed and Lieutenant Commander Manutti's section of M.A.S. torpedoed and sank the cruiser *Manchester*.

On the morning of the 13th the convoy was once again subjected to air attack. In the evening three cargo ships finally reached Malta, and subsequently one tanker and one cargo ship, both damaged, struggled painfully into harbor. On the British side nine merchant ships and several warships had been sunk; so far as the Axis was concerned, this affair, which the Italians called the "Victory of mid-August," had been one of the best handled actions of the entire war.

The operation had been very costly for the British; nevertheless, so valuable was the materiel that did reach Malta that these heavy losses were balanced by the strategic success of enabling the island's air strength to operate effectively. Although Supermarina had disposed its forces well, the decision to withdraw the cruisers can be criticized. The risks were very great but the stakes made them worthwhile, for what was at issue was the fate of the Axis armies in Egypt.

Had Admiral Syfret's air search informed him of the threat from the Italian cruisers, it seems probable that he would have strengthened the convoy's escort, but with cruisers only, for his carriers had suffered heavy punishment and the British were reluctant to send heavy ships into the Sicilian Channel; the Italian cruiser squadron would therefore have been faced only by ships of its own class. On the other hand, it was deplorable to have the Italian battleships kept in port because of lack of fuel. The Germans were stingy in supplying their allies with oil, at first because they had none to spare and subsequently because they had little confidence in the fighting spirit of the Italian High Command. Thus it came about, contrary to all principles of war at sea, that air crews, submarines, and small craft had to bear the brunt of a battle without adequate support from the surface squadrons, a battle in which, despite their bravery, they were unable to gain decisive results.

In September, following the improvement of the fuel situation effected by the August convoy and the ending of air attacks, the British again based a surface force at Malta. This force, commanded by Rear Admiral Power and containing a division of cruisers and two destroyer flotillas, now reinforced the aircraft and submarines which had already returned to the island. From August on, Malta continued to be supplied by submarines and fast minelayers. On 11 November the minelayer *Manxman* reached the island with a cargo of powdered milk which had been so anxiously awaited that, on the arrival of the ship, women kneeled in the streets holding their children up to heaven. Then, when Cyrenaica was retaken by Montgomery, supply again became normal; by December 1942 Malta was definitely saved; in 1944 even the blackout was abandoned. In the course of the war this island underwent 3,215 alerts, received 14,000 tons of bombs, and had 20,000 houses destroyed or damaged. In attacking it the Axis lost 1,126 planes, 236 of which were destroyed by antiaircraft, while the British defenders lost 568.

Although several times the island seemed doomed, it was saved by convoys which, at the price of terrible losses, repeatedly brought in fuel at the last moment. Thus it was able to revive and again to deliver powerful attacks against Axis supply lines. In the course of the war aircraft from Malta alone destroyed or damaged 500,000 tons of Axis shipping. If one can say of Great Britain that that little island saved the world, it can equally well be said that the little island of Malta saved the Mediterranean.

The action of August had been cried up by Axis propaganda. Although the aircrews, the submariners, and the men of the motor torpedo boats deserved the praise they received, it was clear that the Italian battle fleet had failed in the Western no less than in the Eastern Mediterranean. To support Rommel's June advance part of the Italian Fleet should have been sent to Crete and to the Dodecanese where it would have been better situated to strike enemy communications and to protect Axis supply lines. Such a movement had been planned as early as May. It was intended to base cruisers and destroyers, supported by one or two *Cavour* battleships, at Suda Bay, Leros, and Rhodes, but these plans had to be given up because of the difficulty of fueling these forces, and all that was done was to base three light cruisers at Navarino where their presence was far less effective.

Throughout the summer the African front remained stabilized. In August the British attempted to attack Axis lines of communication by an amphibious landing at Tobruk. They arrived off shore without being sighted and succeeded in landing commandos who, however, were unable to destroy the harbor installations and supply dumps that were their objectives. While retiring, the expedition was struck by German aircraft which sank the cruiser *Coventry*, a destroyer, and a fast motor boat. On 31 August Rommel made a new attempt to break through; he failed, and on 2 September retired into his lines. For almost four months the German-Italian forces had been held up at El Alamein, and by September it appeared necessary to fall back on Sollum where there was a very strong position and where the supply line was shorter. But Rommel, against the advice of the Italian command, refused to do this.

The halting of Rommel's advance, which marks one of the turning points of the war, has been generally attributed to lack of supplies and, in particular, to the loss of three tankers in late June, just before the July attacks. But lack of supplies was not the only cause of failure. Rommel himself explained the first halt in July by the following reasons: delay in the attack as a result of minefields, the fact that since the enemy had recovered himself surprise was no longer possible, British air superiority, and lack of fuel.

From July on, the British Eighth Army was rapidly strengthened, thanks in part to the support given Great Britain by the American merchant marine. The United States also sent aerial reinforcements which, under General Brereton, were to share in Montgomery's victory. At the same time Rommel's supplies were inadequate. During the first four months of 1942 Axis losses of materiel in transit had been remarkably small, but beginning in June they became considerable, amounting to thirty or forty per cent of the tonnage shipped monthly. In October, just before the British offensive, losses of fuel reached sixty-six per cent. By this time all Axis convoys were being spotted by planes from Malta and continually attacked both by aircraft from that island and from Egypt. Doenitz was thus able to say that Rommel was lost owing to the failure of the Italian Navy, but this failure itself had causes for which the German command was partly responsible: refusal to give the Italians the indispensable minimum of fuel; transfer of German air strength to the Russian front which, by freeing Malta, contributed greatly to the interruption of Libyan communications; finally, persistence in the Egyptian effort at a time when the growing difficulties of supply dictated a strategic retirement.

Of all these causes the withdrawal of the Luftwaffe was the most serious. Even if not conquered, Malta could have been neutralized by a powerful air force based in Sicily, and transport shipping in the Eastern Mediterranean could have been protected had Rommel possessed a Libyan air force superior to that of the British. The fact is that the Germans attempted more than they could accomplish, and when Doenitz blamed only the Italian Navy he overlooked the deeper causes of defeat. Keitel expressed himself with greater moderation: "One of the greatest opportunities which we lost was El Alamein. I would say that at that moment of the war we were nearer than ever—either before or afterward—to victory. We came very close to seizing Alexandria and to pushing on to Suez, but owing to the disposition of our forces and above all to the war with Russia, we were not strong enough at this particular point."

The Germans may have deceived themselves in thinking that the capture of Suez would have guaranteed victory, but it would most certainly have been a great triumph.

Montgomery's offensive

ON 15 AUGUST 1942 General Alexander, who was to lead the Allied armies to Rome, relieved General Auchinleck in command in the Near East. The area of Persia and Iraq was detached from the Middle East Theater and was formed into a separate command to block a German threat from the Caucasus. At this time an attack by way of Anatolia did not seem imminent, and the Allies did not expect the Germans to present an ultimatum to Turkey before spring of 1943. On 10 August Churchill handed General Alexander the following directive which he had written out in his own hand:

1. Your prime and main duty will be to take or destroy at the earliest opportunity the German-Italian army commanded

by Field-Marshal Rommel together with all its supplies and establishments in Egypt and Libya.

2. You will discharge or cause to be discharged such other duties as pertain to your Command without prejudice to the task described in paragraph 1, which must be considered paramount in His Majesty's interests.

General Auchinleck had exercised command not only over the theater but also over the British Eighth Army. It had been agreed that the Eighth Army was to be given to General Gott, commander of 13 Corps, who had been in every desert battle from the beginning, but he was shot down by enemy fighter planes before taking over command. General Montgomery was sent out from Great Britain to replace him. Thus chance took a decisive part in the selection of Montgomery for the command in which he was to win one of the most important battles of the war.

As soon as he took over command he isued the order, "No withdrawal," an order reflecting the state of mind of all Great Britain: Suez would not be lost. Now at last reinforcements were flowing in, and on 23 October the Eighth Army passed over to the offensive. It had at this time about five hundred first-line planes, a relatively small number, but all were excellent machines manned by picked crews and operating from well-supplied bases. The strength of the attack took the Axis by surprise. Rommel, who was in Germany, returned hastily to discover that his deputy had made serious blunders. After ten days of furious battle Montgomery broke his adversary's front, and Rommel was forced to order a retreat which proved as rapid as his June advance. On 6 November Mersa Matruh was occupied, on the 13th Derna was taken, on the 24th Benghazi, and once again all Cyrenaica was in the hands of the British. Although in July the fuel shortage had not been the principal cause of Rommel's halt, in November it indubitably brought about his downfall. Several Axis tankers had been sunk during October, the German Marshal had fuel for only a few days, and this shortage not only led to his defeat but also prevented him from reestablishing his situation.

Montgomery, on the other hand, had excellent communications. On land his vehicles were numerous, and the Alexandria Fleet ensured free movement of supplies along the coast. Restoration of captured ports had been minutely prepared; a large flotilla of tugs, minesweepers, and light ships had been assembled at Alexandria and went rapidly into action. Three days after the troops entered Tobruk the port was in operation and was unloading 3,000 tons a day, a remarkable feat for that harbor.

The harbor of Benghazi, which the Axis had not had time to destroy completely, was in service on 22 November. At no time was the Navy behindhand in supplying the Eighth Army. After a short halt before El Agheila, where Rommel attempted a stand, Montgomery resumed his advance. El Agheila was taken on 15 December, and Sirte on Christmas Day. And in the west decisive events had taken place; a new phase of the war was beginning in the Mediterranean. The United States now intervened powerfully on the side of Great Britain, and the combined forces of these two powers were to thrust the Axis out of Africa.

PART IV
THE AXIS
DRIVEN FROM AFRICA

11. The Landings in North Africa

The concept

FROM the moment that the United States entered the war the leaders of Britain and America had been in complete agreement that Germany, the strongest and nearest enemy, was to be defeated before Japan. But it is no longer a secret that on the subject of the invasion of Europe deep differences developed between the British and American staffs. The British advocated an attack by way of the Mediterranean; they wished to seize North Africa and use it as a springboard for an invasion of Italy or, better still, of the Balkans, the region that Churchill called the "soft under-belly of Europe." The Americans suspected Great Britain of wishing to gain positions in southeastern Europe in anticipation of post-war problems, and they felt that such an approach was strategically a very difficult one. The Balkan peninsula, exceedingly mountainous, is easy to defend, while from the Balkans to the Rhône Germany is protected by the Alpine barrier, of which General Marshall wrote, "In Europe's innumerable wars no vigorously opposed crossing of the Alps had ever been successfully executed."

Furthermore, an offensive by way of the Mediterranean would have involved very long lines of communication and would have required a vast amount of shipping, and the question of available tonnage was always a determining factor. The American military leaders thought that Germany ought to be attacked by way of the plains of northwest Europe, and they felt that invasion would be possible in 1943. In April 1942 their concept was adopted. But by the middle of the year Russia found herself exceedingly hard pressed by the Germans, while at the same time Rommel's advance threatened the Suez Canal. Something had to be done to reduce enemy pressure without waiting until 1943. Consequently, in late June 1942, Roosevelt and Churchill definitely decided to establish a second front before the end of the year, leaving the time and place to be decided by their staffs.

The discussion of this subject among the Allied military leaders in Washington was very spirited, and the Americans even considered completely reversing overall strategy and concentrating their main effort on Japan, a plan which fortunately was abandoned. Roosevelt strongly favored an attack through North Africa but was reluctant to force his will upon the services. In July the debate was continued at London, where General Marshall and Admiral King represented the American staffs and Harry Hopkins the President. Marshall and King defended to the last the plan of the American Joint Chiefs of Staff which called for a landing in the Cotentin peninsula in the summer or autumn of 1942: the peninsula was to be held so as to draw off German forces and relieve the other fronts, and in 1943 major landings would be carried out in a neighboring region.

The British considered this enterprise premature and unlikely to succeed; they thought that, if the peninsula were conquered, all available German aircraft would concentrate their efforts on the small occupied area and that the position would become untenable. The Americans had to give up their plan, perhaps less from conviction than to avoid acting with such unwilling partners. On this question General Marshall has written with his usual moderation:

After prolonged discussions, it became evident that the only operation that could be undertaken with a fair prospect of success that year was TORCH, the assault on North Africa. Landings there would be a long way from Germany, but should serve to divert at least some German pressure from the Red Army, and would materially improve the critical situation in the Middle East. It was therefore decided, with the approval of the President and the Prime Minister, to mount the North African assault at the earliest possible moment, accepting the fact that this would mean not only the abandonment of the possibility for any operation in Western Europe that year, but that the necessary build-up for the cross-Channel assault could not be completed in 1943. TORCH would bleed most of our resources in the Atlantic, and would confine us in the Pacific to the holding of the Hawaii-Midway line and the preservation of communications to Australia.

It may be seen from this quotation that General Marshall accepted this strategy only reluctantly, and his biographers have confirmed this fact with much less reserve.

The directive for Operation **TORCH** contemplated the following action:

1. Establishment of firm and mutually supported bridgeheads in the Mediterranean between Oran and Tunisia, and in French Morocco, so as to gain bases for continued and intensified action by ground, sea, and air forces.
2. Vigorous and rapid exploitation of these bridgeheads to gain complete control of French Morocco, Algeria, and Tunisia, and to extend the offensive eastward against the rear of Axis forces in Africa.
3. Complete annihilation of Axis forces opposing the British in the Western Desert, and intensification of air and sea operations against the European continent.

It will be noted that the plan made no commitment regarding the direction of future offensives. This question remained to be decided. In France, when news came of the North African landings, many officers completely misjudged the immediate possibilities and expected a speedy arrival of the Allies upon our Mediterranean shore. But at this time the British and Americans had no such intention, let alone the necessary strength.

On 14 August General Eisenhower was named commander in chief of all land, sea, and air forces of the expedition, and Admiral Cunningham was placed in command of the fleet. For several weeks the question of the extent of the landings was discussed in London. As the Allies lacked adequate force for simultaneous attacks on all the ports of Morocco, Algeria, and Tunisia, a choice had to be made. As the dispatch of naval forces to the region of Bizerte and Tunis seemed hazardous, the British having previously suffered very heavy losses in that area from enemy aviation, it was decided not to go beyond the region of Algiers, and to occupy Algiers, Oran, Casablanca, and Safi. Although the landings in Morocco and Algeria were planned to be simultaneous, they were not wholly interdependent. It was agreed that the operations within the Mediterranean would be carried out even in the event of a repulse in Morocco, and vice versa. On the other hand, the landings at Oran and at Algiers were closely linked, and it was understood that abandonment of one of these operations for whatever reason would entail cancellation of the other.

The assault was considered extremely risky and the Allies undertook it only with grave misgivings. During the planning, Eisenhower thought it the kind of adventure in which success depended much more on political arrangements than on military decisions. To begin with, the land forces committed were relatively weak; again, the landings risked being delayed by bad weather, particularly in Morocco, in which case the advantage of surprise would be lost; it was not known what the reaction of the local French forces would be; it was even thought that the Toulon Fleet might intervene; and finally, most dangerous possibility of all, the Axis might react by way of Gibraltar, with or without Spanish assistance. In such an event the expeditionary force in Algeria would be cut off from the ocean at the same time that it would have to face enemy attacks coming from Tunisia.

Nevertheless the situation contained a number of favorable elements. By patient work the Americans had gained intelligence sources in North Africa, where the feeling was generally on their side. The French forces, although determined to resist according to the formula "we will defend North Africa against any aggressor," were uncertain of Marshal Pétain's real wishes and were deeply disturbed in spirit. Even had they been determined to resist, these French forces could not have done so very effectively; they were inadequately armed and they had been unable to keep up with the technical progress of the belligerents. In the Navy, for example, ships had not acquired radar and antiaircraft armament was as inadequate as it had been at the start of the war. The shortage of fuel restricted training, and great ingenuity was required in the Fleet to devise exercises which were realistic and yet called for little oil. The French Command was not equipped to conduct searches and it seemed probable that it could be taken by surprise. The Toulon Fleet had no air strength; although the ships did have fuel they could not replenish their supplies and, had they intervened, the heavy consumption involved in high-speed maneuvers would have rapidly immobilized them. As the war spread and the German armies became bogged down in Russia, the Spanish Government had become less than ever willing to abandon its neutrality and the Axis less and less able to force it to do so. One may conclude that, risky as it was, the Allied enterprise was more likely to succeed than to fail.

Convoy organization

THE EXPEDITION was divided into three groups. The first of these, the Western Task Force or Task Force 34, was wholly American; it contained some thirty transports with 35,000 troops, and was escorted by three battleships, six cruisers, five carriers, about forty destroyers and miscellaneous ships. This force, under command of General Patton and Admiral Hewitt, sailed from the United States for the invasion of Morocco.

The second group, the Center Task Force, contained about 39,000 American troops embarked in Britain. The naval forces of this group under Commodore Troubridge comprised the headquarters ship *Largs*, the battleship *Rodney*, the carrier *Furious*, the escort carriers *Biter* and *Dasher*, the antiaircraft cruiser *Delhi*, thirteen destroyers, six corvettes, eight minesweepers, and various auxiliary ships. The Center Task Force was responsible for the attack on Oran.

In the third group, the Eastern Task Force, were 23,000 British and 10,000 American troops under General Ryder; these had been embarked in Great Britain. The naval forces of this group, commanded by Rear Admiral Burrough, contained the headquarters ship *Bulolo*; three cruisers, *Sheffield*, *Scylla*, and *Charybdis*; two escort carriers, *Argus* and *Avenger*; three antiaircraft ships, *Palomares*, *Pozarica*, and *Tynwald*; the monitor *Roberts*; thirteen destroyers, three sloops, seven corvettes, and auxiliary ships.

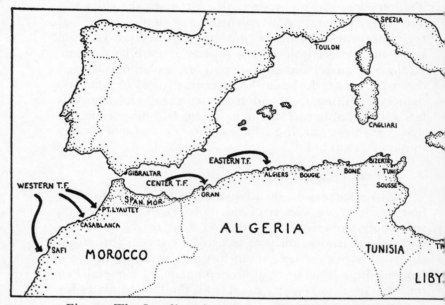

Fig. 17. The Landings in North Africa, 8 November 1942

Once inside the Mediterranean the convoys were protected by a powerful British covering force containing battleships *Nelson* and *Duke of York*; the battle cruiser *Renown*; carriers *Victorious* and *Formidable*; light cruisers *Bermuda*, *Argonaut*, *Sirius*, *Phoebe*; and seventeen destroyers. Gibraltar provided the shore-based aviation.

The Western Task Force, various elements of which had departed from Portland, Norfolk, and the Bermudas, joined on 28 October in 40° N 50° W. From this point it headed southeast until south of the Azores in 27° N, and then

184

turned north again toward Morocco. The Algerian expeditions departed from Great Britain in two large convoys of different speeds. The slow convoy got underway on 22 October, the fast convoy four days later, and during the night of 5-6 November all ships passed the Strait of Gibraltar at which time they were redistributed into groups destined for Oran and for Algiers.

During the voyage strong air patrols in the Bay of Biscay prevented enemy searches, and the entire expedition crossed the Atlantic without being reported.

The attack on Algiers

THE ALGIERS operation was made up of three landings. Group Charlie was to land east of Cape Matifou; Group Beer between Sidi Ferruch and Cape Caxine; Group Apples east of Castiglione. In addition two British destroyers, *Broke* and *Malcolm*, were given the difficult task of landing an American detachment inside the harbor of Algiers so as to prevent sabotage of ships and port facilities.

During the voyage the American transport *Thomas Stone* was torpedoed off Palos by an Axis submarine but continued at slow speed escorted by a destroyer. A second attack barely missed the transport *Samuel Chase*. In accordance with orders the convoy continued ahead without waiting for *Stone*, and successfully made contact with the beacon submarines which were marking the landing points. The landings took place at night with some delay and considerable confusion. While the coastal battery at Cape Matifou made gestures symbolic of resistance, troops of Group Charlie rapidly captured the airfield at Maison Carrée. At Castiglione the troops landed unopposed and headed for Blida against only sporadic resistance. No fighting occurred at Sidi Ferruch.

During the same night the destroyers *Malcolm* and *Broke* came forward to enter Algiers harbor. They missed the entrance and while starting a second approach were picked up by searchlights and fired upon. *Malcolm* was hit in the boilers and forced to withdraw. *Broke* succeeded in breaking the boom and in landing her antisabotage detachment which was surrounded and ultimately taken prisoner; the Americans observed that the French were shooting much more to stop them than to kill. Maneuvering under fire with great skill, *Broke* succeeded in leaving the harbor and was taken in tow by the destroyer *Zetland* which had helped her escape by laying a smoke screen. Heavily damaged, *Broke* sank at sea on 10 November while still in tow.

At noon on the 8th Admiral Darlan, who by chance had happened to be at Algiers, issued orders to cease firing, and by evening all resistance in the Algiers sector was over.

The attack on Oran

THE ORAN operation, like that at Algiers, called for three separate landings in the same region. Group Z, the most important, was to seize the harbor at Arzeu and then march on Oran by way of Saint Cloud. Group Y was to land in the bay at Les Andalouses and then attack Mers el Kébir. Landing at Mersa Bou Zedjar, Group X was to send motorized elements against the airfields at Tafaraoui and La Senia to support the parachute troops charged with seizing them at the outset. Finally the British cutters *Hartland* and *Walney* were given the task of entering Oran harbor and landing commandos to prevent possible sabotage.

At Arzeu surprise was complete. As along the whole Algerian coast the navigational lights were burning, and the harbor boom was open. Allied ships penetrated boldly into the port and the town was rapidly seized. Further to the southward troops went ashore to meet only weak and disorganized opposition. By afternoon of the 8th all resistance in this sector had ceased and unloading was being carried on without difficulty at Arzeu; this was fortunate for the attackers, for the weather had turned bad and the beaches outside the port had become unusable.

Neither at Les Andalouses nor at Mersa Bou Zedjar was there resistance to the landings, but the column moving inland from the latter beachhead had to fight before Lourmel, which was seized only after a fairly severe engage-

186

ment. The troops which had landed at Les Andalouses were held up by fire from the forts at Mers el Kébir, which in turn were engaged by *Rodney*. Having missed their target the parachute troops had been unable to seize the airfields, but once past Lourmel the American motorized columns reached and captured Tafaraoui by midday and La Senia in the evening.

At Oran the attempt of the coast guard cutters *Hartland* and *Walney* had failed. Bravely entering the port during the night of the 8th, they were sunk by the fire of the numerous French ships which were lying moored to the quays. Although taken prisoner, the crews and the commandos were treated much more as friends than as enemies. It is not easy to understand why the Allied Command had decided on these extremely risky ventures at Oran and at Algiers; they could only have succeeded with the complete cooperation of the French, and in such a case they would have been superfluous.

The French destroyers at Oran attempted to sortie but were immediately engaged by Allied cruisers watching off the harbor. *Tramontane, Surprise*, and *Tornade* were sunk on the 8th; *Epervier* and *Typhon* on 9 November. A general attack on Oran had been planned for the 10th, but on that day the armistice went into effect; this was fortunate for the success of the enterprise, for Axis reaction was already beginning to be felt.

In Morocco the fighting had been more severe; in particular the small French squadron had fought a brave and skillful battle under very unequal conditions and had suffered heavy losses.

The landings in North Africa were thus an Allied success: the losses were small, the gains considerable, surprise had been complete. Spain had not moved and seemed fully determined not to abandon her neutrality; no threat weighed upon Gibraltar. With their rear secure, the Allies could hasten their march on Tunisia.

But although it had been a success, Operation TORCH had also shown that major improvements in landing techniques were needed. There had been delays in schedule, mistakes in landing, and general confusion. Even more serious, numerous landing craft had been lost from poor handling. Some, badly loaded, had shipped water and drowned out the engines; others had been beached too soon; some had even been sunk as a result of being maneuvered with open ramps. As a result of these accidents the soldiers evinced considerable resentment against the Navy, and General Ryder recommended that in future the Army should control operations from the time that the troops embarked in the landing craft and that the landing craft themselves should be manned by soldiers. Cunningham and Eisenhower wisely dismissed these revolutionary proposals, placing the blame on inadequate training. The Allies were to profit greatly from experience and to improve their techniques, but it may be questioned whether a landing in the Cotentin at this time would have succeeded in the face of a powerful and determined adversary. Perhaps it was very fortunate that the first attempt was made in North Africa.

Axis reaction

As EARLY AS AUGUST 1942 the Axis had been aware of preparations for a great Allied amphibious operation, and the High Command naturally made great efforts to discover the objective. Anticipating a landing in North Africa, Supermarina urged preparation for a rapid occupation of Tunisia, if such should prove necessary. In September 1942 the German and Italian members of the French Armistice Commissions of Wiesbaden and Turin met with intelligence officers at Venice and discussed the possibilities of an Allied invasion and the probable French reaction. Three assumptions were made: a landing at Dakar, a landing in Morocco before winter, and a landing in the region of Oran. The possibility of a landing in Algeria east of Oran seemed improbable; that of a landing in Italian territory was wholly rejected. The operation against Dakar was considered most likely.

With regard to the probable attitude of the French, the

Germans felt that their forces would offer determined resistance to Allied attempts but the Italians were much more sceptical. Nevertheless it was agreed not to take any precautionary measures which might antagonize them. The findings of these commissions were accepted by the Axis High Command and the distribution of German submarines in the Atlantic was modified so as to take account of the presumed threat to Dakar.

The movement of Force H into the Mediterranean on 4 November at first appeared to Supermarina to be the start of a normal attempt to supply Malta, but on the 6th the discovery of convoys of unprecedented size showed that a great landing operation in the Mediterranean was imminent. As the convoys had not been sighted before reaching the approaches to Gibraltar, the Axis was taken by surprise. Once again the Italian ships of the line were unavailable owing to lack of fuel; in any event they could not have ventured west of the Balearic Islands without air cover, and this they did not have. The light forces and the Air Force were busy protecting the transport of urgent supplies to the Libyan armies. The number of available submarines was inadequate: after TORCH had begun the Axis succeeded in mustering about thirty submarines, but this number could not be maintained, and by the end of November submarine reaction had become very weak. From Spezia, Supermarina brought down battleships *Littorio* and *Vittorio Veneto*, and also *Roma*, which had just entered service; while this movement might have indicated that the Fleet was about to intervene, the lack of fuel made the threat an empty one. On 7 November, believing that they had a Malta convoy to deal with, the Italian Navy had laid new mines of German model in the Sicilian Channel; on the return the new cruiser *Regolo* was torpedoed and damaged by a submarine. All in all these efforts were of small importance and in no way comparable to the offensive with which they had to contend.

Thus the Allies controlled both air and sea in the Western Mediterranean. The Axis leaders now fully realized the terrible error they had made in neglecting the problem of Gibraltar. It was too late. Among themselves they raged against the Spanish government, but their fury was impotent for they lacked the strength to seize the Rock without the consent and assistance of the Spaniards.

Hitler and Mussolini now decided to seize unoccupied France and Corsica, and to dispatch all available air and ground reinforcements to Tunisia. To the Germans the occupation of southern France included the seizure of the Toulon Fleet. On 11 November they entered the unoccupied zone, and on the same day the Italians occupied Nice and landed in Corsica. In North Africa Axis reaction, although improvised, was speedy. On the evening of 8 November eight Junker 88's and Heinkel 111's attacked Allied transports off Matifou, sinking *Leedstown* and damaging several ships. Fortunately for the Allies, the speed with which the French ports were turned over to them gave their ships some degree of protection. On the 9th, German airborne elements occupied the airfield of El Aouina in Tunisia; and on the 13th, German and Italian troops began flowing in. General Barré retired westward with the French forces, passed into the Allied lines, and established himself on the Tunisian Ridge in accordance with orders from General Giraud.

In the meantime the Anglo-American advance guard was hastening eastward. On 9 November a British convoy of twenty-eight ships, escorted by the warships *Roberts, Sheffield, Tynwald*, and *Karanja*, was formed at Algiers. On the 11th the British landed unopposed at Bougie, but as heavy surf prevented their landing at Djidjelli its airfield was occupied only by paratroops, a circumstance which deprived the expedition for some time of effective air cover. During the evening of the 11th, Axis planes sank the auxiliary antiaircraft cruiser *Tynwald* and damaged several ships, and only on the 13th did British Spitfires come into action. Bône was occupied on the 12th by British commandos brought in on the destroyers *Lamerton* and *Wheatland*. On 15 November the British 78 Division landed at Bône; a front was being established but the Allies where unable to reach Bizerte. The Axis had won the race for Tunisia and its ejection was to require six months of fighting.

The scuttling of the French Fleet at Toulon

As EARLY AS 1940 the Germans had planned the seizure of the French unoccupied zone in minute detail. This step was in no way surprising, for it seemed probable that if the war were prolonged the French Mediterranean coast would some day become a theater of hostilities. This operation, known as ATTILA, was to be carried out according to instructions given by Hitler in his Directive 19 of 10 December 1940:

Preparations must be completed for the rapid occupation of the remaining free territory of metropolitan France in the event of attempts at revolt in parts of the French Colonial Empire now under command of General Weygand. At the same time it will be necessary to seize the French Fleet and French aircraft, or at least prevent them from going over to the enemy. Both for military and political reasons these preparations will be disguised, so as to avoid alarming the French.

Entry into the unoccupied zone, if ordered, will be made by heavy motorized elements under adequate air cover proceeding via the valleys of the Garonne and Rhône; they will advance rapidly to the Mediterranean and, if possible, occupy the ports, in particular the important naval port of Toulon, and will cut France off from the sea.

Steps will be taken to prevent the French Fleet from getting underway and joining the enemy; constant watch will be kept on all units of this Fleet. The C-in-C, Navy, will cooperate with the external security forces and will make arrangements for exploiting the possibilities offered by the Armistice Commission. The Cs-in-C, Navy and Air Force, will study methods of gaining possession of the French Fleet. In particular the following points will be considered:

Blocking harbor entrances, especially at Toulon;
Army-Navy cooperation;
Acts of sabotage;
Submarine attacks on ships putting to sea.

Preparations for ATTILA will be kept strictly secret. The Italians are to have no knowledge of preparations made, nor even that action is contemplated.

Whenever relations with France became tense, the question of executing Operation ATTILA was raised, but because the German leaders were hesitant and divided regarding its wisdom this step was not taken until the Allied occupation of North Africa. Throughout 1941 Admiral Raeder opposed such a move; he was an advocate of collaboration with France and hoped to reach an understanding which would give the Germans the cooperation of the excellent French crews as well as the use of French bases. From the German point of view this was clearly the ideal situation and all that was lacking was French assent. But a meeting in January 1942 between Raeder and Admiral Darlan produced no concrete result, and from that time on the Germans thought only of seizing the French Fleet by force. Nevertheless they postponed action until November.

When the Germans entered the unoccupied zone, Admiral Auphan, Minister of the Navy, repeated the instructions that Admiral Darlan had given in 1940:

Secret preparations for sabotage will be made so that no enemy or former ally, seizing a ship by force, will be able to use it. If the German Commissions attempt to violate the rules of the Armistice, ships are either to be taken to the United States or scuttled without further orders. In no case will they be left intact for the enemy.

At the same time Admiral Darlan in Algiers was sending forth signals urging the Fleet to get underway, but these, being contrary to the orders of the government, were not carried out.

The occupation of the southern zone placed the Fleet in a critical situation. If Toulon were occupied by the Germans the safety of the ships would be doubtful. On the other hand the Axis leaders feared their departure. "One fine day," said Ciano, "we will wake up and find the port of Toulon empty." On 11 November on orders from Admiral Raeder, Captain von Ruault-Frappart proposed an agreement to Admiral Marquis, Commander of the Port, and to Admiral de Laborde, the Fleet Commander. This involved the creation of a zone around Toulon which was not to be occupied by the Germans and which was to be protected by French forces. In exchange the French commanders would give their word of honor to take no action against the Axis and to defend Toulon against both Anglo-Saxons and dissident French. Marquis and De Laborde felt that this agreement was consistent with their orders and accepted. Admiral Auphan, consulted by telephone, immediately gave his consent to the proposed arrangement. But the Germans were planning to break their word; they only wanted to gain time to stabilize the situation in the southern zone and to bring their forces up to Toulon, so that when all was ready they could pounce upon the Fleet.

The French staff intended to assemble 50,000 men within the perimeter at Toulon; this would have assured the protection of the Fleet, at least for a considerable amount of time, and would also have reconstituted a small Armistice Army. A Franco-German commission spent the 14th and 15th of November in marking out the perimeter while Auphan struggled to endow the little entrenched camp with appropriate means of defense. On 16 November part of the French troops were in place, but on the 18th the Germans required their withdrawal; Toulon was to be defended only by naval forces. As it was only with great difficulty that the Navy could muster a few battalions, the protection of the encampment became a farce. On 19 November Admiral Auphan, disagreeing with Laval regarding the policy of the government, resigned his ministerial post and was replaced in this unenviable position by Admiral Abrial.

The German plan called for an attack on Toulon by two columns. One coming from the east was first to seize Fort Lamalgue, which contained Admiral Marquis' headquarters, and then occupy the southern part of the Mourillon and the Grosse Tour and emplace artillery so as to control the harbor mouth from the northward. A second column was to approach from the westward through Sanary and make its way through the Navy Yard to where the ships were tied up. Part of this column was to occupy the Saint Mandrier peninsula south of the anchorage, and join its fire with that of the artillery at the Grosse Tour to interdict the channel. At the same time planes were to fly over the anchorage, laying mines, and dropping flares to illuminate the movements of ships. H Hour was set for 0430 on 27 November.

The German members of the Commissions had cut the telephone wires so that the forward elements of the camp were unable to warn the French command. Admiral Marquis was taken prisoner at Fort Lamalgue at 0420 but his Chief of Staff, Rear Admiral Robin, was able to warn Major General Dornon by telephone, and he in turn alerted De Laborde. By parleying, Dornon succeeded for a time in holding up the Germans at the gates of the Navy Yard. By the time they reached the quays the scuttling, for which careful preparations had been made, had begun.

Thus the worst was avoided, but sixty-one ships totalling 225,000 tons were sunk. These included the old battleship *Provence*; two large battleships, *Strasbourg* and *Dunkerque*, which had survived Mers el Kébir; four 10,000-ton cruisers, *Algérie, Foch, Colbert, Dupleix*; three second-class cruisers, *Marseillaise, La Galissonnière, Jean de Vienne*; the aircraft transport *Commandant Teste*; fifteen destroyers; thirteen torpedo boats; fourteen submarines. Five submarines succeeded in getting underway: *Casabianca* and *Marsouin* reached Algiers; *Glorieux* arrived at Oran; *Vénus* had to scuttle herself off Toulon; *Iris* reached Barcelona and was interned. The Germans had tried to persuade Vichy to forbid the scuttling of the ships, an attempt which fortunately did not succeed. At Bizerte, following an ultimatum which allowed only thirty minutes' delay, the Germans obtained delivery of a few light vessels and of nine second-class submarines of doubtful utility, and the Italian San Marco Regiment occupied the forts.

At this stage in the war the port of Bizerte had considerable importance and, had the Italians been able to base a powerful naval force there, the Mediterranean situation might perhaps have been altered in their favor. But they would have had to protect this force effectively against Allied air attack, and this the Axis lacked the strength to do. Bizerte served principally as terminus of the line of communications and was used only by escort ships and minor vessels.

Although improvised, Axis reaction on land had been prompt and energetic. Nevertheless it was insufficient. To counter the invasion of North Africa it was necessary, over and above the steps taken by the German-Italian High Command, to install Axis forces on the Strait of Gibraltar and to close it to the Allies. That Germany had been unable to attempt this was a confession of impotence.

12. The War at Sea During the Tunisian Campaign

The Axis decision to hold Tunisia

AT the end of November 1942 several German leaders, including Grand Admiral Raeder, felt that Tunisia had become the key to the Mediterranean and that by its seizure the Axis had reestablished a situation dangerously imperilled by the Allied landings in North Africa. Raeder's argument was as follows: the lines of communication of the German and Italian armies had been shortened while those of the Allies had become longer and more vulnerable; the occupation of Tunisia had strengthened the Axis situation in the Sicilian Channel and had divided Allied Mediterranean naval forces; so long as the Axis held Tunisia an Allied landing in the Balkans or Italy was improbable. The only advantage that the Allies had gained was in advancing their bases closer to the Central Mediterranean and this, in Raeder's opinion, did not make up for the drawbacks.

Had the Axis possessed adequate military strength the Grand Admiral's optimism might have been vindicated, for in November 1942 the Germans were counting on quick success on the Russian front to enable them to send strong air reinforcements to the Mediterranean. But the fall of Tripoli, which was entered by the Eighth Army on 23 January 1943, coincided with the disaster at Stalingrad, which ended the hope of withdrawing air strength from Russia. Under these circumstances it was necessary to assess the Tunisian situation calmly and to consider a withdrawal from Africa, an action which would have saved a large part of the German and Italian armies.

Before abandoning Tripoli the Italians had destroyed the port facilities and had bottled up the harbor with sunken ships. But the work was not thoroughly done and the port was rapidly entered and cleared. Increasingly the advance of Allied air and naval bases from both west and east offset the advantage of shortened sea communications between Italy and Africa. In point of fact, the situation which had at first glance seemed favorable to the Axis was quite the reverse, given the disproportion of available air and naval strength. At the time of the African landings Italy still had about a million tons of merchant shipping, but part of this tonnage was composed of highly vulnerable liners which could not be employed. Moreover, numerous ships had to be used to maintain communications with the islands and with the Balkans, so that there remained only about 400,000 tons available for the supply of the Tunisian armies, an amount which steadily diminished as a result of losses.

Naval strength was also very unequal. The Italian Fleet did have battleships, but throughout the Tunisian campaign these were immobilized by lack of fuel and by repairs. Such fuel as was available was saved for escort vessels; only after the campaign was over was it made available to the capital ships, whereas the Allies at all times had at least four battleships in fighting condition. The number of Italian cruisers fell from eight on 30 November 1942 to only one in April while the Allies had a dozen. In destroyers the Allies also had a heavy superiority. But so restricted was the theater that naval inferiority would not have prevented the Italians from carrying out cruiser raids had the Axis not been handicapped by weakness in the air. The ratio of aircraft, which had been two to one in favor of the Allies in late November, had by the following spring increased to five to one. As General Marshall observed in his reports, it was very clear that with the arrival of good weather air superiority would play its full role and Axis communications would become very precarious.

In this connection it is worth noting that the German Admiral Weichold has severely criticized the O.K.W. for taking into account, in its strategic thinking, only the apparently favorable geographical situation while ignoring the ratio of available forces. Jodl subsequently attempted to excuse the High Command by saying that they had been forced to fight in Tunisia because an evacuation was impossible. Certainly a rapid evacuation was difficult, but a gradual planned departure would probably have permitted saving an important part of the German-Italian forces, and these, being among the best the Axis had, would have contributed effectively to the defense of Sicily.

As a result of disagreements with the Fuehrer, Admiral Raeder resigned on 30 January and was replaced as Supreme Commander of the German Navy by Admiral Doenitz, commander of the submarine fleet, who was made a Grand Admiral. Doenitz, a submariner of the First World War, was above all a man of action who had great influence over his crews. Although of keen intelligence, he had paid little attention to questions of high strategy, and in such matters Raeder considered him of very limited ability. For the Fuehrer, Doenitz had a limitless admiration and a blind devotion which he maintained even in disaster. Following a conference with Hitler he wrote: "The immense strength radiated by the Fuehrer, his unwavering confidence, and his far-sighted appraisal of the Italian situation, have shown how insignificant we are compared to him, and how fragmentary is our knowledge of the situation. The man who thinks he can do better than the Fuehrer is an imbecile."

In late March 1943 the Axis Command was reorganized and unified. Marshal Kesselring was given control of all German forces of land, sea, and air, and mixed German and Italian staffs were established at Comando Supremo and in all principal echelons of command. This latter was a useful if belated step, but although amalgamation was now accomplished on paper, in spirit it existed less and less. Weichold, who had continually asked for reinforcements, who was suspected of excessive friendship for Italy, and who was blamed for supporting Supermarina's grievances too strongly, was now relieved by Doenitz and replaced by Admiral Ruge. In mid-March, following a visit to Italy, Doenitz reported to the Fuehrer on the malevolence of the Italian staff, which he accused of pretending a lack of fuel to excuse its inertia. But like Weichold, the Grand Admiral stressed the need of sending aerial reinforcements to protect Tunisian communications; like Raeder he complained of the lack of naval aviation; and, again like Raeder, he urged a move against Gibraltar. In short, once having passed from the specialized command of submarine forces to the overall command of the Navy, he embraced the same strategic ideas as his predecessor.

Allied naval dispositions

THE ALLIES had divided their naval forces into several groups. In the west Force H, containing battleships, carriers, and light ships, was stationed at Gibraltar or at Mers el Kébir; it carried out sweeps through the Western Mediterranean and stood ready to intervene if the Italian battleship squadron, which was being kept under surveillance by submarines and aircraft, moved southward.

Force Q, composed of cruisers and destroyers and based at Algiers and Bône, covered the continuous coastal traffic along the Algerian shores and made frequent raids on Axis communications in the Sicilian Strait. At Malta there was a destroyer force whose mission was analogous to that of Force Q. Two British submarine flotillas, the Eighth at Algiers and the Tenth at Malta, were used to attack enemy communications and to watch enemy naval forces. In the harbors of Algeria and Libya and, with the advance of the armies, in those of Tunisia as well, were numerous flotillas of small vessels: minesweepers, escort vessels, trawlers, motor torpedo boats, and the like. And every landing field held a portion of the air strength which was to play the central role. Most of the ships were British. The principal American contributions to the offensive at sea consisted of aircraft and of Motor Torpedo Boat Squadron 15. It is worth noting that although before the war the Americans had placed only slight confidence in these craft, feeling that they could profitably be replaced by torpedo planes, the war had shown their usefulness for night attack.

The dispatch of Force K to Bône had seemed hazardous,

for that port was at first poorly defended against air raids. The decision was nevertheless taken, owing to the advantages of the location, but Force K suffered serious losses. Similarly, the risks run by cargo vessels east of Algiers made it necessary to transfer supplies to small ships for the final stage of the voyage. This coastal traffic was very heavy, for the capacity of the land routes, both rail and road, was inadequate.

On 20 February 1943 the command structure was reorganized. General Eisenhower, hitherto Commander in Chief of the Allied Expeditionary Force in North Africa, received the title of Commander in Chief of Allied Forces in the Mediterranean. His command included the whole Mediterranean north of a line running south of Tunisia and north of Syria, while the area southeast of this line remained part of the Middle East Command. The Mediterranean Theater also extended through Spain and Africa into the Atlantic so as to include the Cape Verde and Azores Islands. Under Eisenhower, all naval forces of the theater were commanded by Admiral Sir Andrew Cunningham. In the Middle East, according to British custom, the naval, land, and air forces remained under their respective commanders, cooperating simply by mutual understanding without one being subordinated to another. After Montgomery's army entered Tunisia, the Middle East Theater declined in importance and became essentially a rear area responsible for logistic support of the Mediterranean Theater proper.

From the naval point of view the line which separated the two Mediterranean theaters was a fairly arbitrary one, but Admiral Sir Andrew Cunningham and his namesake, Admiral Sir John Cunningham, who was in command in the Middle East, cooperated perfectly. Ships were continually exchanged between the two zones, combined missions were often carried out, especially in the Central Mediterranean, and all went smoothly. In any case such theater boundaries have only relative importance in naval warfare, for navies are accustomed to the constant movement of forces from one area to another.

The fighting

THE FIGHTING at sea involved no major naval engagement but rather a host of small actions, incessant mine warfare, and continuous air effort. At Bône, where the ships of Force K were exposed, aircraft seriously damaged the destroyer *Ithuriel* in November and the cruiser *Ajax* at the end of 1942, and sank several cargo ships. Nevertheless the maintenance of Force K at Bône was justified by its success against enemy shipping. On the night of 1-2 December it intercepted and sank a whole Italian convoy, including the destroyer *Folgore*; on the return, however, the destroyer *Quentin* was torpedoed and sunk by an Axis plane.

On the afternoon of 4 December Allied aircraft heavily bombed the Italian fleet at Naples. The cruisers *Eugenio di Savoia, Montecuccoli, Attendolo,* and four destroyers were hit, and *Attendolo* capsized. Following this raid, the battleships *Vittorio Veneto, Littorio,* and *Roma,* and several cruisers were transferred on 7 December to Spezia. On 9 December the cruisers *Gorizia* and *Trieste* were withdrawn from Messina to La Maddalena. This retirement northwards made more difficult the intervention of Italian forces and, indeed, the heavy ships never again appeared, leaving the weight of the battle to be borne by aircraft, light ships, and submarines.

On 11 December the Italian submarine *Ambra* succeeded in passing the nets of the roadstead of Algiers. It carried three piloted torpedoes and ten "gamma" scouts, divers who were equipped to fasten explosive charges under ships' hulls. The divers and piloted torpedoes left the submarine at about 2300, and the latter, leaving a boat on the surface to serve as a marker, settled to the bottom to await the return of the assault machines. The harbor was alerted as the divers were returning and *Ambra* was attacked while hurriedly getting underway. But the Italians had succeeded in sinking one merchant ship and in damaging three others, two of which had to be run ashore. Once again the assault forces had performed a fine feat of arms, although in view of the great strength of the Allies its influence on the struggle was negligible.

In mid-December the British cruiser *Argonaut* was torpedoed by Axis planes, having both bow and stern blown off; but astonishingly enough it was still able to maneuver, and succeeded in reaching Algiers under its own power. In March the British returned the visit of the Italian assault machines to Algiers: a piloted torpedo boldly entered the harbor at Palermo and torpedoed the cruiser *Traiano* which was just being completed. On 10 April four American B24's attacked the Italian cruiser division at La Maddalena, sinking *Trieste* and heavily damaging *Gorizia*. A few days later, on 14 April, Allied bombers made a night attack on shipping at anchor at Spezia, and the attack was repeated on the 19th by sixty planes. The battleship *Littorio* had a turret damaged; the destroyer *Alpino* and three patrol vessels were sunk; one destroyer, one submarine, and various minor ships were damaged.

In April 1943, after more than two years in command, Admiral Iachino was relieved by Admiral Bergamini, hitherto the second in command of the Italian Fleet. For various reasons Bergamini had no chance to lead his ships to battle and show his abilities, but in September, at the time of the armistice, he acted decisively and promptly.

On 17 April the destroyer *Pakenham* was sunk by coastal batteries while patrolling in the Strait of Messina. Such engagements with the shore were frequent, and it is impossible to list the countless actions which took place in the course of the campaign. Little by little, with the development of Allied airfields, the Axis situation became more serious and the percentage of ships destroyed increased. In March 1943 forty per cent of the merchant ships sailed were sunk or seriously damaged; in April the figure reached seventy per cent. Despite the employment of some sixty French ships, which had been captured in the ports of southern France, the Italian merchant fleet was unable to fulfill its tasks, and the same was true of the escort flotillas. In Italy the Axis used the ports of Naples, Taranto, Leghorn, and Reggio Calabria, and for small ships Trapani, Marsala, and Termini; in Tunisia, Bizerte, Tunis, and Sousse were employed. Not only did the continuous bombing of these ports cause work to be frequently interrupted and make it more difficult by destroying the harbor facilities, but operations were further hindered by the bad winter weather. In the course of the Tunisian campaign, from the time of the Allied landings down to the surrender, the Italians lost 243 warships and merchant ships sunk and 242 damaged, a total of 33,500 tons of warships and 325,000 gross tons of merchant shipping. Naval losses included the following: one cruiser, fourteen destroyers, fourteen torpedo boats sunk; six cruisers, twenty-four destroyers, and thirty-eight torpedo boats damaged. Of the 485 ships sunk or damaged, 324 or sixty-seven per cent were sunk or damaged by air attack, thirty-seven by submarines, twenty-three by surface ships, thirty-eight by mines, and sixty-three by various agents.

As the Allied Command had foreseen, the coming of good weather enabled the air forces to play their full role and the situation of the Axis troops became extremely critical. On 26 March 1943 Mussolini, foreseeing defeat, made radical proposals to Hitler. In the belief that Russia was so weakened as to be no longer a threat and that peace with her was desirable and possible, the Duce advocated ending the Russian war. Thinking that repulse of the North African invasion would have considerable effect on the United States, he urged entry into Spain, closure of the Strait of Gibraltar, and occupation of the Balearic Islands. But it was easier to recommend peace with the U.S.S.R. than it was to make it, and in any event Hitler was not yet convinced of defeat. On 30 April Mussolini sent him this anguished telegram:

Fuehrer,
If, as I have frequently stated, the Mediterranean air question is not solved by the immediate dispatch of sufficient air

strength to cancel the crushing enemy superiority, it will be no longer possible to send to Tunisia either a warship, or a transport, or an airplane. This means losing Tunisia at once without being able to save anything.

Even the use of destroyers as transports is doomed to failure.

Today we lost three destroyers, two carrying German troops and one carrying ammunition, as a result of continuous attacks by large enemy formations escorted by 70 to 120 fighter planes.

Fuehrer, this question is of the greatest urgency. The troops in Tunisia are fighting splendidly, as the enemy is forced to admit, but if they cannot be supplied their fate is sealed.

On 2 May Hitler replied that the Second Air Fleet, which prior to 1 March possessed 1,012 planes, had received 574 in March and 669 in April. He could do no more. He was surprised that the Italians were unable to supply Axis armies across a ninety-mile strait, whereas in Norway the German Navy protected a much greater volume of traffic over a route ten times as long. Unfortunately for the Italians, conditions in the North Sea were very different from those in the Sicilian Strait, where the enemy had air bases on the edge of the zone of operations.

In any case it was too late. Air weakness had brought with it the collapse of sea communications and this had led to the defeat of the Axis in Tunisia. Nevertheless the fight had been a hard one and the German-Italian armies had defended themselves bitterly. Up to 24 February 1943 they gained ground, but on that date their defeat in Kasserine Pass marked the change in the tide, and March saw the Allies advancing from the west. In the south the Mareth Line, called with some exaggeration the Tunisian Maginot Line, fell on the 27th after holding out against a first attack in the middle of the month. In early April Sfax and Sousse had to be abandoned by Axis troops; Tunis and Bizerte were seized by the Allies on 7 May. An attempt at evacuation by the Italian Fleet was expected, and Admiral Cunningham had deployed his forces so as to effect a very tight blockade. He had given the order: "Sink, burn, and destroy. Let nothing pass." But no attempt at evacuation was made. As the British reported, "Two features of the occupation are prominent. Firstly, the complete absence of any Axis men of war or shipping, which was very disappointing, and, secondly, the manner in which the Axis Air Forces deserted the theatre of operations and left our destroyer patrols to operate without inconvenience." On 10 May the Italians dispatched fast motor boats from Marsala to Tunisia but bad weather forced them to turn back. A few small contingents of troops attempted to escape in small boats, most of which were captured or sunk. General von Arnim, commander of the German forces, and Marshal Messe, the Italian commander in chief, surrendered on 12 May. The Allies had taken 248,000 prisoners. So ended the war in Africa after three years of fighting.

As has been seen, the landings in North Africa were not originally intended to lead to an attack on Germany by way of the Mediterranean but were rather in the nature of a counteroffensive, intended to assist the Russian ally and to relieve a situation which had been compromised by German initiative. The results were nevertheless brilliant: the Axis driven from Africa, the threat to Suez removed, excellent German-Italian armies destroyed and the Germans forced to reinforce their Mediterranean front, a strong French army on the Allied side, Italy demoralized and almost defeated, and the resistance movement encouraged in all occupied countries. On the other hand, the Allied offensive in northwest Europe had been delayed by more than a year. What would have been the results if the invasion of Normandy had taken place in the spring of 1943? What would have been the course of the war? What the consequences for the postwar situation? To some, this invasion would have been premature and would have failed. To others, the war would have ended a year earlier and the meeting with the Russians would have taken place in eastern Germany. From these wholly conjectural opinions one can conclude, with similar lack of proof, that the landings in North Africa were either an operation of genius or an unlucky error. What can be said without fear of contradiction is that the Axis made a major error in not obtaining a favorable solution of the Mediterranean question in the first months of the war, for on the one hand this would have made an Allied attack by way of the Mediterranean impossible, and on the other it would have permitted an economy of force which would have strengthened the resistance to an invasion from the Atlantic.

PART V
THE INVASION
OF ITALY

13. The Conquest of Sicily and the Italian Surrender

The seizure of Pantelleria

THE island of Pantelleria lies about 150 miles west of Malta, on the route from Gibraltar to Alexandria. Its shores are steep; its area small; it has no natural harbor. These unfavorable factors detract from the importance it would otherwise possess owing to its location, and according to Mussolini he had the greatest difficulty in persuading his technicians that it both should and could be fortified and improved. But the Duce's will overcame resistance and, when the task was completed, Pantelleria became known as "Mussolini's island." Work was begun in 1937 and by 1943 the island was strongly fortified with about forty batteries, a small port for light vessels, underground shelters for aircraft, a plant for distillation of sea water, and a garrison of about 12,000 men. This number was also roughly that of the island's inhabitants, many of whom could have been evacuated had the opportunity not been let slip.

In view of the pending invasion of Sicily and, more important, so as to suppress a threat to the Gibraltar-Alexandria line of communications, the Allied Command decided to take the island. Aerial bombing, far more dreadful than any that Malta had undergone, was begun in May, and on the 13th the cruiser *Orion* and some destroyers carried out a naval bombardment which was repeated at the end of the month and in early June. On 8 June a squadron of five cruisers with destroyers and motor torpedo boats attacked the island in order to ascertain the location of the batteries, the torpedo boats approaching to within rifle range. Italian reaction was weak and the assault was set for the 11th. Extremely heavy bombing was continued and on the night of 10-11 June the assault force, under Rear Admiral McGrigor, got under way from Sfax and

Sousse covered by cruisers *Newfoundland, Aurora, Orion, Penelope,* and destroyers. General Eisenhower and Admiral Cunningham had embarked in *Aurora* to observe the operation.

Repeated flights of aircraft pounded the island, from which arose heavy clouds of smoke. At 1000 the landing craft were in position and at about 1100 the covering squadron began an intense bombardment. Batteries in the harbor replied and a few shells fell near *Newfoundland.* About 1130 the destroyers approached the shore to engage the batteries at short range, but within a few minutes white flags began to appear here and there on the island. At 1245, as the boats were landing, Malta relayed a signal from Admiral Pavesi, commanding the garrison: "Pantelleria desires to surrender owing to lack of water." Sporadic fighting nevertheless continued in various parts of the island; two Italian motor boats were destroyed while attempting to escape; and during the afternoon some thirty German aircraft appeared and attacked the Allied ships, their bombs barely missing the targets. By about 1600 tanks and heavy artillery were ashore and were advancing against negligible opposition. By evening all was over.

More than 12,000 prisoners were taken on Pantelleria. Occupation of the island disclosed that there were still reserves of water but that the distillation plant had been destroyed, and while resistance might have been continued by severe rationing, the end was nevertheless near. The town of Pantelleria had gone for three days without food or water.

On the next day the island of Lampedusa was subjected to a violent bombardment, and on the evening of the 12th the garrison of 3,000 men surrendered. On the 13th Linosa was occupied without fighting, and the last Italian outpost south of Sicily passed into the hands of the Allies.

The landings in Sicily

THE INVASION of Sicily had been decided upon at the Casablanca conference in January 1943. The conquest of this island had a double purpose: first, to provide a base of operations for future attacks against southern Europe, and second, to free maritime communications in the Central Mediterranean. This operation, known as HUSKY, was to be undertaken only after the end of the Tunisian campaign; this was expected by 1 May, and the attack on Sicily was consequently scheduled for July.

Sicily is very mountainous, its single extensive plain being the area southwest of Catania which is dominated by Mount Etna. A narrow strip of low-lying country extends all around the coast; through this strip runs the main road which encircles the island. Capes of varying prominence divide the shoreline into numerous bays, most of which have gradually sloping beaches. None of the island's principal ports—Messina, Palermo, Catania, and Syracuse—has very large capacity.

It was estimated by Allied intelligence that the island would be defended by eight mobile divisions, six Italian and two German, and by five Italian coastal divisions. On Sicily the Axis had about thirty airfields located in three principal groups, one in the east, one in the southeast, and one in the west. The operation was considered very difficult and hazardous. After studying the problem the Joint Planning Staff in England concluded, "We are doubtful of the chance of success against a garrison which includes German formations."

Plans for the operation underwent frequent modification during the preparatory phase. The original concept had contemplated landings in the southeast followed by another in the Palermo area; in this way it was hoped that the ports of Syracuse, Palermo, and Catania could all be quickly captured, but as this plan required excessive dispersion of strength the early occupation of Palermo was given up. The result was a plan which called for landings in the southeast, on both sides of Cape Passaro, and which designated as the initial objectives the seizure of neighboring airfields, of the ports of Syracuse and Augusta, and of the

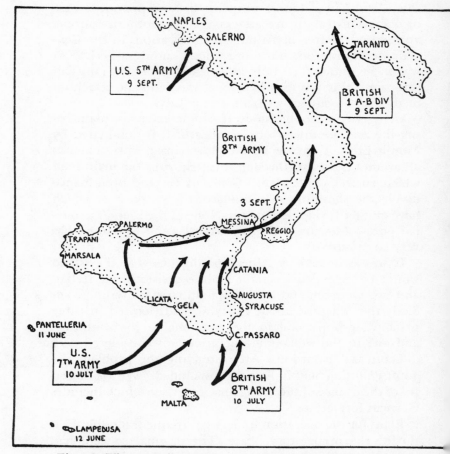

Fig. 18. The Invasions of Sicily and Southern Italy, July to
September 1943

small harbor at Licata. The occupation of Catania was to
follow with the least possible delay.

The expeditionary force was commanded by General
Alexander, deputy to Eisenhower, and included ten divisions formed into two armies of roughly equal strength:
the British Eighth Army under Montgomery, which was to

attack on the east coast, and the American Seventh Army under General Patton, which was to land on the southern shore. In addition to these forces Alexander had two divisions in reserve under his own control. D-Day was set for 10 July.

The Allied navies were given the tasks of protecting the operation against an intervention by the Italian Fleet, of escorting the convoys, and of supporting the landings. Admiral Cunningham consequently divided his forces into three groups. The Naval Covering Force, with four battleships, two aircraft carriers, four cruisers, and eighteen destroyers, operated in the Ionian Sea so as to intercept either Italian ships from Taranto or the Spezia fleet, should it approach by way of the Strait of Messina. An advance force of cruisers and destroyers watched the exit from the Strait of Messina and protected the northern flank of the Eighth Army. An additional covering force, based on Algiers and containing two battleships, two cruisers, and six destroyers, provided protection to the westward. The whole expedition contained 2,775 ships, including 280 warships, and more than 4,000 planes. The Eighth Army embarked in Near Eastern ports, in Libya, and on the eastern coast of Tunisia, while certain elements came directly from Great Britain. The Seventh Army embarked from Algerian ports and from the northern shore of Tunisia. Eighth Army headquarters were at Cairo prior to departure and subsequently moved to Malta; Seventh Army headquarters were at Oran during the planning stage and subsequently at Bizerte; General Alexander's headquarters were at La Marsa near Carthage; Cunningham's staff was at Malta. It will be seen that the operation covered the whole Mediterranean and required perfect liaison.

Aerial preparation was begun upon completion of operations in Tunisia. Since many planes required overhaul following the Tunisian campaign, the bombing was at first on a moderate scale, but its intensity steadily increased. Strategic bombardment was first extended into Italy and into southern France and then concentrated on the Sicilian airfields; as a result of continuous attacks on the island the Allies gained almost complete mastery of the air. The Strait of Messina was also subjected to violent bombing which destroyed most of the ferry boats and harbor facilities; enemy traffic across the Strait had to be carried on by small craft and lighters.

On 9 July the Allies were momentarily alarmed by a violent storm from the northwest. Although the wind fell somewhat during the night of the 9th-10th, the parachute troops were scattered and their efforts seriously hindered. Nevertheless the landings were carried out quite easily. At 2100 on 10 July Syracuse was occupied by British forces, while during the day airfields at Pachino, Licata, and Gela were seized by the Allies. Augusta, strongly fortified on the sea front but weakly defended from the interior, was surrounded and fell on the 14th. It was plain that strategic surprise had been attained; the German-Italian Command had been awaiting an attack in the west. Furthermore, the Allies had greatly profited from the use of Dukws, amphibious trucks, which were here used for the first time. These machines revolutionized landing techniques, for they made possible the rapid landing of supplies without the use of port facilities. In addition to giving fire support to the landings, the Allied fleet bombarded the Sicilian ports of Trapani, Marsala, and Augusta on 12 July, and Catania on the 17th.

Axis inertia at sea

STRANGE to say, the Axis made only the most insignificant efforts at sea to hinder an operation on which depended the fate of Italy, and perhaps of Germany as well. As will be seen, the German-Italian High Command was at this time in a state of uncertainty and confusion.

Following the defeat in Tunisia, German intelligence had acquired an Allied order which indicated that the invasion of Europe would begin in Sardinia or in the Peloponnese, and Hitler believed the document to be authentic. In May Doenitz returned to Italy to see what steps should be taken. Comando Supremo felt that the threat to Sardinia was greater than that to Sicily, and this opinion was shared by the Naval High Command. Doenitz insisted on the need of reinforcing and supplying both these great islands, and for this purpose proposed to use warships including cruisers and submarines, an idea which surprised the Italian staff, for its adoption would make it difficult for the Fleet to intervene immediately in the event of a landing. "A fleet engagement at sea," said the Grand Admiral, "might have perhaps been useful a few months ago; it can no longer be so today owing to the enemy's crushing air superiority." This statement, which, it must be added, was badly translated by the interpreter, gave rise to a violent reaction on the part of the Italian admirals, who saw in it criticism of their past conduct, and Doenitz, whatever his private feelings, was forced to appease them with soft words.

Subsequently he saw Mussolini, who, wiser than his advisers, considered a landing in Sicily as most probable. The Duce was confident that as soon as the soil of the homeland was invaded, the Italian people would rise and find the strength to drive out the enemy. But Kesselring, who also expected an attack in Sicily, was less optimistic. Returning from an inspection there, he described the situation to the Grand Admiral in somber colors and gave it as his opinion that only heavy bombing of the embarkation ports and capture of Gibraltar could prevent invasion. This was the point at which these discussions always ended and, inevitably, on his return to Berlin Doenitz again proposed reviving the Gibraltar operation. But Hitler objected, saying that the enterprise required shock troops which he could not provide; furthermore, the Fuehrer feared that the Spaniards, "the only fighting Latin people," would start a guerilla war which might extend beyond Spain. Once again the conquest of Gibraltar, the only real reply to the Allied advance, was put aside. Since this was impossible, Doenitz suggested attacks on Gibraltar by radio-controlled glider bombs, mining of Port Said and Alexandria, commando landings in Africa, sending new Walther-

THE INVASION OF EUROPE

type submarines south via the Rhône. But time was lacking and nothing was ready. The Axis therefore attempted no preventive attacks and, in view of their uncertainty regarding Allied intentions, such defensive measures as were taken were inadequate.

Although it had received fuel by the time of the invasion, the Italian Fleet made no move, and its inactivity led to impassioned discussion throughout the country. British doctrine requires that any invasion attempt must be opposed by the Fleet without regard to loss and that British ships are to attack the enemy even if locally outnumbered. In the Pacific in 1944, when the Americans attacked the Philippines, a position which the Japanese considered vital, the Nipponese fleet flung its whole strength into battle in a great suicide operation; and in 1945 such of the remains of this fleet as could find fuel sacrificed themselves in desperate battle at Okinawa. Even in Italy Mussolini had once spoken bold words, for on 30 March 1935 he told the Senate: "To those who in discussing naval strategy suggest that in a future conflict battleships will remain in harbor as in the World War, I reply that for Italy it will not be so. It is not a question of the cost of ships, it is a question of the type of men and of the orders they receive."

Nevertheless on the evening of 10 July, a dramatic council of war at Comando Supremo decided, on the motion of the Chief of Staff of the Navy, not to commit the fleet. The decision was based on the following reasoning: the new battleships, then at Spezia, would require twenty-five hours to reach the landing points south of Augusta; they would certainly be sighted by enemy aircraft and attacked before reaching their objectives; it was impossible to give them adequate air cover; and finally, even if they miraculously escaped air attack, they would run into a crushing concentration of naval force. These are very powerful arguments. The battleships should have been sent to Taranto ahead of time, but even had this been done it seems probable that the whole fleet would have been destroyed by Allied air and sea forces before reaching its objectives in the transport area. Yet this sacrifice might have held up the Allied offensive for several hours and thus eased the task of the defending troops. It might also have encouraged their resistance: in the Pacific the destruction of the Japanese Fleet in the Philippines produced a flood of volunteers for the Kamikaze forces.

Within the Italian Navy, staffs and crews were expecting orders for a general engagement, and reports indicate that the decision of Supermarina and of Comando Supremo ran counter to the general feeling. Had Mussolini remembered his earlier words he could himself have given the order for battle which the Fleet Command clearly could not bring itself to do. The Italian Government had followed a policy of saving its battleships—after the sabotage at Toulon Ciano had said, "The necessity for carefully preserving our own Navy becomes more and more evident"—but such a policy would only have been justified in the event of a compromise peace, and by July 1943 such a hypothesis was becoming increasingly improbable.

Without committing their capital ships the Italians could have sent light vessels. On the night of the landings, while hundreds of Allied ships, sailing without lights and in bad weather, were headed for the Sicilian shores, an attack by Axis destroyers and motor torpedo boats might have thrown the armada into confusion and inflicted losses. Nothing was attempted. Not only was the Axis surprised, but Italian morale had by this time been severely affected. Events in Sicily made this plain, for the Italian Army, which had fought very bravely in Tunisia, did less well on the soil of the homeland. The defense of Sicily had been confided largely to troops from that province in the thought that they would fight fiercely for their native soil. But the soldiers were demoralized by the suffering of their families and, while there were brave deeds, many failed in their duty.

At sea the only opposition to the Allies was provided by planes and submarines. Air attacks were on a rather modest scale and caused only slight losses. The Italian submarines did, however, enter the fight, and between 10 July and the first days of August *Flutto, Bronzo, Nereide, Acciaio, Remo, Romolo, Ascianghi,* and *Argento* were sunk off Sicily, sacrifices which at least saved honor.

Although he had earlier advocated holding back the Italian surface fleet, Doenitz had now changed his mind and was infuriated by its inaction. On 17 July he sought out the Fuehrer and stated that the attitude of the Italian High Command regarding the employment of the Fleet was "infamous." Doenitz had failed to get Admiral Riccardi to use his light ships to drive Allied units from the Strait of Messina; when the Chief of the German Navy had said that this was feasible, Riccardi had replied that he needed his ships for a possible sortie of the Battle Fleet. The Grand Admiral felt that the Germans should take over the Italian Fleet, the younger elements of which were full of spirit and opposed to Supermarina. He therefore proposed to dismiss the Fleet Command, to entrust the Navy to a young rear admiral, either Manfredi or Legnani (who later became Minister of the Navy under the Fascist Republican Government), and to provide it with a German staff. The Fuehrer answered evasively that he would consider the matter. Even the Japanese now took a hand, and in Berlin General Oshima, seething with excitement, shouted at Alfieri, the Italian ambassador, that the Allies had to be driven out of Italy and that the Italians once and for all should take some action. But the Italians themselves were not lacking in subjects for complaint, for they thought that the Germans had deserted them.

The fall of Mussolini

TWO DAYS after the invasion of Sicily, Mussolini, at the insistence of Comando Supremo, again sent Hitler an urgent appeal for more help: "I beg of you, Fuehrer, to give the defense of Sicily maximum assistance, particularly in fighter aircraft." On the 14th Hitler replied with a message in which, after having expressed a certain lack of faith in the efficiency of Italian troops, he promised to send some aerial reinforcements and a division of parachutists and, for the more distant future, conditionally promised an armored division. On the same day General Ambrosio, Chief of the General Staff, handed Mussolini a disillusioned memorandum on the situation: "If the establishment of an Allied second front in Italy cannot be prevented, I ask the high political authorities to consider whether the country should not be spared future fighting and ruin by a termination of hostilities, given the fact that the end result will be worse after one or more years of fighting." Thought of surrender had begun to haunt the military leaders.

On the 19th Mussolini met Hitler at Feltre. Anticipating urgently needed assistance, Mussolini received instead a long remonstrance from the Fuehrer. The latter delivered himself of comments on the inevitable vicissitudes of all important wars, and then went on to expound his theories on how to protect airfields, on convoys, and on the need of using warships for transport purposes. Like the beggar in the fable, Mussolini could have replied that he needed help and not advice. As things turned out, Hitler was unable to send any more planes than he had promised on the 14th, and Keitel announced that, as he would have no new troops available for two months, it was up to the Italians to move such divisions as they had available into Sicily.

Mussolini knew that he was lost; he returned to Rome a man without hope. On the 16th Milan and Bologna were bombed; on the 19th it was the turn of the capital; on the 22nd the Americans entered Palermo. The Italian leaders were despondent. On the 24th the Fascist Grand Council met, and the majority insisted that Mussolini return all his military powers to the King. On the 25th the King, proceeding with necessary but regrettable duplicity, placed Mussolini in confinement.

Marshal Badoglio, the head of the new government, announced that the struggle would be continued at the side of the Germans. The people and the Army were profoundly disappointed, for all had interpreted the disappearance of the Duce as heralding the end of hostilities. The Sicilians were suffering from bombing and starvation. Food and munitions no longer arrived across the Strait of Messina, which was under continuous attack by Allied air and sea forces. Nevertheless the struggle continued; the terrain was difficult, and only on 17 August, after thirty-eight days of steady fighting, did the Americans reach Messina.

At sea the men of the assault machines continued their exploits up to the last moment. On board the merchant ship *Olterra*, which had taken refuge at Algeciras, the Italians had organized a secret base in violation of Spanish neutrality. On 8 May, after several fruitless attempts, piloted torpedoes from *Olterra* sank several ships in the roadstead at Gibraltar. On 4 August, a month before the armistice, three more ships were sunk at Gibraltar by the same method. But in the boundlessness of the Italian disaster these brave deeds passed unnoticed.

The Surrender of Italy

WHEN the Badoglio government assumed power the Italian military situation was very precarious. The Army possessed sixty-one mobile divisions, twenty-five of which were outside the peninsula; counting the personnel manning fixed defenses, it contained about two million rather badly armed men. There were only three armored or motorized divisions in Italy; the troops were poorly officered and trained; anti-tank weapons were scarce; the Army was short of antiaircraft artillery, and the antiaircraft defenses of railway junctions, industrial centers, and airfields were very inadequate. The Navy still had considerable strength: it possessed seven battleships, eight cruisers, forty-five destroyers, and about sixty submarines. The Air Force was weak: of a total of about a thousand aircraft, many of which were out of commission, seven hundred were in Italy and the remaining three hundred scattered about the Balkan peninsula and the Aegean.

Of the seventeen German divisions in Italy seven were either armored or motorized. The Germans had 600 aircraft locally available including 240 bombers and 220 fighters. In the Mediterranean they had about twenty submarines in addition to motor torpedo boats and small auxiliary vessels.

The Italian transport system was disorganized. The nature of the railway system made it very vulnerable to the Allied air offensive which was directed against the junctions of Bologna, Genoa, Naples, and Foggia, the coastal railroad lines, and the transverse lines between Bari and Battipaglia. Motor transport was scarce, and the lack of fuel prevented its being used to replace the railroads. Coastal navigation was harassed by Allied submarines and aircraft, and lack of tonnage prevented the coasting trade from fulfilling its important function in Italian economic life. The disorganization of transportation, the bombing, and the lack of raw materials reduced production; the war industries were slowing down and German help was becoming increasingly inadequate. The situation, as described by the Minister of Armaments, was "tragic from every point of view."

In the Navy and Air Force morale and discipline were still good, but the Army was giving way. The people were despondent. They suffered under all kinds of restrictions. In the bombed cities the shelters, indeed all passive defense measures, were inadequate, and evacuation of the inhabitants was carried out without planning and in confusion. These hardships and sufferings would have been better borne had the country had confidence in its cause, but the war had never been well understood—"*la guerra non è sentita*"—even before it had brought defeat and invasion. The Germans had been unable to make themselves liked; they were accused of being harsh, overbearing, and suspicious, of taking credit for success and throwing responsibility for defeat upon their allies, of having abandoned Italians during retreats in Libya and in Russia. The Alpini, returning from the eastern front, were saying that they would fight anywhere except alongside the Germans.

The King, Marshal Badoglio, and most civil and military leaders expected that the peninsula would be rapidly invaded and conquered. These views were perhaps pessimistic. Kesselring was to demonstrate that this very mountainous country was easy to defend. With the support of determined Italian forces the German Marshal could probably have held the Allies for a long time. But the Italian leaders also thought, and with more justification, that the Axis would ultimately be defeated and that to prolong the fighting meant only useless sacrifice. Article V of the German-Italian Alliance of 1939 had provided that "The high contracting parties bind themselves in the case of a jointly waged war to conclude an armistice and peace only in full concord with one another." But the Italians felt that the Germans had observed neither the spirit nor the letter of the alliance: they had begun the war prematurely, they had never kept their partners informed regarding their intentions, they had invaded Russia without consulting their allies. Finally, Badoglio voiced the general feeling when he said that the welfare of the country constituted the supreme law which took precedence over all other considerations.

In fact, although they had announced their intention of continuing the war, the King and the head of the Government had only done so to win time, having decided to end the struggle at the time of Mussolini's fall. In early August they made contact with the Allies, and on the 12th General Castellano met representatives of General Eisenhower at Lisbon. After considerable bargaining, a provisional armistice, the *corto armistizio*, was signed on 3 September, the day the British landed in Calabria, and was made public on the 8th, the day of the Salerno landings. The text of the armistice was as follows:

1. Immediate cessation of all hostile activity by the Italian armed forces.

2. Italy will use its best endeavors to deny, to the Germans, facilities that might be used against the United Nations.

3. All prisoners or internees of the United Nations to be immediately turned over to the Allied Commander in Chief, and none of these may now or at any time be evacuated to Germany.

4. Immediate transfer of the Italian Fleet and Italian aircraft to such points as may be designated by the Allied Commander in Chief, with details of disarmament to be prescribed by him.

5. Italian merchant shipping may be requisitioned by the Allied Commander in Chief to meet the needs of his military-naval program.

6. Immediate surrender of Corsica and of all Italian territory, both islands and mainland, to the Allies, for such use as operational bases and other purposes as the Allies may see fit.

7. Immediate guarantee of the free use by the Allies of all airfields and naval ports in Italian territory, regardless of the rate of evacuation of the Italian territory by German forces. These ports and fields to be protected by Italian armed forces until this function is taken over by the Allies.

8. Immediate withdrawal to Italy of Italian armed forces from all participation in the current war from whatever areas in which they may now be engaged.

9. Guarantee by the Italian Government that if necessary it will employ all its available armed forces to insure prompt and exact compliance with all the provisions of this armistice.

10. The Commander in Chief of the Allied Forces reserves to himself the right to take any measure which in his opinion may be necessary for the protection of the interests of the Allied Forces for the prosecution of the war, and the Italian Government binds itself to take such administrative or other action as the Commander in Chief may require, and in particular the Commander in Chief will establish Allied Military Government over such parts of Italian territory as he may deem necessary in the military interests of the Allied Nations.

11. The Commander in Chief of the Allied Forces will have a full right to impose measures of disarmament, demobilization, and demilitarization.

12. Other conditions of a political, economic and financial nature with which Italy will be bound to comply will be transmitted at a later date.

This armistice was succeeded by the "long-term armistice," which enumerated and defined the conditions imposed upon Italy. Marshal Badoglio received the even more severe "long-term armistice" on 20 September and, after an unhappy discussion, signed it on board the battleship *Nelson* at Malta, in the presence of General Eisenhower. Its provisions were for the time being kept secret.

The German reaction and the fate of the Italian Fleet

IT WAS CLEAR that fulfillment of the conditions imposed upon Italy would lead to war with the Germans; on this point Marshal Badoglio's government had no illusions. With the idea of having the naval forces take part in the resistance against the Germans, the government planned to send those in the Upper Tyrrhenian to Corsica and Sardinia, and those in the Adriatic to Sebenico and Cattaro. The Allies, however, required that they be sent to Malta. Moreover, Eisenhower had been unwilling to state in advance either the place or the precise date of the projected landings in central Italy. While security reasons justified this refusal, the uncertainty was terribly disturbing to the Italians. "You distrust us," said General Rossi to the Allied Commander in Chief. "How could we do otherwise," the latter replied, "since only a few hours ago we were still enemies." As the Italian Command had kept its preparations secret to avoid alerting the Germans, the troops were understandably confused. The terrible situation in which the Italian forces found themselves must not be lost sight of when forming a judgement on the vigor of their resistance to their former allies.

These latter, however, had wasted no time. From 26 July, the day after Mussolini's fall, German troops had been flooding in. Whereas at Feltre the Germans had declared themselves unable to assist Italy, the inhabitants of the peninsula now saw with amazement the arrival of a dozen divisions within the space of a few days. These reinforcements, which entered into Italy in battle array as if into an enemy country, were divided into two main groups, one in the north under Marshal Rommel and another in central Italy under Kesselring. In August the Italian and German commanders met, first at Tarvisio and subsequently at Bologna, each group attempting to throw the other off the scent and neither being deceived. Under these circumstances they discussed problems of organization of their combined command, a wholly pointless procedure for all were on guard and none was concerned with mutual assistance.

At the end of July the Germans prepared four plans to guard against Italian collapse. The first, Operation EICHE, had as its object the rescue of Mussolini; the second, STUDENT, concerned the restoration of Fascism and occupation of Rome; the third, called with perhaps involuntary humor ACHSE or AXIS, involved seizure of the Italian Fleet and occupation of ports; the last, SCHWARZ, provided for taking over key positions in the peninsula. By 27 July it had been decided to take control of the warships and merchant vessels with the aid of Fascist crews; to station German submarines off the harbor entrances with orders to torpedo any ship departing without permission; and to prepare to evacuate Sicily and Sardinia.

On the question of evacuation the German commanders were not in agreement. Jodl and Kesselring, expecting the Allies to land on the Ligurian coast, urged that the islands be abandoned at once and that strong defensive positions be established in Calabria and in northern Italy. Rommel and Doenitz, on the other hand, wanted to hold on in Sicily so as to bring pressure against Allied navigation and protect the whole of Italy. They hoped to be able to keep Italy in the alliance, at least for some time. But word came from Admiral Ruge at Rome that the situation was degenerating and that Supermarina seemed to him to be increasingly hostile. He warned that seizure of the Fleet would require considerable strength and pointed out that stationing submarines off Spezia involved grave risk of compromising the plans.

For Hitler, the first thing to do was to rescue Mussolini,

who was thought by the Germans to be on Ventotene Island. Plan EICHE contemplated his abduction by parachutists arriving at dawn. The operation was to be supported by fast light ships, submarines were to surround the island, and the Duce was to be taken off by seaplane. But the Italians were suspicious. Sent first to Ventotene, the dictator was then ordered moved to Ponza Island. On 7 August a torpedo boat carried him to La Maddalena in Sardinia, whence subsequently he was taken to the Grand Sasso. For the time being the Badoglio government had won; the operation no longer concerned the Navy, and Mussolini was only to be delivered on 12 September, following the armistice. This disappointment did not prevent Rommel and Kesselring from carefully planning their counterstroke, which was vigorously executed as soon as the armistice was announced. The Italian Command, whose difficulties have been noted, succeeded in saving the Fleet but lost a large part of the Army along with Rome, northern Italy, and the entire Dodecanese.

On his return from Rome on the afternoon of 8 September, Admiral Bergamini summoned the admirals and captains of the Spezia Squadron on board *Roma* and informed them that an armistice had been signed with the Allies and that he had been ordered to take the Fleet south to join the British. The officers were surprised; they had expected to sortie for a final battle. Nevertheless they accepted the decision with discipline and there were no desertions from the squadron.

There were no Germans at Spezia. The Italian troops which surrounded the port at a distance of some miles had, during the crucial days, succeeded in preventing any German infiltration. The Fleet left harbor without difficulty; it was joined offshore by a group of torpedo boats from Genoa; and the whole force, three battleships, six cruisers, ten destroyers, and five torpedo boats, headed southward. The Germans reacted quickly and their bombers attacked the Fleet while it was passing west of Sardinia. Glider bombs hit the battleships *Italia* and *Roma*, and the latter sank with the loss of a great part of her crew including Admiral Bergamini, the Fleet Commander. A few light vessels picked up survivors and carried them to Port Mahon, where the torpedo boats *Pegaso* and *Impetuoso* scuttled themselves offshore. The cruiser *Regolo*, the destroyers *Fusiliere* and *Carabiniere*, and the torpedo boat *Orsa* were interned by the Spaniards, who released them in January 1945. But the main body of the Fleet, after having been joined and escorted by a British squadron, proceeded to Malta.

At Taranto matters were simplified by the absence of German forces, and Admiral da Zara's squadron, battleships *Doria* and *Duilio*, two cruisers, and a torpedo boat, reached Malta on 10 September. The battleship *Cesare* and the seaplane carrier *Giuseppe Miraglia* succeeded in descending the Adriatic from Trieste despite German air attacks and reached Malta the 13th; other ships also arrived singly or in small groups. German coastal batteries on the Strait of Bonifacio sank the torpedo boat *Vivaldi* and damaged *Da Noli*, which was subsequently sunk by a mine. A dozen other ships, torpedo boats, V.A.S., gunboats, and the like, were lost in the course of local actions with the Germans.

Italian ships in Japan were ordered to scuttle themselves. The colonial sloop *Eritrea*, which at the time of the capture of Somaliland by the Allies in 1941 had succeeded in reaching the Far East, once again was able to evade enemy observation and reached a British port, as did the submarine *Cagni* and some small vessels. Forty-nine other ships, caught in ports under German or Japanese control, scuttled themselves. The Tenth M.A.S. Flotilla, which was commanded by a Prince Borghese, remained faithful to Mussolini and fought bravely to the end both at sea and on land, but the great majority of the Italian Navy obeyed the Royal Government. In all, five battleships, eight light cruisers, seven destroyers, twenty-four torpedo boats, forty submarines, nineteen corvettes, thirty-two motor torpedo boats, an aircraft supply ship, three minesweepers, and various auxiliary ships went over to the Allied side, along with about a hundred merchant ships totalling 170,000 tons. Once again Admiral Cunningham showed himself to be a great commander: he avoided all vexatious requirements, required no purging of the staffs, and took only essential security measures.

After his deliverance by the Germans, Mussolini established the Italian Socialist Republic, which continued the struggle at the side of Germany. Marshal Graziani took command of the Fascist armed forces and Rear Admiral Legnani became head of the Navy. The latter was subsequently killed in an automobile accident of a rather suspicious nature.

In addition to the sufferings of defeat the Italian people were now subjected to those of a civil war, which inevitably brought with it great excesses and much injustice. A special tribunal was set up by Mussolini's government to judge so-called traitors. Among many other officers tried by this tribunal were the Governor of the Aegean, Admiral Campioni, who had commanded the Italian Fleet at the battle of Punta Stilo, and Admiral Mascherpa, who had been in command of the island of Leros. These officers, who had gone over to the Allies on 8 September and had subsequently been captured by the Germans, were condemned to death and executed for having surrendered the Aegean. This act of vengeance was shocking, for it took place not under the stress of the moment but six months after the armistice, and the crime of which the victims were accused was that of having obeyed a government recognized as legal by the majority of Italians.

The special tribunal also condemned *in absentia* Admirals Pavesi and Leonardi, the one accused of having surrendered Pantelleria and the other the stronghold of Augusta without having exhausted the fighting strength at their disposal. Mussolini was particularly enraged against Pavesi, whom he blamed for having initiated the surrender of home territory. Actions like these were not calculated to bring to the support of the Socialist Republic the naval officers and sailors who, already little inclined to serve at the side of Germany, were hiding in northern Italy.

The Germans succeeded in refitting some of the ships that had been scuttled in shallow water or sabotaged in port; and as the Italian Republic lacked the necessary crews, these were manned by Germans. But the Germans themselves were short of trained naval personnel, and confined their efforts to the formation of squadrons of light units. Unable to use the heavy ships, they were forced to discontinue work on the aircraft carriers *Aquila* and *Sparviero*. In 1944 the cruiser *Bolzano* was sunk and the *Gorizia* damaged by British and Italian assault machines in a brilliant action at Spezia.

In the Ligurian Sea the Germans organized the Tenth Torpedo Boat Squadron, based at Spezia and composed of three destroyers and nine torpedo boats, and the Twenty-second Escort Squadron, which contained about ten ships. In the upper Adriatic they formed another Torpedo Boat Squadron with a few units that were completed by the Monfalcone yards and some old Italian and Yugoslav vessels, and the Second Submarine Chaser Squadron, which was composed of corvettes. In the Aegean they seized and manned five Italian destroyers. Most of the ships taken over by the Germans were either destroyed in minor actions or scuttled as the Allies advanced, and in any case these efforts had little importance. The great naval struggle in the Mediterranean had ended with the Italian armistice; from that time on the Allied fleets were employed in the protection of convoys and, above all, in the attack against Fortress Europe from the south which constituted the last act of the Mediterranean drama.

Italian naval cooperation with the Allies was begun on local initiative shortly after the armistice. On 12 September the officer commanding the M.A.S. at Capri placed his ships at the disposal of the Allied command in the Salerno-Naples region. At Malta on 13 September Admiral Cunningham requested Da Zara to transport an urgent shipment of arms and munitions to the Italian troops fighting beside the

French in Corsica. Appreciating the importance of this request for the development of relations with the Allies, the Italian admiral hastily acquiesced, and the departure next day of two torpedo boats, *Legionario* and *Oriani*, marked the formal entry of the Italian Navy into the struggle. Such action was clearly dependent on good discipline, but it is no less certain that the change in sides corresponded to the real feelings of most Italian naval personnel.

Balance sheet

IT is interesting to compare the losses suffered by the British and Italian navies up to the time when the latter abandoned the struggle against the Allies. The losses of the Italian Fleet between the outbreak of the war in the Mediterranean and 8 September 1943 totalled 193 warships divided as follows:

Cruisers	12
Destroyers and escort vessels	75
Submarines	65
M.A.S.	41
Total	193

Ships sunk at Taranto in November 1940 and subsequently refloated are not included in this list.

In personnel, out of a total strength of 220,000 men, the Italian Navy lost 1,364 officers and 23,476 men killed, and 607 officers and 5,369 men wounded.

In this same period, British losses in the Mediterranean were as follows:

Battleship	1
Aircraft carriers	2
Cruisers	14
Destroyers and escort vessels	89
Submarines	50
Motor torpedo boats	35
Total	191

The two battleships sunk at Alexandria in December 1941 and subsequently refloated are not included in this list.

The following table shows the percentage of British losses incurred from Germans and Italians and from ships and aircraft.

Causes	Ships sunk by Germans	Ships sunk by Italians	Un-determined	Total
By ships	8%	42%	—	50%
By aircraft	20%	13%	—	33%
Various or unknown agents	—	—	17%	17%
Total	28%	55%	17%	100%

It will be seen from these tables that the Italian Navy accounted for forty-two per cent of the British warships lost in the Mediterranean prior to 8 September 1943, and that the British Navy suffered as heavily as did the Italians. But the British were far better able to replace their losses, and they had behind them the whole American Navy. These figures come from Italian documents; they have been checked in so far as possible and seem to be correct.

Between 8 September 1943 and 8 May 1945 the Italians lost many more ships. As has been noted, the battleship *Roma* was sunk by a German plane on 9 September 1943. In February 1945 the battleship *Cavour* was sunk at Trieste by Allied aircraft. The battleship *Impero*, which was being completed at Trieste, was seized by the Germans and was found to have been sunk at the time of liberation. At Genoa the aircraft carrier *Sparviero*, the former liner *Augustus*, was scuttled by the Germans in October 1944 before its conversion had been completed. The following additional ships were lost: eight cruisers, *Bari, Bolzano, Caio Mario, Cornelio Silla, Guilio Germanico, Gorizia, Ottaviano Augusto, Taranto*; twenty-two destroyers; thirty-nine torpedo boats; thirty corvettes; about fifty submarines; and motor torpedo boats, minelayers, minesweepers, and auxiliary ships, to make a total of 413 vessels. Many of these, scuttled first by the Italians at the time of the 1943 armistice, were raised by the Germans and again destroyed in 1945.

The tragic fate of the Italian merchant marine is summarized in the following table:

Existing 10 June 1940	770 ships totalling 3,310,584 tons
New construction	45 ships totalling 255,531 tons
Total	815 ships totalling 3,566,115 tons
Ships lost before 8 September 1943	395 ships totalling 1,594,112 tons
Ships lost after 8 September 1943	197 ships totalling 837,968 tons
Ships seized by the Allies	105 ships totalling 605,465 tons
Ships seized by Germany and Japan	33 ships totalling 152,697 tons
Total loss	730 ships totalling 3,190,242 tons
Ships remaining in Italian hands	85 ships totalling 375,893 tons

Wartime new construction was wholly inadequate. Prior to the armistice Horst Venturi, the Minister of the Merchant Marine, said, "For every ship that we build we have six or seven sunk." In the table given above, the losses include those of Italian ships used by the Axis and sunk by the Allies, and also those used by the Allies and sunk by the Axis. As has been seen, in June 1940 about a third of the Italian merchant marine had taken refuge in neutral ports; most of these ships were put back into service when the neutrals entered the war on the side of Great Britain. All in all, including ships seized by other nations, the Italian merchant fleet had lost ninety per cent of its tonnage by May 1945.

14. The Invasion of Italy

The concept of Operation AVALANCHE

IN August 1943 President Roosevelt, Mr. Churchill, and the British and American Chiefs of Staff met at Quebec for a discussion of overall Allied strategy. At this time, unknown to Germany, Marshal Badoglio's government was taking steps to bring about the surrender of Italy. It was consequently decided to undertake Operation AVALANCHE, the invasion of Italy proper, in order to exploit the Italian capitulation to the maximum, to aid the Russians by keeping German forces in the peninsula, and to acquire air bases in southern Italy and in the area about Rome from which to exert pressure by bombing on Germany and the Balkans. A further subordinate purpose of this invasion was to assure complete freedom of sea communications in the Mediterranean, an objective already largely accomplished by the conquest of Sicily. General Eisenhower was also ordered to occupy Corsica and Sardinia.

Finally, the proposal for a landing in southern France, Operation ANVIL, was accepted in order to create a diversion in the Toulon-Marseilles region which would assist Operation OVERLORD, the landing in northwestern France. Allied Mediterranean strategy was now firmly settled for the first time since the decision to land in North Africa had been made. But, as will subsequently be seen, the projected landing in southern France was more than once to be reconsidered.

For the invasion of Italy it was decided to land both in southern Calabria and at Salerno, and the dates of the two operations were slightly staggered. The choice of Salerno was disappointing to the Italians; they had hoped that the expected offensive would take place far to the northward, if not in Liguria at least in the region of Rome, but Salerno was chosen so that fighter aircraft based in Sicily could help to protect the beachhead. Had the landing been made farther north it would have been necessary to rely wholly on carrier aviation.

In Marshal Badoglio's opinion, the Allied Command made a major error by insufficiently separating the dates of the Calabrian and Salerno operations. The terrain of the Calabrian promontory is particularly difficult, and Kesselring was able to slow the Allied advance with very few troops while holding back the greater part of his forces to counterattack at Salerno. Badoglio, who is quite critical of Allied strategy, feels that the whole Italian campaign was mismanaged. In his view Sardinia rather than Sicily should have been taken, for Sardinia is no farther than Sicily from Tunisia and, as the Allied Command must have known, it was less strongly garrisoned. Not only would its capture have been easier but it offered greater possibilities for exploitation, for it would have permitted the landing in Italy proper to have been made much farther to the north. A landing between Civitavecchia and Leghorn, which could have been supported by fighters based on the good Sardinian airfields, would have eliminated all Axis forces in southern Italy, and the Allies would thus have avoided the terrible climb up the peninsula. But, as we have seen, by first attacking in Sicily the Allies expected to free their Mediterranean communications at the earliest possible moment and thus save valuable merchant tonnage and diminish the load on escort vessels, a calculation which was fully justified.

Furthermore, according to the Italian Marshal, the advance was delayed by excessive care for economy in human life, a prudence which was at cross purposes with the desired goals. He felt that the Allied army was over-mechanized, and that while this was an excellent thing in the Libyan Desert it was a drawback in a region of steep mountains. It was his belief that the Italian troops, who clearly did not suffer under this particular handicap, could have provided important assistance, but that their help was scorned.

The Italians complained constantly that although the

Allies obliged them to declare war on Germany, they made no calls upon them. They wanted to take a larger part in the expulsion of the Germans, and believed that their knowledge of the country was a valuable asset which might have been put to better use. Indeed, as the fighting dragged on, it became necessary to call upon Italian supply columns which were skilled at operating on the steep Apennine trails, and ultimately mountain warfare schools were set up with officers of the Alpini as instructors. But since no complete plan for an Allied invasion of Europe from the south had been set up prior to the North African landings, each successive stage was decided upon only after long discussion, and inevitably both planning and execution felt the effects of this lack of foresight.

The Germans believed the invasion of southern Italy to be merely a step in an Allied advance towards Greece. Fifteen days after the Salerno landings, Doenitz wrote: "The enemy's next strategic moves will evidently be directed against the Balkans." The German Command expected that prior to invading the Balkan peninsula the Allies would attempt to capture the important group of airfields at Foggia, and they hoped to prevent seizure of this important position.

The landings in Calabria and at Salerno

IN THE FIRST hours of 3 September, the first day of the fifth year of the war, troops of the British Eighth Army landed in Calabria between Catona and Reggio. These landings were protected by aircraft and by a naval force composed of cruisers *Mauritius* and *Orion*, monitors *Abercrombie*, *Roberts*, and *Erebus*, and gunboats and destroyers. At about 1000 battleships *Valiant* and *Warspite* bombarded enemy positions at Cape Armi. Opposition was very weak. The Germans had only small forces in Calabria, the Italians offered no resistance, and the British advanced amidst the enthusiasm of the populace. At Salerno things were to be very different.

The landing at Salerno had as its object the seizure of

Naples, a first-class port, possession of which would facilitate the supply of Allied armies in Italy. Salerno was at the limit of the operating range of fighter planes based in Sicily. Spitfires from the nearest Sicilian bases could remain only twenty minutes over the landing area, and Lightnings only about an hour. The plan provided for a standing patrol of forty fighters to protect the troops. But to fight, the planes had to drop their auxiliary fuel tanks which greatly decreased their range of action, and it took thirty minutes for reinforcements to arrive from Sicily. It was therefore necessary to employ carrier aircraft until such time as captured airfields could be placed in operation.

The troops employed were from General Clark's Fifth Army. The landings in the Gulf of Salerno, south of the harbor, were to be made by two groups, the British 10 Corps on the north and the American VI Corps on the south. Northwest of Salerno two British Commandos and three battalions of American Rangers were to attack, the former at Vietri sul Mare, the latter at Maiori. The expedition contained more than 600 ships including 230 warships, and was organized in sixteen convoys which departed from Oran, Algiers, Bizerte, Tripoli, Palermo, and Termini. Command at sea was exercised by Admiral H. Kent Hewitt, USN, in *Ancon*.

The ships of the landing force were divided into two groups, the British Northern Attack Force under Commodore Oliver in *Hilary* and the American Southern Attack Force under Rear Admiral Hall in *Samuel Chase*. Force V, under Admiral Vian in *Euryalus*, which was to provide air cover in cooperation with shore-based aviation, contained five British escort carriers, *Unicorn*, *Hunter*, *Attacker*, *Stalker*, *Battler*, and cruisers and destroyers. Finally Force H, under Admiral Algernon Willis, with battleships *Nelson*, *Rodney*, *Valiant*, *King George*, and *Howe*, carriers *Illustrious* and *Formidable*, and light ships, was to provide distant cover for the expedition against a possible diversion by the Italian Fleet. With the exception of *Nelson*, all these battleships were shortly detached to meet and escort the Italian Fleet to Malta, and to take part in the occupation of Taranto.

On the night of 8-9 September the expedition was discovered and scouted by German aircraft. Their attacks were unsuccessful but surprise was lost. Shortly after midnight Allied aviation violently bombed enemy positions in the Gulf of Salerno. Two hours later the ships joined in and were promptly engaged by shore batteries. At Maiori the American Rangers went ashore at 0300 without opposition. At Vietri, where there were shore batteries, the reaction was more lively but the British Commandos nevertheless landed successfully. The main landings south of Salerno took place at about 0400. German resistance was very strong, the bay was bristling with batteries and machine gun nests, and enemy tanks appeared shortly after the first troops reached the beaches. On the 9th alone the ships fired on 132 different objectives and the advance was extremely difficult. Nevertheless by evening the bridgehead had been temporarily secured.

Although he was busy liquidating Italian resistance at Rome, Kesselring was also preparing a counteroffensive which he fully intended would throw the Allied troops back into the sea. While waiting for it to be launched, German units continued to offer strong resistance. On the days following the landing the Allied ships were continually in action, supported by day by fighters from Force V and by Lightnings and Spitfires, and at night by Sicily-based Beaufighters. The plan had envisaged seizure of the Monte Corvino airfield on the day of the landing, but it was far out in its reckoning. The Allies entered Salerno on the 10th but the 11th was a day of very heavy fighting. On the night of the 11th-12th the enemy launched violent attacks, and on the 13th almost reached the shore, causing the Allies great anxiety. Although it had been hoped that the carriers could be sent back on the 12th, not only did they have to be retained, but cruisers had to be used to rush reinforcements from Sicily.

The situation, which remained critical until the 16th,

was finally saved by the 15-inch guns of *Valiant* and *Warspite*, by heavy Allied air attacks, and by reinforcements from the Eighth Army. On the 16th the Allies again assumed the offensive, on the 17th Monte Corvino was finally occupied, and on the same day Montgomery's troops, coming up from southern Italy, joined with those of Clark. The pressure which they had applied from the south had finally relieved the bridgehead.

At sea, attacks by German planes using remote-controlled glider bombs had caused serious losses to the fleet. *Warspite* was damaged by a bomb exploding close to the hull, her boilers were flooded, and she had to be taken in tow. With some difficulty she managed to pass the Strait of Messina and reach Malta whence, after temporary repairs, she returned to Great Britain, thus ending her long and glorious wartime career in the Mediterranean, where she had taken part in all important operations. She was to be restored to active service in time for the Normandy landings. The cruiser *Uganda* was also seriously damaged and had to retire under tow, the hospital ship *Newfoundland* was sunk, *Albacore* hit a mine, and several minor ships were sunk or damaged.

The Eighth Army, which was advancing in the east, entered Potenza on the 21st and on the 27th captured the great air base at Foggia. Aided by Italian partisans, the Fifth Army entered Naples on 3 October to find that marvellous city in a state of terrible disaster. It had undergone 120 bombings and the departing Germans had completely destroyed the port. There was neither water nor electricity, the harbor was clogged with wrecks, the channel was blocked and mined. In their ruined houses the inhabitants were starving, while typhus had reached epidemic proportions. Working furiously, the Allies restored the port, raising more than fifty wrecks within a month. The people of Naples helped eagerly in this work, and the Italian Navy provided four submarines which supplied electricity. Thanks to the great resources of the Allies and the intense activity shown by all, Naples was enabled to fulfill her role as a great supply base for the armies.

After the capture of Naples the Germans withdrew in the west to a line along the Volturno, which was broken in mid-October. In the east the British carried out a minor landing at Termoli. In November the Germans dug in on their Winter Line, which roughly followed the Garigliano and Sangro Rivers. Bad weather came ahead of time, in mid-November. The Allies found themselves in extremely difficult country and confronted by a tenacious, energetic, and skillful enemy. For long months their progress was to continue at what German propaganda called a snail's pace.

Sardinia and Corsica

As THE principal force in Sardinia consisted of about two Italian divisions which immediately rallied to the Royal Government, the Germans speedily evacuated the island and moved across into Corsica. On 17 September American officers landed at Cagliari and were welcomed by the inhabitants. Sardinia possessed four airfields, Alghero, Elmas, Monserrato, and Oristano; two seaplane bases, Cagliari and Elmas; and nine landing strips. Its occupation made it possible to improve air coverage of the Tyrrhenian Sea and of the Western Mediterranean.

Corsica was held by about 40,000 Italians and 12,000 Germans. The Maquis had been supplied and reinforced by earlier daring operations of French ships, in particular by the submarine *Casabianca* commanded by the heroic Lherminier. On the nights of 13-14 and 16-17 September French troops landed at Ajaccio which had already been abandoned by the enemy. With the help of the Maquis and the Italians, these French troops rapidly occupied western Corsica. At the end of September the Germans held only Bastia and were evacuating their last troops to Leghorn and Elba. On 4 October Bastia was retaken and all of Corsica was free. These operations had been continually supported by a French squadron containing cruisers *Montcalm* and *Jeanne d'Arc*, destroyers *Le Fantasque* and *Le*

Terrible, and submarines *Casabianca, Perle,* and *Aréthuse.*

Corsica possessed three good airfields, Campo del Oro, Bastia Borgho, and Ghisonaccia, and in view of the planned invasion of southern France the Allies proceeded to build others. They also found Bastia an excellent base from which light coastal forces could continually attack the heavy enemy traffic along the shores of Liguria and Tuscany. By mid-September the Allies had seized without difficulty the islands of Capri, Ischia, Procida, Ventotene, and Ponza, off the Campanian coast.

At this time a notable change in the naval command took place. Sir Dudley Pound, the First Sea Lord, was seriously ill, and Admiral Sir Andrew Cunningham, who was chosen to replace him, gave up his Mediterranean command in October. For three years he had directed British and Allied naval forces in masterly fashion. To Frenchmen, he will remain one of those foreign commanders who best understood France's mournful situation. His successor as commander of Allied naval forces was Admiral Sir John Cunningham, who had previously commanded the British naval forces in the Middle East. Unlike his predecessor, the latter did not have to fight against a powerful enemy fleet, but he was to be faced with difficult landing operations in which he showed himself worthy to succeed his namesake.

The Dodecanese

AT THE TIME of the Italian armistice General Maitland Wilson, the British commander in the Middle East, had completed plans for capture of the Dodecanese, and a British division was ready to embark to attack Rhodes and Scarpanto, the two islands having the best airfields. But lack of shipping forced the Allies to cancel this operation at the last minute. The Italians were left largely on their own, and the Germans, who had foreseen the defection of their ally, rapidly executed their own plans and took possession of these two islands, the key positions of the archipelago. Then between 8 and 18 September weak British forces occupied the islands of Castelrosso, Cos, Leros,

Samos, Icaria, Simi, and Stampalia. To the German Command, which was preoccupied with the prospect of an attack through the Balkans, these operations appeared to herald a major invasion.

Marshal von Weichs, commanding in southeastern Europe, was an advocate of complete evacuation of the Aegean Islands, and his view was strongly supported by Doenitz. The latter urged upon Hitler all the reasons which he thought justified abandoning these islands: although of considerable importance from an offensive viewpoint, they were far less so defensively; they were difficult to defend owing to Germany's lack of air and sea strength; a considerable tonnage of shipping was required to keep them supplied; and finally, since in the event of a Balkan offensive the enemy could mask these islands without attacking them and thus render the garrisons useless, it was important to withdraw the troops first if they were not to be wasted.

While granting the strength of these arguments, Hitler believed that to abandon the islands would have serious political repercussions, especially in Turkey. Not only therefore did the Germans not withdraw from the positions that they held, but they decided to retake the entire Dodecanese. Their fields on Crete and Rhodes gave them control of the air; and the British forces on Cos, with its small and inadequate airfield, were unable to hold out for long. The garrison, amounting to about a battalion, was surprised on 3 October by German airborne troops which were followed by landing forces. On 4 October the Germans controlled the island, loss of which cost the British their only fighter field in the archipelago.

The struggle then became a repetition of the Greek and Cretan campaigns of 1941, with British ships fighting alone against German aviation. By rapid night raids they attempted to prevent German troop movements and succeeded in sinking some German ships and caïques. But they were unable to stop all movement, and they suffered heavy losses. On 26 September the British destroyer *Intrepid* and the Greek *Vasilissa Olga* were sunk by German aircraft at Leros. On 7 October *Penelope* was damaged; on the 8th the destroyer *Panther* was sunk; on the 9th the cruiser *Carlisle* was hit and had to be towed back to Alexandria. In early November cruisers *Sirius* and *Aurora* were seriously damaged, as were destroyers *Belvoir* and *Rockwood*. In the same month two destroyers, *Eclipse* and *Hurworth*, were sunk by mines off Cos, while the Greek *Adrias* had its bow blown off but was successfully towed away. With such heavy losses it was clear that the British squadron in the Aegean, composed of only a few cruisers and a dozen destroyers and handicapped by having to base at Alexandria, would be unable to interdict German communications.

On 7 October the Royal Navy destroyed a German convoy; this delayed the assault on Leros and enabled the British to send in some reinforcements. Continuous effort by the R.A.F., by American planes, and by the Fleet Air Arm made itself felt despite the distance between their bases and the objectives. Nevertheless the Germans methodically continued to occupy these islands. Naxos and Paros were taken on 12 October and Simi on the 15th. On 26 October Leros and Samos were heavily bombed. Supported by planes and small ships, the Germans attacked Leros at dawn on 12 November using both ship-borne troops and parachutists. The Italian and British garrison resisted fiercely but was forced to surrender after a four-day struggle. Samos fell a few days later.

The speed with which the Germans overcame the Italian forces and reestablished their situation in the Aegean, together with the failure of British endeavors, was not calculated to strengthen Allied prestige in the Near East. Fortunately the victories in Italy palliated the untoward effect of these repulses, and the resistance movement in Greece, Albania, and Yugoslavia grew steadily throughout the rest of the war, causing increasing difficulties for the Germans. This resistance in the interior, together with their fear of an Allied attack, forced the Germans to maintain in the Balkans forces which were needed elsewhere. Parenthetically, it is worth noting that Doenitz's ideas on the certainty of an Allied offensive in the Balkans were in accordance with British intentions; at Teheran in November 1943 Churchill once again vainly attempted to turn Allied strategy in this direction.

In October 1943 the Allies established a motor torpedo boat base on the island of Lissa in the Adriatic, which had been occupied by Marshal Tito's partisans. From Lissa these boats were able to enter the Dalmatian channels to attack shipping, and their activity became so disturbing to the enemy that in the following spring Doenitz advocated recapture of the island. But Jodl and Goering opposed this move. They thought that the operation would be difficult, that it would be hard to supply the island after its seizure, and that its possession would not ensure them freedom of communications because of the strength of Allied aviation in the Adriatic. Hitler, who had favored Doenitz's idea, abandoned it with the statement that, "If the Army is opposed to begin with, and inner conviction is lacking, then nothing will come of it anyway," a comment which gives rise to some doubt regarding the oft-proclaimed omnipotence of the Fuehrer.

15. The Struggle for Rome

The decision to continue the Italian offensive

WITH the arrival of their forces before the Winter Line the Allies came up against serious difficulties. Winter had come early; heavy rains were falling; streams turned into torrents; the engineers had constantly to repair bridges; vehicles bogged down in the mud. The Germans had mined positions, roads, airfields, and rivers, and had organized an impenetrable net of deep defenses, a task made easier by the rugged and mountainous terrain.

The Allies might have considered that the goals of Operation AVALANCHE had been attained: Italy had declared war on Germany on 13 October; the forces of the Fascist Republic were weak and in northern Italy the resistance movement was being organized; the Germans had been forced to maintain twenty-four divisions in the peninsula; finally, the Allies were developing airfields in the south, particularly at Foggia, from which their strategic aviation could reach out to the summit of the Alps, southern France, southern Germany, and the Balkans. Airfields in central Italy were not required for the invasion of southern France: Corsica, Sardinia, and the carriers were sufficient.

Nevertheless the Allied Command decided to take Rome. The continuation of the offensive gave the additional advantage of forcing the Germans to send further reinforcements to Kesselring, thus relieving the Russian front. Another consideration was the belief of the Allies, particularly the British, that capture of Rome would have a powerful moral effect, and that so long as the city remained in enemy hands all victories in Italy seemed only partial successes. These were important reasons, but it is possible that the British strategists had others which were undisclosed. At Teheran Churchill had once again unsuccessfully attempted to direct the Allied offensive toward the Balkans. Were central Italy to be quickly conquered, the Americans might let themselves be drawn towards the plain of the

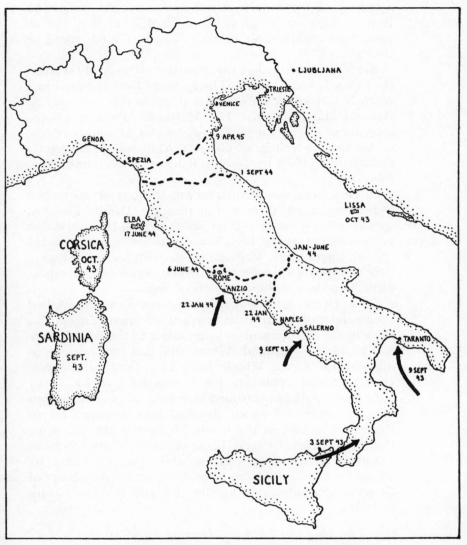

Fig. 19. The Italian Campaign, 1943-1945

Po, and thence towards Yugoslavia and Hungary. Thus for a variety of reasons the Allies undertook the march on Rome, which was to prove far more difficult than the already very considerable obstacles had indicated would be the case.

Before the end of 1943 the American Fifth Army reached the valley before Cassino. The Second Moroccan Division, recently arrived in Italy, was sent up to this position. As General Marshall said, "The Moroccan Division was the forerunner of the *Corps Expéditionnaire Français* which, under the leadership of General Alphonse Juin, greatly distinguished itself in the hard fighting of the months that followed."

In December the Mediterranean theaters of operations were reorganized. Prior to this time the Middle East had constituted a separate theater under British command. On 10 December General Eisenhower's authority was extended over all forces in the Mediterranean, with the single exception of the strategic air force which continued to report directly to the Combined Chiefs of Staff.

On 24 December Eisenhower was named Supreme Allied Commander of the invasion forces of northwest Europe, his place in the Mediterranean being taken by the British General Sir Henry Maitland Wilson, who had previously been in command of the Middle East. The American General Devers became deputy to the Commander in Chief. Sir John Cunningham continued in command of Allied naval forces, a command which also had been enlarged on 10 December to take in the whole Mediterranean including the Middle East. General Leese replaced Montgomery in command of the Eighth Army while General Clark remained at the head of the Fifth, both under the orders of General Alexander, commanding the Allied Army Group in Italy.

The plan for the Anzio landing

In October General Alexander urged a landing behind the German lines. The Allies had been held up along a line running from the Garigliano valley in the west to Pescara in the east, and it seemed necessary to turn the enemy's flank by sea and to threaten his lines of communication. The operation was decided on; the landing beaches selected were near the port of Anzio, about thirty miles south of Rome. At Anzio the harbor is protected from southwest winds by a small breakwater about 600 yards long and can receive ships drawing up to ten feet. But with southerly or southeasterly winds there is a considerable swell and in bad weather ships cannot lie alongside. North of Anzio the coast is sandy with low dunes sloping gently to the sea; to the south the region is bounded by the Pontine marshes. There were three possible landing beaches: one inside the harbor itself, a second five miles to the eastward, and a third five miles to the west. All three had fairly steep gradients and were obstructed by sandbars 150 feet and 500 feet off shore.

The assault forces contained about 50,000 men and about 5,000 vehicles. The amphibious force, commanded by Rear Admiral Lowry, USN, was divided into two groups. The British group, designated Task Force P, contained one headquarters ship, four cruisers, eight destroyers, six destroyer escorts, two antiaircraft ships, two Dutch gunboats, eleven minesweepers, six minelayers, and landing craft. The American group, known as Task Force X, contained one headquarters ship, a cruiser, eight destroyers, two destroyer escorts, twenty-four minesweepers, and patrol boats and landing craft. In these amphibious operations the determining factor, which took precedence over all other considerations, was always the number of landing craft available, and in this instance the assembly of a sufficient number had involved numerous difficulties. For the Anzio operation there were available eight LSI's, eighty-eight LST's, ninety LCI's, sixty LCT's, 250 Dukws, and four Liberty ships.

The Allied Command expected only weak enemy air reaction. The bombers of the Second Luftflotte had been withdrawn from Italy while the Allies had within range of the beachhead some 700 aircraft, based in the Naples area from which the landing craft convoys were to sail. A simulated landing at the mouth of the Tiber River had originally been planned as a feint, but since German reinforcements were concentrated north of this river this ruse would only have drawn them closer to the actual scene of the landings. The diversion was therefore cancelled and replaced by naval bombardment of the port of Civitavecchia which was carried out on the day of the landings and repeated the next day. The Anzio landings were set for 0200 of 22 January. To help gain surprise naval bombardment was limited to a five-minute rocket barrage. Rear Admiral Lowry, commanding Group X, was to land an American division on the beach east of Anzio and Rear Admiral Troubridge's Group P was to land British troops in the bay west of the harbor. Finally American Rangers, transported by the British ships *Royal Ulsterman, Princess Beatrix*, and *Winchester Castle*, were to seize the port.

Preliminary operations

ON 12 JANUARY the Fifth and Eighth Armies attacked all along the front. Although prior to the landing these attacks were not as successful as had been hoped, the Germans were nevertheless forced to commit their reserves. Allied aviation undertook the tasks of cutting the enemy's lines of communication in the north, and of destroying as much as possible of the Luftwaffe before the landings took place. Strategic and tactical air forces attacked targets at Florence, Pisa, Arezzo, and Terni, as well as bridges in the enemy's rear. The four airfields in the Rome area were attacked with explosive and incendiary bombs. The three airfields at Perugia, where German reconaissance units were based, were so heavily damaged that no search flights could be made until 25 January. On 21 January a final pre-landing air attack was made against airfields in southern France, where enemy torpedo and glider-bomb units were based.

On 20 January the British ships *Orion, Spartan, Jervis,*

Janus, Laforey, and *Faulknor* bombarded coastal batteries in the Terracina area, safe passage through the Gulf of Gaeta being insured by the 12th Minesweeping Flotilla. During the night *Dido, Inglefield,* and the French destroyer *Le Fantasque* bombarded Civitavecchia. At daylight on the 21st these forces withdrew to the southward and bombarded the coast near Formia and Terracina in order to prevent the movement of reinforcements towards Anzio. In the meantime ships had been steadily gathering at Naples and Salerno, loading of supplies began on the 19th, and personnel was embarked on the 20th. At 1600 on 20 January General Maitland Wilson, feeling that all preliminary conditions had been fulfilled, decided that the operation would be launched as scheduled at 0200 on the 22nd.

The landing and its consequences

WEATHER conditions were perfect and the forecast was favorable as the amphibious force, commanded by Admiral Lowry, got underway from Naples at 0500 of the 21st. The convoy was made up of 243 warships, transports, landing craft, and miscellaneous vessels of the American, British, French, Dutch, Greek, and Polish navies. To mislead the enemy the expedition sailed southward for a time before heading towards Anzio. The passage was uneventful, no German planes appeared, and at midnight the first ships arrived off Anzio under cover of darkness. The British submarines *Ultor* and *Uproar* had been stationed as beacons off the landing beaches to the west and east of the harbor. Naval detachments went ashore to mark the landing points while minesweepers swept the bay. On shore all was quiet. At 0150 a rocket barrage was laid down for five minutes and at 0200, before moonrise, the first assault waves touched down on the beaches. The cruisers *Brooklyn* and *Penelope* and five destroyers stood off the eastern beaches to give fire support, and to the west similar assistance was provided by *Orion* and *Spartan*. Two Dutch gunboats, *Flores* and *Soemba,* stood by in reserve.

On the east the American Third Division rapidly over-

ran a few enemy patrols, at Anzio the Rangers easily overcame a weak enemy defense, but to the west difficulties were
somewhat more serious. Some mines had to be cleared from
the beaches, sandbars hindered unloading and made pon-
toons necessary, and a few enemy mobile batteries offered
slight resistance. But losses were light and before day-
break most of the infantry was ashore and antiaircraft units
had been landed and set up to protect the beachhead.

By early afternoon Anzio and Nettuno were in the hands
of the Allies, and before dark the channel had been swept
of mines and the port opened to landing craft. During the
day the two divisions had advanced almost unopposed for
a distance of four miles into the interior and had consoli-
dated their lodgement. The beach to the westward of
Anzio, where conditions proved far worse than had been
expected, was abandoned and unloading was carried out
within the port.

During the 22nd, the tactical air forces flew 840 sorties
while the strategic air force attacked enemy airfields in
southern France to prevent intervention by the Luftwaffe.
Similarly the movement of enemy reinforcements back
northward was slowed by bombardment of the Formia
region by the cruiser *Dido*. Enemy air attacks on the day of
landing were very weak, although one LCI was hit and
sunk. The next day they grew in intensity and at dusk
glider bombs sank the destroyer *Janus* and so damaged
Jervis that she had to withdraw to Naples. On the 24th
three hospital ships, *Saint David, Leinster*, and *Saint Andrew*, although fully illuminated, were deliberately attacked; *Saint David* was sunk and *Leinster* damaged. Between the 22nd and the 24th, the headquarters ship *Palomares* and the destroyer *Mayo* were damaged by mines
and the minesweeper *Portent* was sunk. Nevertheless the
landings at Anzio were a magnificent success: careful preparation, very skillful planning by experienced staffs, perfect
cooperation of the various services, and enthusiasm on the
part of all had made this operation a model. The bombings
which had preceded the landings had cut enemy communi-

cations in three places between Rome and the Pisa-Rimini line, had rendered the airfields of the capital unusable, and had prevented enemy reconnaissance so that the Germans, unaware of Allied preparations, only tardily realized the importance of the landing. The naval feint against Civitavecchia had succeeded in deceiving the Germans until dawn of the 22nd. Finally, the attacks on the Fifth Army front had led Kesselring to commit a large part of his reserves to the southward.

But if the landing was a success, the exploitation which followed was a failure. The enemy rapidly brought in reinforcements and contained the beachhead. On 24 January a special order from Hitler was captured which clearly showed enemy intentions: "The Gustav Line must be held at all costs for the sake of political consequences which would follow a completely successful defense. The Fuehrer expects the bitterest struggle for every yard." To hamper the heavy build-up of enemy forces at Anzio, Allied air and naval forces continually bombarded the main roads. On 23 January the British ships *Dido, Kempenfelt, Inglefield, Mauritius,* and the French *Le Fantasque* and *Le Malin* kept the Formia-Terracino road under constant fire. Nevertheless the Germans succeeded in occupying the high ground at Colli Laziali from which they could bombard the beachhead. Prior to the operation the Allied planners had been greatly worried by the problem of supplying the beachhead in the event that a junction with the southern front was not rapidly achieved. This problem was solved more easily than had been feared, despite the gales which on the 24th and 26th washed a dozen landing craft ashore. By the 29th, more than 68,000 men, 500 guns, and about 240 tanks had been landed.

But the Germans were also feverishly active. They recalled several air groups from the Balkans and, by preventing the Allies from basing air strength ashore, made it necessary to continue to protect the troops by planes from the Naples area. On 29 January a Liberty ship and the cruiser *Spartan* were sunk by glider bombs, the latter being probably destroyed by a magazine explosion. On 18 February the cruiser *Penelope*, an old veteran of the Mediterranean campaigns, was sunk in the Bay of Naples by a German submarine, disappearing in forty seconds. On 25 February the destroyer *Inglefield* was in turn sunk by a plane in the Anzio roadstead. Throughout the month of February the situation was extremely critical and withdrawal was considered. Eventually the Allies did succeed in maintaining their positions, but for several months the supply problem laid a heavy task upon the fleet. Only at the end of May was a victorious general offensive launched on the Italian front, and only on 7 June, two days before the Normandy landings, did the Allies enter Rome.

Thus was seen the unusual spectacle of Rome falling to an army coming from the southward. The policies of Mussolini, who had dreamed of reestablishing the Eternal City in its former grandeur, ended with its conquest by a cosmopolitan army made up of British, Americans, Poles, Italians, Irishmen, Moroccans, Greeks, Basutos, and various other races, an army in which more than forty languages were spoken. In Rome they called it the return of Hannibal.

After the capture of Rome the Allies undertook a vigorous pursuit of the enemy army which by September had carried them to the Gothic Line north of Pisa and Florence. Naval forces supported the flanks of the advance both in the Tyrrhenian and in the Adriatic, and carried out continual attacks on enemy coastal communications, operations which involved numerous minor actions between small ships. On 17 June the Allies entered Leghorn, where they found the port in a melancholy state; the Germans had sunk sixteen cargo ships in the channel and the harbor was clogged with wrecks. Nevertheless emergency measures restored the port to use, and it proved of great importance for logistic support of the armies.

It had been decided to capture the island of Elba, which commands the southern approaches to Leghorn. Elba is separated from the mainland by the Piombino Channel which, only six miles wide, is completely commanded by the island's guns. An amphibious operation was organized composed of French troops under General Martin and a naval force of British, French, and American vessels under Admiral Troubridge, the whole placed under the authority of General de Lattre de Tassigny. The landings began at dawn on 17 June, and by evening the French flag floated over the villa of Napoleon. The island was secured after fifty-five hours of fierce fighting in the course of which the French troops in general, and the *Bataillon de Choc* in particular, greatly distinguished themselves.

16. The Landings in Southern France

The operation plan

THE plans for the landing in southern France were worked out only with great effort and amid many difficulties. Conceived at the time of the QUADRANT Conference at Quebec, Operation ANVIL was re-studied at the SEXTANT Conference at Cairo in November 1943. At that time the operation was envisaged merely as a diversion which would hold enemy forces in southern France while the invasion of Normandy was taking place. But even for such a limited effort the question of available landing craft was an acute one: the lack of these ships, wrote General Marshall, "was to plague us to the final day of the war." In order to provide the landing craft needed for the attack in Provence, the Combined Chiefs of Staff had to put off until 1945 an operation in the Bay of Bengal which had been planned for 1944.

In December 1943 the plans for ANVIL were modified and expanded. No longer was it to be simply a maneuver to fix enemy troops, but rather an invasion in the grand style which was to take Allied forces to the Rhine by way of Lyon and Vichy, and which was to be carried out at the same time as the invasion of northwestern France. The execution of this plan was predicated on a rapid advance in Italy, for the capture of Rome and an advance to the Pisa-Rimini line, where the Germans had established a strong defensive position, were considered essential prerequisites. Consequently, when delays in the Italian campaign forced postponement of the landings in southern France, General Maitland Wilson, Allied Commander in Chief, Mediterranean, recommended that ANVIL be cancelled. In its place he suggested breaking the Pisa-Rimini line, continuing into the Po Valley, and then branching off with a landing in the Istrian peninsula followed by exploitation through the Ljubljana Gap into the plains of Hungary.

As always, the British idea was to reach southeastern Europe as rapidly as possible.

On 19 June, thirteen days after the Normandy landings, Maitland Wilson officially suggested this audacious plan. The British Chiefs of Staff, who could hardly have been surprised by the proposal, gave their immediate approval and support. But the American commanders, Eisenhower in particular, felt that all resources should be devoted to the Battle of France, which they considered the decisive operation. Furthermore they thought that the ports captured in Normandy would not suffice for the deployment of Allied reserves and that additional ports would have to be acquired in southern France. Their views prevailed.

But even this did not end the hesitation. Before ANVIL could be launched Eisenhower's American armies had entered Brittany; as it was hoped that Brest would be quickly taken the occupation of Marseilles no longer seemed essential, and the whole problem of the landings in southern France was reopened. On 4 August London asked Maitland Wilson for his views regarding a rapid movement of his expeditionary force from the Mediterranean to Brittany. After hastily consulting his commanders in chief, the General replied that such a change in program would involve long delays and, at long last, ANVIL was irrevocably decided upon.

Despite these tergiversations, which continued up to the last moment, the Mediterranean Supreme Command had thoroughly planned the landings in southern France and had carefully considered all possible objectives. Seizure of the port of Sète was ruled out because its small cargo handling capacity would not have permitted speedy supply of the armies. Port Vendres was not worth consideration. Only Marseilles fulfilled the desired requirements, and it was estimated that demolition by the departing Germans would not critically reduce the capacity of the port. For the landing, the region west of Marseilles was ruled out because the prevailing winds are much stronger than they are east of Hyères, and also because this area, being beyond range of Corsica-based fighter cover, would have required complete dependence on carrier aircraft. Three landing zones were studied. The first, at Hyères, had an excellent sheltered anchorage and an airfield which could have been quickly used; this alternative was abandoned because of the advantage afforded the defense by the islands which protect the roadstead. The beaches near Cannes were eliminated because they were too far from the ports of Toulon and Marseilles, because of the surrounding high ground which might delay the Allied advance, and because they were strongly fortified. Consequently the choice fell upon the region between Cavalaire and Saint Raphaël, despite the fact that there were no airfields available.

The expeditionary force was made up of ten reinforced divisions and, counting rear echelon personnel, totalled 450,000 men. The Americans, with their extensive experience in landing operations, were to furnish the initial main strength, but subsequently the proportion of French troops was to increase to seven-tenths of the total force.

The naval forces, under Admiral Hewitt of the U.S. Navy, included the American battleships *Nevada, Texas,* and *Arkansas,* H.M.S. *Ramillies,* the French *Lorraine,* and the British monitor *Abercrombie;* the British carriers *Attacker, Searcher, Khedive, Emperor,* and *Pursuer,* and the American *Tulagi* and *Kasaan Bay;* British cruisers *Orion, Aurora, Ajax, Dido, Black Prince, Achilles, Argonaut,* and *Sirius,* the American cruisers *Brooklyn, Philadelphia, Augusta, Tuscaloosa, Quincy, Omaha, Marblehead,* and *Cincinnati,* and the French cruisers *Montcalm, Georges Leygues, Gloire,* and *Emile Bertin.* The force contained a hundred destroyers from the Allied nations, including British, American, French, Polish, Dutch, and Greek ships. Finally, about a hundred minesweepers and a mass of miscellaneous vessels made up the total of 800 warships. Admiral Hewitt commanded the naval force at sea; the naval commander in chief, Sir John Cunningham, had established his headquarters on the command ship *Largs* in the Gulf of Ajaccio.

The Allied Mediterranean Command had about 5,000 aircraft. In Corsica, which was being used as an advance base, fourteen airfields had been established on which some forty squadrons were based. Each aircraft carrier had twenty-four planes, and once again experience was to show that the mobility of the carrier multiplied the strength of ship-borne aviation by a factor which would have been difficult to imagine before the war.

As in the Atlantic, the Germans had here strongly reinforced the coast defenses, but at the time of the landing their available forces were rather weak. South of the Lyons-Bordeaux line they had about ten divisions, considerably weaker than those of the Allies and including only one armored division. They had to guard the whole country against sabotage; they had no navy; most important of all, their air strength had fallen to 200 planes, with the result that the Allies had overwhelming superiority in the air. The German command expected a landing but did not know where it would take place. To deceive the enemy, Allied bombing was extended until it covered the region from Sète to Genoa. In accordance with the operation plan this effort began on 1 August, but southern France had in fact been undergoing heavy bombardment since April. At the last moment the movement of convoys was organized so as to indicate an invasion in the Gulf of Genoa. These measures were successful, and the Germans were surprised by the choice of landing beaches.

The convoys sailed from Naples, Taranto, Brindisi, and Oran, while Ajaccio served as a staging base. The total number of ships taking part in the operation, including the warships, totalled more than 2,000, and the coordination of their movements called for very accurate staff work. After the requirements of antisubmarine and antiaircraft protection and of minesweeping had been taken into account, the expedition was routed as follows: convoys from Naples proceeded to Ajaccio through the Strait of Bonifacio; convoys from Taranto, Brindisi, and Oran followed the main Alexandria-Gibraltar route along the African coast and then turned northward passing west of Sardinia and Corsica; a diversionary convoy headed for Genoa through the Tyrrhenian Sea. All of these movements were carried out with remarkable precision.

The assault

ON 15 AUGUST, shortly after midnight, an airborne and parachute division took off from the neighborhood of Rome. Although visibility was poor, the use of radar and direction-finding apparatus made the landings a complete success, and the percentage of accidents was very small. Once on the ground, the division was aided by members of the French resistance, and the villages of Le Mitin, La Motte, Castron, and Les Serres were occupied by noon. At Le Muy the German defense was vigorous and the town was not taken until the 16th, but by evening of the 15th the airborne division had made contact with the troops that had come ashore.

Thirty minutes after midnight the American Special Service Force went ashore on Port Cros and Levant Islands and a French Commando landed on the mainland, seizing its objective, the battery on Cap Nègre, by about 0830. By 0920 the Americans had the situation in the islands under control although some enemy groups continued to resist until the 17th.

Between 0700 and 0800 the naval forces carried out an extremely violent bombardment which proved to be one of the most effective ever made in the Mediterranean: in one hour 45,000 shells of 5-inch and above were fired, while at the same time the bombers were pulverizing the defenses. Except at Saint Raphaël, enemy artillery was for all practical purposes silenced and the Germans opposed the landings with small arms alone. At Saint Raphaël, however, the assault had to be abandoned and the troops of the American 36th Division were landed at Agay. By noon of the 16th this division had captured Fréjus and Saint Raphaël; in the center the 45th Division seized Sainte Maxime before 1700 on the 15th; on the left the 3rd Division landed at Cavalaire and Pampelonne, and reached Lavandou on the 16th.

The landing was a complete success. As one Allied officer put it, "Compared to Salerno, the landing in Provence was just guerrilla warfare." The Germans had expected an attack near Genoa and were surprised both by the time and place of the operation. Losses were small. At sea one

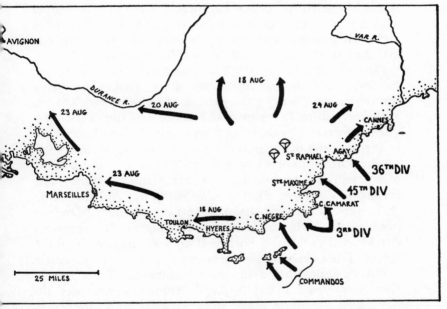

Fig. 20. The Landings in Southern France, 15 August 1944

LST and two LCVP's were sunk by glider bombs and nine LCT's and a dozen smaller craft were damaged. The air forces had made 11,000 sorties at a cost of forty-two planes. After two days of fighting ashore casualties totalled 1,500 killed and a similar number wounded.

By noon of the 16th the three American divisions were ashore with all their equipment. General de Lattre de Tassigny's French forces were following and assembling in the Bormes-Cogolin area prior to advancing on Toulon and Marseilles, their first objectives. Throughout their advance the French troops were supported by naval units, notably at Toulon, where the sea front was strongly defended by batteries which could assist the ground defense. The strongest of these were the two twin turrets of 13.4-inch guns on the Saint Mandrier peninsula, which flanks the Toulon roadstead on the south. The guns emplaced there before the war had been disabled in November 1942 but had been replaced by weapons of the same caliber and with a range of 38,000 yards which the Germans had salvaged from the scuttled battleship *Provence*.

On the 18th Allied bombing attacks on Toulon hit the battleship *Strasbourg* and capsized the cruiser *La Galissonnière*, which was in the process of being raised. On the 19th battleships *Lorraine* and *Nevada* and the cruiser *Augusta*, protected by destroyers and aircraft, bombarded the heavy batteries of the port. French troops began the assault on the 20th, supported by a powerful naval force made up of battleships *Lorraine* and *Nevada*, cruisers *Quincy*, *Aurora*, *Black Prince*, *Augusta*, *Philadelphia*, and numerous destroyers. Resistance lasted longest on the Saint Mandrier peninsula, which was taken on 28 August. On the same day Marseilles fell and Port de Bouc was captured by F.F.I. forces. The operation was running well ahead of schedule.

On 15 September a squadron composed of the cruiser *Georges Leygues*, flying the flag of Admiral Lemonnier, the battleship *Lorraine*, and eight cruisers and destroyers, made a stirring entry into Toulon. As a gesture of Allied friendship these French units were accompanied on this occasion by the Commander in Chief of Allied Mediterranean naval forces, Admiral Sir John Cunningham, in cruiser *Sirius*, and by the American Admiral Davidson in cruiser *Philadelphia*.

Toulon and Marseilles had been conscientiously destroyed by the Germans. At Toulon both arsenals had been blown up, the docks had been destroyed, and the roadstead was clogged with wrecks; ten German submarines had been sunk at their moorings. Marseilles had been sacked: 2,000 mines had destroyed five miles of wharfs and almost half the sheds; of some 200 cranes only four were in working condition; seventy sunken ships blocked the harbor and the channels; the drydocks were out of commission and all harbor craft had been destroyed.

Although the landings in Provence and the Allied invasion of southern France were brilliantly successful operations, their importance was greatly diminished by the delay in their execution. "The success of the Northern invasion," wrote General Maitland Wilson, "and particularly the break-through into Brittany had actually drawn off forces from the southern invasion area, which for the moment made the original mission assigned to our forces appear almost superfluous." Although the General writes with great reserve, one can detect in his report a regret that the move towards Hungary, which he had suggested in June, had not been approved. On the other hand Marshal von Rundstedt felt that if the Allies had followed up the attack in Normandy by a second major landing in the north, the war would have ended in 1944. But in August of that year it was not possible to move the Provence expeditionary force rapidly to the north.

17. The End of the Mediterranean War

Final operations

RUMANIA deserted the Axis on 23 August 1944 and declared war on the Reich two days later. The final armistice with the U.S.S.R. was not signed until 12 September, but by the end of August Russian armies had crossed Rumania and reached Bulgaria. The threat of being outflanked forced the Germans to evacuate Greece. Once again British ships flocked into the Aegean Sea, where they had suffered so many trials and had shown such steadfastness in adversity. Now at last the situation was completely reversed. The Luftwaffe was very weak and Admiral Rawlings, commanding the naval forces of the Levant, had not only numerous cruisers and destroyers but also four escort carriers, *Stalker, Attacker, Hunter,* and *Emperor*. The fleet bombarded German positions and attacked both single ships and weakly protected evacuation convoys.

These operations began on 9 September and continued until the liberation of Greece. The Allies sank three torpedo boats, destroyed forty-five miscellaneous vessels, and damaged about sixty more. On 4 October the British occupied Patras, on the 12th they entered Corfu, on the 13th they reached the Piraeus, already freed by the Greeks, and on 1 November they were in Salonika. On 17 October the Greek Government returned to the Piraeus on board *Averof*. In the various islands of the Aegean, particularly in Crete, there remained about 20,000 Germans whose surrender was only a matter of time. There was no need to undertake costly operations to seize these German-held islands, for their garrisons, lacking naval and air forces, had no offensive power and could do nothing to hinder the Allies. Nevertheless on 1 May 1945, without awaiting the imminent end of hostilities, the Greeks seized Rhodes after heavy fighting. Doubtless they thought it wisest to occupy this island before the diplomatic discussions began.

In November 1944 the Germans evacuated the islands of

southern Dalmatia and withdrew into those of the Gulf of Quarnero—Pago, Rab, Cherso, Krk, and Lussin—where they were to remain on the defensive until April 1945. Here they were barely strong enough to protect their coastal and inter-island traffic, which indeed was frequently interrupted by combined attacks of Allied planes and light units based at Zara. In the upper Tyrrhenian the struggle continued with minor actions off the Ligurian coast, and with frequent bombardment of enemy positions in which the French cruisers *Jeanne d'Arc, Emile Bertin, Montcalm, Duguay-Trouin, Georges Leygues, Gloire*, and numerous French torpedo boats and frigates took part.

At Genoa on 6 January 1945 the British destroyer *Lookout* and the American destroyer *Woolsey* bombarded and set on fire the aircraft carrier *Aquila*; and this ship, on which the Italians had founded such hopes, ended its career in port with its conversion still incomplete. *Sparviero*, work on which had been begun in 1943 and halted that same September, had been sunk at Genoa by the Germans on 15 October 1944.

The surrender

BY LATE OCTOBER 1944 Allied ground forces in Italy had reached a line running from Rimini to north of Lucca. Winter halted operations, but on 4 April 1945 an offensive was launched on the Fifth Army front, and on the 10th on that of the Eighth Army. Progress was rapid; by the 25th the enemy armies were collapsing and revolt had broken out all over northern Italy. On 29 April Allied troops entered Milan and Venice, and at noon the same day Radio Milan announced that Mussolini, his mistress Claretta Petacci, and various members of the government of the Fascist Republic had been shot at Dongo in the province of Como. Mussolini, together with a group of fascists and a few German soldiers, had been captured by partisans while making for the Valtellina, where they hoped to establish a redoubt based on Austria and Bavaria. Neither Italians nor Germans had offered resistance.

It was said that before dying Mussolini cried out, "A tree cannot reach the sky." In truth he had attempted the impossible. To hope within the space of a few years to restore modern Italy to the grandeur of Rome was to forget not only that that city was not built in a day but also that times had changed. Had the Axis been victorious, Mussolini would not have found himself back in the empire of Augustus, but rather in fifth-century Rome, protected and dominated by Odoacer; for Hitler, in a conference with the leaders of the German Navy, had spoken threateningly of the fate which he planned for Italy.

On 29 April German emissaries appeared at General Alexander's headquarters at Caserta to accept unconditional surrender. One of the representatives signed in the name of General von Vietinghoff Schell, Commander in Chief of German Army Group C and of all naval, air, and land forces in the so-called Southwestern Region. The other signed in the name of Obergruppenfuehrer Karl Wolff, Commander of the S.S. and of the German police forces in the same area. The surrender included all German and Fascist forces in northern Italy, in the Austrian provinces of Vorarlberg, Tyrol, and Salzburg, and in certain parts of Carinthia and Styria.

This capitulation became effective at noon on 2 May, thus preceding the general German surrender by a few days. The execution of the Caserta armistice involved the surrender of about a million men: the fragments of twenty-two German and six Fascist divisions; a few score almost useless aircraft; and a number of small vessels—escort ships, torpedo boats, and motor torpedo boats—which either reached Allied bases flying a white flag over the swastika or were seized in harbor.

The garrisons of the islands of the Aegean Sea were included in the general surrender of German forces which was signed on 7 May at Rheims.

Reflections on the Mediterranean War

IN THE STRUGGLE for the Mediterranean, which thus ended with the complete collapse of Germany, the Axis had twice been on the point of driving Great Britain from Suez, first in June 1941 after the conquest of Crete, and again in the summer of 1942. In 1941 the Germans voluntarily halted their advance in order to send forces against the Russians, and the departure of the Luftwaffe saved the British. Again in 1942 the reduction of Mediterranean air strength in order to reinforce the Russian front made possible the victory of Montgomery's Eighth Army. The question thus arises: Would Great Britain have been defeated if the Axis had reached Suez?

In 1941, when she stood alone in the face of a coalition which dominated most of Europe, such might have been the case. But even then the help being given by the United States would have enabled the British Empire to hold out for a long time. By 1942 it was very doubtful that the Axis, then fighting not only Great Britain but also Russia and the United States, would have succeeded in defeating its enemies by dominating the Mediterranean.

It is of course true that Grand Admiral Raeder had founded the highest hopes on the conquest of the Suez Canal. "We would," he said, "have been able to reach the Indian Ocean and join forces with Japan." But this would have been a very precarious union: the Italian Fleet was not designed for oceanic operations; it had few supply ships and, generally speaking, had an inadequate fleet train. The Italian merchant fleet was very weak. How effective would the Italian naval forces have been in the Indian Ocean when faced by well-supplied Allied squadrons containing aircraft carriers? And how would the Italians have managed to support large armies in Egypt and Asia Minor? It would seem that Raeder labored under some remarkable misconceptions. As for the Japanese, they had wisely limited their ambitions to the conquest and defense of a perimeter which did not extend westward of Burma, and by June 1942 their momentum had been broken and they could no longer contemplate great operations in the Indian Ocean. If today the Japanese leaders blame themselves for anything it is for having overextended their conquests. It therefore seems highly probable that a union between the Axis and Japan, even following the conquest of Suez, would have been productive only of minor exchanges of goods. In 1942 the loss of the Canal would have been a very serious defeat for the Allies, but not a decisive one.

The naval war in the Mediterranean falls naturally into two great periods divided by the surrender of the Axis armies in Tunisia—first the Battle for Africa, and then the Battle for Europe—and these two phases differ not only in their objects but also in the nature of the struggle. The first phase was almost entirely dominated by the problem of sea communications, above all of Axis communications with Africa. After the conquest of Africa by the Allies the struggle for sea communications remained important although no longer primary. Allied navigation became increasingly safe and the Anglo-American air forces concentrated their attacks much more on land routes than on enemy sea communications which, indeed, were reduced almost entirely to coastal traffic. In this phase the principal mission of the Allied naval forces became the assault against the shore.

The principal cause of the defeat of the Axis armies in Libya and Tunisia was the inadequacy of German-Italian communications in the Mediterranean, an inadequacy which was much more the result of inferiority in the air than of inferiority at sea. Important and glorious though the role of the British surface fleet had been, it was very nearly destroyed during the first half of 1942 and was unable to maintain control of the Central and Eastern Mediterranean. The weight of the struggle then fell upon the submarines and, above all, upon the aircraft of the R.A.F. and of the Fleet Air Arm, aided by the U.S. Army Air Force, which appeared in Egypt well before the landings in North Africa. With the arrival of Anglo-American forces in Algeria and Morocco, Allied air and sea supremacy was established in the western basin, whence, growing ever stronger, it was subsequently extended over the whole Mediterranean. The first part of the war ended for the Axis with the catastrophe in Tunisia.

At the start of the war it might logically have been thought that, in a narrow sea which each of the adversaries needed to control, the presence of large opposing fleets would lead to great battles of annihilation. Nothing of the kind occurred. Matapan does not rank as a great battle; it was in essence a chance night encounter, in no way comparable to the furious battles fought between the Americans and Japanese at Midway and in the Philippines. The chief reason for this was that the Italians followed the general policy of the "fleet in being"; they tried to avoid risking their battleships except in circumstances promising very great chances of success. As these circumstances did not occur, the war in the Mediterranean became one of small actions. The heavy ships destroyed in this sea were lost in scattered encounters: the battleship *Barham*, the carriers *Eagle* and *Ark Royal* were sunk by German submarines; the Italian battleship *Roma* by German planes; *Cavour* by an attack of Allied aircraft while at anchor. But although no great battle took place at sea, the struggle was none the less deadly. In all categories except battleships, the Italian Fleet lost the greater part of its units. The submarines suffered particularly severely; including those operating outside the Mediterranean, a total of 116 was lost. "They departed," as one Italian chronicler wrote with somber brevity, "they departed and they did not return." The fate of the destroyers and escort ships was no more enviable.

One of the characteristics of this war was the importance of actions in harbor. The events at Mers el Kébir and at Toulon had, of course, special causes. But the Italian Fleet lost many ships at anchor, a fact easily explained by the progress of aviation and the restricted size of the theater. So, too, the British Fleet not only received very heavy blows in harbor from the actions of the Italian assault machines, but was also hard hit by enemy aircraft, particularly at Malta. Nevertheless Alexandria and Gibraltar were rarely attacked by Axis planes; the Italian Fleet had no aircraft carriers, and both Germany and Italy lacked long-range fighters for bomber escort.

Throughout the second phase of the war—the invasion of Europe—the efforts of naval forces were largely occupied in attacks against the shore. As Admiral Nimitz has rightly observed, naval action against the land has been historically as important as that against enemy fleets in the open sea, despite the fact that the latter, being more dramatic, has drawn much more attention from historians and navalists. As in the Pacific, the war in the Mediterranean confirmed these lessons of the past, and today the United States Navy is emphasizing this aspect in its preparation for a possible future conflict.

On the level of the overall conduct of the war, the Mediterranean struggle provides much food for thought. Marshal Badoglio has written that Anglo-Saxon strategy cannot be considered as a model, but such a judgement should first be applied to the Axis which committed the most serious errors, errors which can be attributed to the German High Command, to the Italian High Command, and often to both of them at once. The most serious of these mistakes, the mistakes which brought about defeat, were the attack on Russia in June 1941 and the attack on Pearl Harbor which catapulted the United States into the war. Neither the Italians nor Mussolini were responsible for these two principal blunders; so far as the Duce is concerned they may be looked upon as extenuating circumstances, for in June 1940 he could hardly foresee that his partners would commit such unprovoked assaults before having eliminated Great Britain. Nevertheless it was very risky to assume that the conflict would remain localized.

At the time of the French armistice, North Africa was neglected both by Germans and by Italians. Mussolini gave up his claims to Tunisia, and Hitler, although admitting the great theoretical importance of the Mediterranean in a world war, did nothing about North Africa. Nor did he move against Gibraltar, and only in 1942, when it was too late, did the Germans undertake a determined offensive against Suez. Given the erroneous information which Hitler had regarding the strength of the Russian Army, one may concede that it seemed logical to him to attack the U.S.S.R. before defeating Great Britain, but it is less easy to understand why he did not attempt decisive action in the Mediterranean during the winter of 1940-1941.

As for Italy, Mussolini had gone to war intending to get the greatest possible profit at the smallest possible cost, the limitation on cost to be achieved principally by inaction. At the outset no real plans existed; subsequently both strategy and policy were vacillating. After having ordered a defensive strategy on the Alpine front, Mussolini went over to the attack without preparation. He prepared for an invasion of Yugoslavia, subsequently demobilized the forces intended for this operation, then called back some of them and, unknown to his partner, plunged into the Greek campaign. Weak and poorly prepared for war though he was, he scattered his forces, rashly sending submarines to the Atlantic and to the Black Sea, planes against Great Britain, armies to the Russian front. It might have seemed sensible to send forces to help the Germans attain primary objectives, but Italian weakness in the Mediterranean already held serious risks for the Axis, risks which it was imprudent to increase by dispersal of Italian forces. Nor were these dangers diminished by the fact that the principle of parallel war, which both nations followed by tacit agreement, led them to act without coordination, without overall control, and, for the greater part of the war, without a common staff. Mussolini can also be blamed for having poorly organized the evacuation of bombed cities, a failure which increased the sufferings of their inhabitants. It is only fair to recognize that, more quickly and clearly than Hitler, he saw the necessity of ending the struggle with Russia, but all in all his influence on the conduct of the war, on both the political and the strategic levels, was an unfortunate one.

He often assigned impossible tasks to the staff of Comando Supremo, but this staff itself was responsible for numerous blunders. It had little understanding of the problems of naval war; it thought that it could control the

Central Mediterranean by adopting a wholly defensive attitude; and in three years of conflict it was unable to establish satisfactory liaison between the Navy and the Air Force.

The instructions which Comando Supremo gave Supermarina were very questionable. And Supermarina in turn issued to the Fleet Commander general orders so contradictory that they can be summed up in the words, "Do and don't do." Perhaps on certain occasions the Fleet Commander would have been well advised to have thrown these orders overboard and to have employed his utmost efforts against the enemy. A Roger de Lauria, a Doria, or a Nelson would have done this, but the Italian commanders remained within the limits of the cautious instructions which they received from Rome. Doubtless the Italian High Command could show good reasons for its guarded strategy: it could not possibly replace its heavy units should they be destroyed; it was often hindered by lack of fuel; it had to bear in mind the technical inferiority of its ships, an inferiority which was apparent in various fields and which, since it resulted from an inadequate industry, could not be blamed upon the Italian sailors. But the historian must state the following facts. The British sailed some twenty convoys from Gibraltar to Malta and Alexandria, convoys whose passage was of the most fundamental importance for the success of their operations in Libya. These convoys generally passed the Sicilian Strait protected only by light cruisers and destroyers. Not once did the Italian Command succeed in throwing against these convoys the powerful mass of its battle fleet, and never did the Italian battleships destroy either an escort vessel or a single transport. Whatever the difficulties of the task with which the Italians were faced, a consideration of these operations makes it difficult to avoid criticism of Comando Supremo, Supermarina, and the Commanders in Chief of the Fleet.

Having made these reservations regarding the Italian High Command, a sufficient estimate of the way in which the Navy fought may be gained from the opinion of the German Admiral Weichold. After two years of collaboration Weichold knew this Navy well, and, as his statement was made after the war, it cannot be suspected of prejudice in favor of the former ally turned enemy. "The crews," he said, "proved that the caution shown in high places was not caused by lack of courage among the men. As was shown by the personnel of the destroyers and of the assault machines during their attacks, all, officers and men alike, did their duty and were a credit to their country." History, we believe, will support this judgement and will correct the impression of wartime propaganda which attributed the defeats of the Italian Navy to a general lack of fighting spirit.

On the Allied side, so long as the British were alone in the Mediterranean they continued the struggle at sea, despite all obstacles and with admirable steadfastness of spirit, in order to assure the supply of their armies in Egypt. By tradition they attributed the most fundamental importance to the Mediterranean, realizing from the beginning that it would be one of the major theaters of operations of the war. They made the decision to hold Malta and without hesitation accepted the risks of sending their Fleet, at times with the weakest of air support, close to the Italian coasts. Tenaciously they attempted to eliminate the Axis from Libya: Wavell failed because he was forced to go to the assistance of Greece; Auchinleck subsequently failed because his reserves had to be taken from him for the defense of the Far East; finally Montgomery succeeded, but the glory which he thus justly acquired should not lead one to forget those who fought on sea, on land, and in the air during the period of adversity.

When the Allies went over to the offensive against the Axis, first in North Africa and then in Europe, the British were no longer alone and the plans which were adopted were the result of compromise between the differing views of the British and American staffs, differences which lasted until the eve of the landings in southern France. With great perseverance Great Britain attempted to draw the Allied armies toward the Balkans. Advocates and opponents of this concept still differ today, and the rivalry between Russia and the Western powers has given the discussion new life. Some feel that an attack on Europe from the southeast would have limited the westward advance of the Russians and that consequently the position of the Anglo-Saxon powers would today be far better. Others, on the contrary, think that if the main Allied effort had been made in the Balkans rather than in France, the Russians would have advanced in the north well beyond the Elbe. These arguments concern only the postwar situation. So far as the defeat of Germany is concerned, it is very hard to say, even in retrospect, whether it was preferable to land in the Balkans or in southern France. One can only say that Allied Mediterranean strategy was not based on any firm plan, completely established in advance and followed with perseverance; rather it groped its way along. Such indecision almost always appears in the strategy of coalitions, especially when the allies are of comparable strength. In the Pacific the assault against Japan followed a much more coherent concept; but there, on the Allied side, the dominant strength of the United States gave it, to all intents and purposes, complete control of the direction of the war.

In the Mediterranean Allied strategy bogged down in a terrible struggle for the possession of Rome, a struggle resulting in delays which considerably diminished the benefits of the landing in Provence. Thus great efforts, much blood, and much heroism were expended for results which. while certainly very important, conformed neither to the hopes which had been built upon them nor to the abundance of the sacrifices made. To say this is not to blame the distinguished leaders who directed Allied strategy. Doubtless it was beyond human ability to wage such a war without making mistakes.

Sources

IN ADDITION to French and foreign eyewitness accounts gathered by the author, the following published materials have been used.

OFFICIAL DOCUMENTS

BRITISH

d'Albiac, Air Vice-Marshal J. H. *Air Operations in Greece, 1940-1941.* Supplement to *The London Gazette,* 9 January 1947.

Alexander of Tunis, Field Marshal Viscount. *The African Campain from El Alamein to Tunis, from 10th August, 1942 to 13th May, 1943.* Supplement to *The London Gazette,* 5 February 1948.

—— *The Conquest of Sicily from 10th July 1943 to 17th August, 1943.* Supplement to *The London Gazette,* 12 February 1948.

Auchinleck, General Sir C. J. *Operations in the Middle East from 1st November 1941 to 15th August 1942.* Supplement to *The London Gazette,* 15 January 1948.

Cunningham, Admiral Sir A. B. *Report of an Action with the Italian Fleet off Calabria, 9th July, 1940.* Supplement to *The London Gazette,* 28 April 1948.

—— *Fleet Air Arm Operations against Taranto on 11th November, 1940.* Supplement to *The London Gazette,* 24 July 1947.

—— *Battle of Matapan, 27th-30th March, 1941.* Supplement to *The London Gazette,* 31 July 1947.

—— *Report of an Action against an Italian Convoy on the Night of the 15th/16th April, 1941.* Supplement to *The London Gazette,* 12 May 1948.

—— *Transportation of the Army to Greece and Evacuation of the Army from Greece, 1941.* Supplement to *The London Gazette,* 19 May 1948.

—— *The Battle of Crete, 15th May-1st June 1941.* Supplement to *The London Gazette,* 24 May 1948.

—— and others. *Mediterranean Convoy Operations.* Supplement to *The London Gazette,* 11 August 1948.

Harwood, Admiral Sir Henry H. *The Battle of Sirte of 22nd March, 1942.* Supplement to *The London Gazette,* 16 September 1947.

273

Somerville, Vice Admiral Sir James. *Action between British and Italian Forces off Cape Spartivento on 27th November, 1940.* Supplement to *The London Gazette,* 4 May 1948.

Wavell, General Sir Archibald P. *Operations in the Middle East from August, 1939 to November, 1940.* Supplement to *The London Gazette,* 13 June 1946.

—— *Operations in the Western Desert from December 7th, 1940 to February 7th, 1941.* Supplement to *The London Gazette,* 26 June 1946.

—— *Operations in the Middle East from 7th February, 1941 to 15th July, 1941.* Supplement to *The London Gazette,* 3 July 1946.

Wilson, General Sir H. Maitland. *Report by the Supreme Allied Commander Mediterranean to the Combined Chiefs of Staff on the Italian Campaign, 8th January to 10th May, 1944.* London, H.M. Stationery Office, 1946.

—— *Report by the Supreme Allied Commander Mediterranean to the Combined Chiefs of Staff on the Operations in Southern France, August 1944.* London, H.M. Stationery Office, 1946.

GERMAN

"Fuehrer Conferences on Naval Affairs" in *Brassey's Naval Annual, 1948,* ed. W. G. Thursfield. London and New York, Macmillan, 1948.

International Military Tribunal, *Trial of the Major War Criminals.* 42 vols. Nuremberg, 1947-1949.

Weichold, Vice Admiral Eberhard. *War in the Mediterranean.* London, Admiralty Publication; Washington, U.S. Navy Department.

UNITED STATES

U.S. Department of State. *Peace and War: United States Foreign Policy, 1931-1941.* Government Printing Office, Washington, 1942.

U.S. Strategic Bombing Survey. *Reports* on the European War. Washington, 1945.

The War Reports of General of the Army George C. Marshall, General of the Army H. H. Arnold, Fleet Admiral Ernest J. King. Foreword by Walter Millis. Philadelphia and New York, Lippincott, 1947.

PERIODICALS

BRITISH: *Journal of the Royal United Service Institution.*

FRENCH: *Revue de Défense Nationale, Revue Maritime, Bulletins de l'Académie de Marine.*

ITALIAN: *Rivista Aeronautica, Rivista Marittima, Rivista Militare.*

UNITED STATES: *Army and Navy Journal, United States Naval Institute Proceedings.*

MISCELLANEOUS[1]

The Air Battle of Malta. London, H.M. Stationery Office, 1944.

Amadori-Virgili, Giovanni. *La guerra e la pace.* Rome, O.E.T., Edizioni del secolo, 1945.

Amicucci, E. *I 600 giorni di Mussolini.* Rome, Faro, 1948.

Armellini, Quirino. *Diario di guerra; nove mesi al comando supremo.* Milan, Garzanti, 1946.

Auphan, Gabriel. *La lutte pour la vie.* Paris, Iles d'or, 1947.

Badoglio, Pietro. *L'Italia nella seconda guerra mondiale (memorie e documenti).* Milan, Mondadori, 1946.

—— *Italy in the Second World War; Memories and Documents.* London, New York, Oxford University Press, 1948.

Bartimeus (pseud.). *East of Malta, West of Suez. The Official Admiralty Account of the Mediterranean Fleet, 1939-1943.* London, H.M. Stationery Office; Boston, Little Brown, 1944.

Bernotti, Romeo. *La guerra sui mari nel conflitto mondiale.* Leghorn, Società editrice tirrena, 194-.

Bragadin, Marc' Antonio. *La marina italiana nella seconda guerra mondiale, 1940-1943.* A cura della lege navale italiana, Rome, 194-.

Brondi, A.-M. *Un generale e "otto milioni di baionette."* Rome, Atlantica, 1946.

Canevari, Emilio. *Graziani mi ha detto.* Rome, Magi-Spinetti, 1947.

Capellini, *Prima di andare a Malta.*

Caracciolo di Feroleto, Mario. *"Ei Poi?" La tragedia dell' esercito italiano.* Rome, Corso, 1946.

[1] Works written in English but used by the author in French translation are here listed in the original edition only; foreign language works which have been translated into English are listed in both the original and in translation.

Carboni, Giacomo. *L'Italia tradita dall' armistizio alla pace.* Rome, E.D.A., 1947.

Chassin, L.-M. *Histoire militaire de la seconde guerre mondiale.* Paris, Payot. 1947.

Churchill, Winston S. *The Second World War: the Gathering Storm.* Boston, Houghton Mifflin, 1948.

Ciano, Galeazzo, *Diario.* Milan, Rizzoli, 1946.

—— *The Ciano Diaries,* ed. Hugh Gibson. Garden City, Doubleday, 1946.

De Guingand, Sir F. W. *Operation Victory.* London, Hodder and Stoughton, 1947.

Edwards, Kenneth. *The Royal Navy and Allies.* London, New York, Hutchinson, 1947.

Eisenhower, Dwight D. *Crusade in Europe.* Garden City, Doubleday, 1948.

Fedeli, Enzo. *1940-1945, L'Italia e il suo esercito.* Turin, Fiorini, 1946.

Fioravanzo, Giuseppe. *Il Mediterraneo, centro strategico del mondo.* A cura del ministero della marina. Verona, Mondadori, 1943.

Fuller, J. F. C. *The Second World War.* London, Eyre and Spottiswoode, 1948.

Garofalo, Franco. *Pennelo Nero; la marina italiana dopo l'8 settembre.* [Rome], Edizioni della Bussola, 1945.

Giamberardino, Oscar di. *La marina nella tragedia nazionale.* Rome, Polin, 1945.

Guedalla, Philip. *Middle East, 1940-1942: a Study in Air Power.* London, Hodder and Stoughton, 1944.

Hitler e Mussolini: lettere e documenti. Milan, Rizzoli, 1946.

Iachino, Angelo. *Gaudo e Matapan; storia di un operazione della guerra navale nel Mediterraneo, 27-28-29 marzo 1941.* Milan, Mondadori, 1946.

James, Sir William M. *The British Navies in the Second World War.* London, New York, Longmans, Green and Co., 1946.

Kammerer, Albert. *La tragédie de Mers-el-Kébir, l'Angleterre et la flotte française.* Paris, Editions Médicis, 1945.

Langer, William L. *Our Vichy Gamble.* New York, Knopf, 1947.

Le Masson, Henri. *Les flottes de combat.* Paris, Editions Maritimes et Coloniales.

Maraldi, Ugo. *Storia della seconda guerra mondiale.* Milan, Cebes.

Maugeri, Franco. *Mussolini mi ha detto.* The material in this pamphlet appears also in the larger work:
—— *From the Ashes of Disgrace,* ed. Victor Rosen. New York, Reynal and Hitchcock, 1948.

Morison, Samuel Eliot. *Operations in North African Waters.* Boston, Little Brown, 1947.

Mussolini, Benito. *Storia di un anno: il tempo del bastone e della carota.* Milan, Mondadori, 1944.

O'Neill, Herbert C. (Strategicus). *The Tide Turns: the Battles of Stalingrad, Alamein, and Tunisia.* London, Faber and Faber, 1944.

Orlando, T. *Vittoria di un popolo.* Rome, Corso.

Pricolo, F. *Ignavia contro eroismo.* Rome, Nicola Ruffolo.

Puleston, William D., *The Influence of Sea Power in World War II.* New Haven, Yale University Press, 1947.

Romat, Etienne. *Au large de Malte.* Paris, J. de Gigord.

Roosevelt, Elliott. *As He Saw It.* New York, Duell, Sloan and Pearce, 1946.

Simoni, L. (pseud.). *Berlino–Ambasciata d'Italia 1939-1943.* Rome, Migliaresi, 1946.

Spigo, Umberto. *Premesse techniche della disfata: dall'euforia al disastro.* Rome, Faro, 1946.

Stitt, George. *Under Cunningham's Command, 1940-1943.* London, G. Allen and Unwin, 1944.

Visconti Prasca, Sebastiano. *Io ho aggredito la Grecia.* Milan, Rizzoli.

Zanussi, Giacomo. *Guerra e catastrofe d'Italia.* Rome, Corso, 1945-1946.

Index

INDEX

INDEX

Mers el Kébir, 26-31, 186-7, 199, 267
Messe, Marshal Giovanni, 205
Messina, 48, 69, 101, 201, 211, 220
Mid-August, Victory of, 168-71
mines and mine warfare, 13, 63, 100, 148, 189, 242, 250
Montgomery, General Sir B. L., 171, 173-6, 200, 212, 238, 246, 271
Morocco, 21, 181-3, 185, 188, 266; landings in, 187
Mountbatten, Captain Lord Louis, 120-1
Mussolini, Benito, 3-4, 8-10, 13, 15-7, 20, 31, 35-6, 40, 43-6, 50-1, 72-6, 88, 93, 110, 139, 142, 146-7, 157, 190, 203, 209, 215-20, 222, 224-8, 252, 263-4, 268-9

Naples, 48, 69, 82, 88, 95, 101, 152, 201, 203, 221, 236, 248-50, 257; taken by Allies, 238-9
Netherlands: *Flores*, 249; *Isaac Sweers*, 144; *Slamat*, 119; *Soemba*, 249
Nile, Army of the, 73, 87, 114, 139; *see also* Eighth Army
Nimitz, Admiral Chester W., 59, 268
Normandy, landings in, 254-5; *see also* OVERLORD
Norway, 204; *Talabot*, 159, 163

Oberkommando der Wehrmacht (O.K.W.), 45, 50, 93, 113, 156-7, 197
Oliver, Commodore G. N., 236
Oran, 11, 13, 181-3, 185, 188, 213, 236, 257; landings at, 186-7
Oshima, General Hiroshi, 218
OVERLORD, 233; *see also* Normandy, landings in

Pact of Steel, 3, 222
Palermo, 14, 48, 144, 152, 202, 211, 219, 236
Pantelleria, 170, 209-10, 228
Parona, Admiral, 160
Patton, Lieutenant General George S., Jr., 183, 213
Pavesi, Admiral Gino, 210, 228
Pearl Harbor, attack on, 83, 268

Perim, 57
Persia, 140
Persian Gulf, 54, 134
Petacci, Clara, 263
Pétain, Marshal Philippe, 58, 182
Pietromarchi, Luca, 9
Piraeus, 103, 116-7, 122, 262
Pisa, Captain de, 109
Poland: *Kujawiak*, 167
Port Said, 61, 215
Port Sudan, 56
Pound, Admiral Sir Dudley, 240
Power, Rear Admiral Arthur, 171
Pozzi, Jean, 31
Pridham-Wippel, Vice Admiral H. D, 83, 103-5, 110, 163
Punta Stilo, Battle of, 65-8, 86

QUADRANT Conference, 254

radar, 40, 111, 153-4, 183
Raeder, Grand Admiral Erich, 16, 19, 21-2, 38, 100, 143-4, 156, 192, 196, 198, 265
Rashid Ali el-Gailani, 133
Rawlings, Rear Admiral H. B., 128, 138, 262
Red Sea, 48-50, 56-7, 135
Rhodes, 71, 74, 133, 172, 240-1, 262
Ribbentrop, Joachim, 4, 9, 15
Riccardi, Admiral Arturo, 88, 100, 218
Rielkhoff, General Karl, 127
Roatta, General Mario, 75
Rome, 48, 226, 233, 237, 244-8, 254, 264, 272; taken by Allies, 252
Rommel, Field Marshal Erwin, 31, 58, 113-5, 141-2, 155-6, 164-5, 167, 172-6, 179, 225-6
Roosevelt, Franklin D., 10, 45, 179-80, 233
Ruault-Frappart, Captain von, 192
Ruge, Admiral, 198, 225
Rumania, 5, 115-6, 131, 262
Rundstedt, Field Marshal Gerd von, 261
Russia, 8, 21-2, 94, 131-4, 140, 151, 156, 158, 164, 167, 174, 179, 183, 196, 203, 205, 262, 265, 268, 272

285

286